FIFTH EDITION

Focus on Grammar 3

Marjorie Fuchs
Margaret Bonner
Miriam Westheimer

Focus on Grammar 3: An Integrated Skills Approach, Fifth Edition

Pearson Education, 221 River Street, Hoboken, NJ 07030

Staff credits: The people who made up the *Focus on Grammar 3, Fifth Edition* team, representing content creation, design, manufacturing, marketing, multimedia, project management, publishing, rights management, and testing, are Pietro Alongi, Rhea Banker, Elizabeth Barker, Stephanie Bullard, Jennifer Castro, Tracey Cataldo, Aerin Csigay, Mindy DePalma, Dave Dickey, Warren Fischbach, Pam Fishman, Nancy Flaggman, Lester Holmes, Gosia Jaros-White, Leslie Johnson, Barry Katzen, Amy McCormick, Julie Molnar, Brian Panker, Stuart Radcliffe, Jennifer Raspiller, Lindsay Richman, Robert Ruvo, Alexandra Suarez, Paula Van Ells, and Joseph Vella.

Text design and layout: Don Williams
Composition: Page Designs International
Project supervision: Bernard Seal
Contributing editors: Françoise Leffler and Bernard Seal

Cover image: Andy Roberts / Getty Images

Library of Congress Cataloging-in-Publication Data

A catalog record for the print edition is available from the Library of Congress.

Printed in the United States of America

ISBN 10: 0-13-582310-2
ISBN 13: 978-0-13-582310-1

2 2021

Contents

Contents (continued)

WELCOME TO
FOCUS ON GRAMMAR
FIFTH EDITION

BUILDING ON THE SUCCESS of previous editions, *Focus on Grammar* continues to provide an integrated-skills approach to engage students and help them understand, practice, and use English grammar. Centered on thematic instruction, *Focus on Grammar* combines comprehensive grammar coverage with abundant practice, critical thinking skills, and ongoing assessment, helping students accomplish their goals of communicating confidently, accurately, and fluently in everyday situations.

New in the Fifth Edition

New and Updated Content

Focus on Grammar continues to offer engaging and motivating content that appeals to learners from various cultural backgrounds. Many readings and activities have been replaced or updated to include topics that are of high interest to today's learners.

Updated Charts and Redesigned Notes

Clear, corpus-informed grammar presentations reflect real and natural language usage and allow students to grasp the most important aspects of the grammar. Clear signposting draws attention to common usage, the difference between written and spoken registers, and common errors.

New Assessment Program

The new edition of *Focus on Grammar* features a variety of new assessment tools, including course diagnostic tests, formative and summative assessments, and a flexible gradebook. The assessments are closely aligned with unit learning outcomes to inform instruction and measure student progress.

Revised MyEnglishLab

The updated MyEnglishLab offers students engaging practice and video grammar presentations anywhere, anytime. Immediate feedback and remediation tasks offer additional opportunities for successful mastery of content and help promote accuracy. Instructors receive instant access to digital content and diagnostic tools that allow them to customize the learning environment to meet the needs of their students.

The *Focus on Grammar* Approach

At the heart of the *Focus on Grammar* series is its unique and successful three-step approach that lets learners move from comprehension to communication within a clear and consistent structure. The books provide an abundance of scaffolded exercises to bridge the gap between identifying grammatical structures and using them with confidence and accuracy. The integration of the three skills allows students to learn grammar holistically, which in turn prepares them to understand and use English more effectively.

STEP 1: Grammar in Context integrates grammar and vocabulary in natural contexts such as articles, stories, dialogues, and blog posts. Students engage with the unit reading and theme and get exposure to grammar as it is used in real life.

STEP 2: Grammar Presentation presents the structures in clear and accessible grammar charts and notes with multiple examples of form and meaning. Corpus-informed explanations and examples reflect natural usage of the target forms, differentiate between written and conversational registers whenever appropriate, and highlight common errors to help students avoid typical pitfalls in both speaking and writing.

STEP 3: Focused Practice provides numerous and varied contextualized exercises for both the form and meaning of the new structures. Controlled practice ensures students' understanding of the target grammar and leads to mastery of form, meaning, and use.

Recycling

Underpinning the scope and sequence of the *Focus on Grammar* series is practice that allows students to use target structures and vocabulary many times, in different contexts. New grammar and vocabulary are recycled throughout the book. Students have maximum exposure, leading them to become confident in using the language in speech and in writing.

Assessment

Extensive testing informs instruction and allows teachers and students to measure progress.

- **Diagnostic Tests** provide teachers with a valid and reliable means to determine how well students know the material they are going to study and to target instruction based on students' needs.

- **Unit Review Tests, Mid- and End-of-Term Review Tests, and Final Exams** measure students' ability to demonstrate mastery of skills taught in the course.

- The **Placement Test** is designed to help teachers place students into one of the five levels of the *Focus on Grammar* course.

The Importance of Context

A key element of *Focus on Grammar* is presenting important grammatical structures in context. The contexts selected are most relevant to the grammatical forms being introduced. Contextualized grammar practice also plays a key role in improving fluent use of grammar in communicative contexts. It helps learners to develop consistent and correct usage of target structures during all productive practice.

The Role of Corpus

The most important goal of *Focus on Grammar* has always been to present grammar structures using natural language. To that end, *Focus on Grammar* has incorporated the findings of corpus linguistics,* while never losing sight of what is pedagogically sound and useful. By taking this approach, *Focus on Grammar* ensures that:

- the language presented reflects real, natural usage

- themes and topics provide a good fit with the grammar point and elicit the target grammar naturally

- findings of the corpus research are reflected in the syllabus, readings, charts, grammar notes, and practice activities

- examples illustrate differences between spoken and written registers, and formal and informal language
- students are exposed to common errors in usage and learn how to recognize and avoid errors in their own speech and writing

Focus on Grammar Efficacy

The fifth edition of *Focus on Grammar* reflects an important efficacy initiative for Pearson courses—to be able to demonstrate that all teaching materials have a positive impact on student learning. To support this, *Focus on Grammar* has been updated and aligned to the **Global Scale of English** and the **Common European Framework** (CEFR) to provide granular insight into the objectives of the course, the progression of learning, and the expected outcomes a learner will be able to demonstrate upon successful completion.

To learn more about the Global Scale of English, visit www.English.com.

Components

Student Books with Essential Online Resources include access codes to the course audio, video, and self-assessment.

Student Books with MyEnglishLab offer a blended approach with integration of print and online content.

Workbooks contain additional contextualized practice in print format.

Digital Teacher's Resources include printable teaching notes, GSE mapping documents, answer keys, audio scripts, and downloadable tests. Access to the digital copy of the student books allows teachers to project the pages for whole-class instruction.

FOG Go app allows users to access the student book audio on their mobile devices.

* A principal resource has been Douglas Biber et al, *Longman Grammar of Spoken and Written English*, Harlow: Pearson Education Ltd., 1999.

The *Focus on Grammar* Unit

Focus on Grammar introduces grammar structures in the context of unified themes. All units follow a four-step approach, taking learners from grammar in context to communicative practice. Thematic units add a layer to learning so that by the end of the unit students will be able to discuss the content using the grammar points they have just studied.

STEP 1 GRAMMAR IN CONTEXT

Before You Read activities create interest and elicit students' knowledge about the topic.

Vocabulary exercises help students improve their command of English.

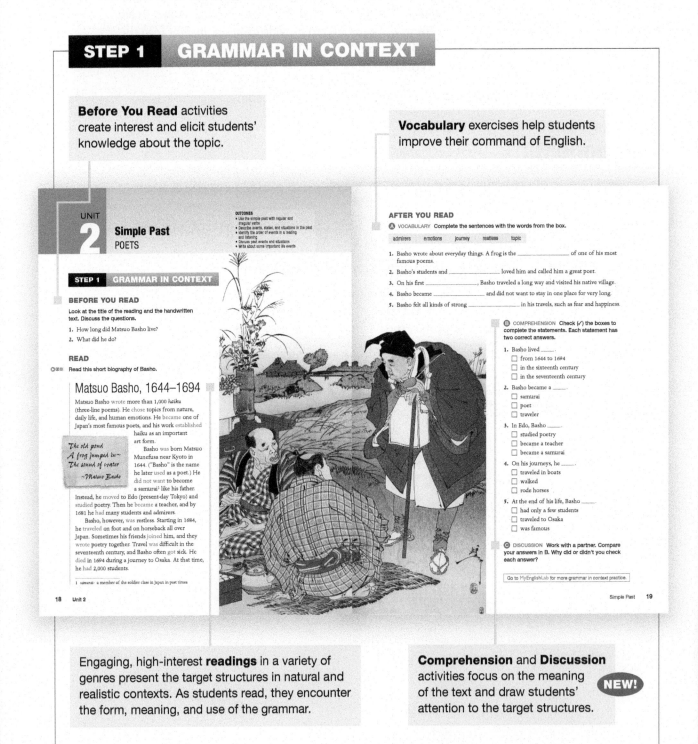

Engaging, high-interest **readings** in a variety of genres present the target structures in natural and realistic contexts. As students read, they encounter the form, meaning, and use of the grammar.

Comprehension and **Discussion** activities focus on the meaning of the text and draw students' attention to the target structures.

NEW!

Grammar Charts present the structures in a clear, easy-to-read format.

NEW!

The newly designed **Grammar Notes** highlight the main point of each note, making navigation and review easier. Simple corpus-informed **explanations** and **examples** ensure students' understanding.

STEP 2   GRAMMAR PRESENTATION

PRESENT PROGRESSIVE

Affirmative Statements

Subject	Be	Base Form of Verb + -ing	
I	am		
You	are		
He She It	is	traveling	now.
We You They	are		

Negative Statements

Subject	Be	Not	Base Form of Verb + -ing	
I	am			
He	is	not	traveling	now.
We	are			

Yes/No Questions

Be	Subject	Base Form of Verb + -ing	
Is	he	traveling	now?

Short Answers

Yes,	he	is.
No,		isn't.

Wh- Questions

Wh- Word	Be	Subject	Base Form of Verb + -ing	
Where	are	you	traveling	now?

SIMPLE PRESENT

Affirmative Statements

Subject		Verb
I You		travel.
He She It	often	travels.
We You They		travel.

Negative Statements

Subject	Do	Not	Base Form of Verb	
I	do			
He	does	not	travel	often.
We	do			

Yes/No Questions

Do	Subject	Base Form of Verb	
Does	he	travel	often?

Short Answers

Yes,	he	does.
No,		doesn't.

Wh- Questions

Wh- Word	Do	Subject		Base Form of Verb
Where	do	you	usually	travel?

GRAMMAR NOTES

1 Referring to Future Events

There are **several ways to refer to future events**. Sometimes only one form is appropriate, but in many cases more than one form is possible.

• be going to	They're going to have a meeting.
• will	I think I'll go. Will you be there?
• present progressive	It's taking place next week.
• simple present	It starts at 9:00 a.m. on Monday.

Past   **Now**   meeting   Future

2 Future Facts

For facts or events that you are **certain will happen in the future**, you can use *be going to* or *will*.

• be going to	The sun is going to rise at 6:43 tomorrow.
• will	The sun will rise at 6:43 tomorrow.

3 Predictions

For predictions about things you are **quite sure will happen in the future**, you can also use *be going to* or *will*.

• be going to	I think a lot of people are going to travel to space.
• will	I think a lot of people will travel to space.

USAGE NOTE We often use *I think* before a prediction.	*I think* tickets are going to get cheaper.
WRITING We use *will* more in formal writing and *be going to* more in conversation.	Prices will drop in time. *(formal writing)* Prices are going to drop in time. *(conversation)*
BE CAREFUL! Do not use *will* when something you notice right now makes you almost certain that an event is going to happen. Use *be going to*.	A: Look at that car! B: Oh, no. It's going to crash! NOT It'll crash.

4 Future Plans

For plans or things that are **already decided**, use *be going to* or the present progressive.

• be going to	I'm going to fly to Chicago next week.
• present progressive	I'm flying to Chicago next week. NOT I'll fly to Chicago next week.

USAGE NOTE We often use the **present progressive** for plans that are already arranged.	I'm flying to Chicago next week. I already have a ticket.
USAGE NOTE When the main verb is *go*, it is more common to use the **present progressive** (*be going*) than *be going to go*.	I'm going to Paris tomorrow. *(more common)* I'm going to go to Paris tomorrow. *(less common)*

NEW!

Clear signposting provides corpus-informed notes about common usage, differences between spoken and written registers, and common errors.

PRONUNCIATION NOTE

Pronunciation of Going to

In **informal conversation**, we often pronounce *going to* as "gonna."	A: What time are you **going to** be home? *(gonna)* B: I'm **going to** get home late. *(gonna)*
WRITING Sometimes people use *gonna* in informal notes, text messages, and email to friends.	Hi Lyn, I'm **gonna** be late. *(email)*
BE CAREFUL! Do not use *gonna* when you write to people you have a formal relationship with. Also do not use *gonna* in formal writing.	Professor, I'm **going to** be late. *(email)* NOT Professor, I'm gonna be late. According to scientists, Mars is **going to** become a tourist destination. *(paper)* NOT According to scientists, Mars is gonna become a tourist destination.

Pronunciation Notes are now included with the grammar presentation to highlight relevant pronunciation aspects of the target structures and to help students understand authentic spoken English.

NEW!

STEP 3 FOCUSED PRACTICE

Discover the Grammar activities develop students' recognition and understanding of the target structures before they are asked to produce them.

Controlled practice activities lead students to master form, meaning, and use of the target grammar.

STEP 3 FOCUSED PRACTICE

EXERCISE 1 DISCOVER THE GRAMMAR

GRAMMAR NOTES 1–7 Read this notice from a university bulletin board. Underline the adjectives and circle the adverbs. Then draw an arrow from the adjective or adverb to the word it is describing.

APARTMENT FOR RENT
140 Grant Street, Apt. 4B

Are you looking for a place to live? This amazing apartment is in a new building and has two large comfortable bedrooms and a small sunny kitchen. The building is very quiet—absolutely perfect for two serious students. It's near the campus on a peaceful street. There's convenient transportation. The bus stop is an easy, pleasant walk, and the express bus goes directly into town. You can run or ride your bike safely in nearby parks. The rent is very affordable. Small pets are welcome. The apartment is available on June 1. Interested students should call Megan at 555-5050. We're sure you'll be satisfied. Don't wait! This beautiful new apartment will rent fast. Nonsmokers, please.

EXERCISE 2 ADJECTIVE OR ADVERB

GRAMMAR NOTES 1–4 Circle the correct words to complete Maggie's email to her brother.

Hi Roger!

I wasn't sure I'd like living in a **large** / largely city, but I **real** / **really** love it! Maybe that's
because my **new** / newly neighborhood is located in such a **beautiful** / beautifully residential
area with lots of nice old trees.

Last Saturday, I worked **hard** / hardly and unpacked all my stuff. Then I spent Sunday
happy / happily exploring my new neighborhood. I couldn't believe the **gorgeous** / gorgeously
houses on these streets. I feel very **lucky** / luckily to live in one of them.

EXERCISE 2 COMPARISONS WITH *AS ... AS*

GRAMMAR NOTE 1 Look at the consumer magazine chart comparing three brands of pizza cheese. Complete the sentences. Use *(just) as ... as* or *not as ... as* and the correct form of the words in parentheses.

PIZZA CHEESE		Better ←→ Worse	
Brand	Price (per serving)	Taste	Smell
X	45¢	◑	●
Y	30¢	◑	◑
Z	30¢	○	◑

1. Brand Z ___is as expensive as or is just as expensive as___ Brand Y.
   (be / expensive)
2. Brand Y _____ Brand X.
   (be / expensive)
3. Brand X _____ Brand Y.
   (taste / good)
4. Brand Z _____ Brand Y.
   (taste / good)
5. Brand Y _____ Brand X.
   (smell / delicious)
6. Brand Y _____ Brand Z.
   (smell / delicious)

EXERCISE 3 COMPARISONS WITH *THAN*

GRAMMAR NOTES 2–3 Look at the menu on the next page. Then complete these sentences comparing items on the menu. Use the appropriate comparative form of the adjectives in parentheses and *than* where necessary.

1. The sweet-and-sour shrimp is ___more expensive than___ the steamed scallops.
   (expensive)
2. The beef with red pepper is _____ the beef with broccoli.
   (hot)
3. The pork with scallions is _____ the sweet-and-sour shrimp.
   (expensive)
4. The chicken with orange sauce is _____ the steamed scallops.
   (spicy)
5. The steamed vegetables are _____ the pork with scallions.
   (salty)
6. The steamed vegetables are _____ the beef with red pepper.
   (healthy)
7. The broccoli with garlic is _____ the chicken with broccoli.
   (cheap)
8. The shrimp dish is _____ the scallop dish.
   (sweet)

A **variety of exercise types** engage students and guide them from recognition and understanding to accurate production of the grammar structures.

Editing exercises allow students to identify and correct typical mistakes.

EXERCISE 8 EDITING

GRAMMAR NOTES 1–6 Read this student's report on space travel. There are eleven mistakes in the use of the future. The first mistake is already corrected. Find and correct ten more.

travel
Both astronauts and space tourists will ~~traveling~~ in space, but tourists is gonna have a much different experience. Space tourists is going to travel for fun, not for work. So, they will no have to worry about many of the technical problems that astronauts worry about. For example, space tourists will need not to figure out how to use tools without gravity. And they isn't going to go outside the spaceship to make repairs. For the most part, space tourists will just going to see the sights and have a good time.

Still, there will be similarities. Regular activities be the same for astronauts and space tourists. For example, eating, washing, and sleeping will turned into exciting challenges for everyone in space. And on long trips, everyone is going to doing exercises to stay fit in zero gravity. And both astronauts and space tourists will going to have many new adventures!

MyEnglishLab delivers rich online content to engage and motivate **students**.

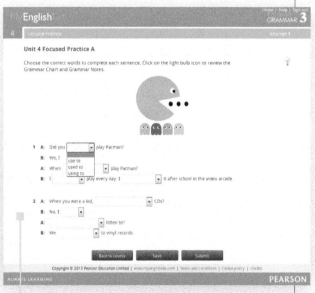

Grammar Coach videos give additional grammar presentations.

NEW!

MyEnglishLab provides students with:

- rich interactive practice in grammar, reading, listening, speaking, and writing
- immediate and meaningful feedback on wrong answers **NEW!**
- remediation activities
- grade reports that display performance and time on task

MyEnglishLab delivers innovative teaching tools and useful resources to **teachers**.

With **MyEnglishLab**, teachers can:

- view student scores by unit and activity
- monitor student progress on any activity or test
- analyze class data to determine steps for remediation and support

MyEnglishLab also provides teachers with:

- a digital copy of the student book for whole-class instruction
- downloadable assessments, including the placement test, that can be administered on MyEnglishLab or in print format
- printable resources including teaching notes, suggestions for teaching grammar, GSE mapping documents, answer keys, and audio scripts

Scope and Sequence

UNIT	GRAMMAR	READING
PART 1 **Present and Past**		
1 **Present Progressive and Simple Present** Page 4 THEME Different Cultures	■ Can tell when to use the present progressive and the simple present to distinguish actions that are ongoing and actions that are habitual ■ Can use non-action verbs to describe states and situations PRONUNCIATION *What do you* and *What are you*	Information Article: *What's Your Cross-Cultural IQ?* ■ Can derive the meaning of unknown words in a simple text ■ Can recognize the main points in a straightforward text on a familiar topic
2 **Simple Past** Page 14 THEME Poets	■ Can refer to past actions, states, or situations using regular and irregular past forms	Biography: *Matsuo Basho, 1644–1694* ■ Can follow chronological sequences in a short biography
3 **Past Progressive and Simple Past** Page 24 THEME Reporting Events	■ Can use the past progressive to focus on the duration of a past action ■ Can use the past progressive with the simple past to describe an action interrupted by another action	Newspaper Article: *Disaster at Sea* ■ Can follow chronological sequences in a short news article
4 ***Used to* and *Would*** Page 33 THEME Changes	■ Can use *used to* and *would* to refer to past habits and actions that are no longer happening and to convey contrast with the present	Information Article: *Dubai: Then and Now* ■ Can get the gist of a straightforward, familiar text about a popular location
5 **Wh- Questions** Page 42 THEME In Court	■ Can ask *wh-* questions about the past	Court Transcript: *State of Illinois v. Harry M. Adams* ■ Can scan an interview transcript for key information
PART 2 **The Future**		
6 **Future** Page 52 THEME Space Travel	■ Can use *be going to* and *will* to refer to future facts or predictions ■ Can use *be going to* and the present progressive to describe future plans ■ Can use *will* to express quick decisions, offers, and promises ■ Can use the simple present for scheduled events PRONUNCIATION *Going to* or *gonna*	Radio Program Transcript: *Space Tourism: Not Just Science Fiction* ■ Can identify relevant information in an interview transcript

PART **2** CONTINUES ▼

LISTENING	SPEAKING	WRITING	VOCABULARY
Interviews with foreign students ■ Can distinguish a present action from a habitual activity in short interviews	■ Can express beliefs and opinions about cultural topics and identify the opinions of others	■ Can write a basic description of a new experience, using a model for support if needed	abroad culture AWL distance (n) event misunderstanding native (adj)
An interview with a poet ■ Can recognize the main points of an interview that addresses familiar topics	■ Can convey simple biographical information to others, emphasizing the most important point	■ Can write a basic description of some important life events, using a model for support if needed	admirer emotion journey (n) restless topic AWL
A witness's description of a traffic accident ■ Can identify the main points of a description of an unfamiliar event	■ Can ask or answer questions about an unfamiliar event	■ Can write a basic description of an unfamiliar past event	alarmed area AWL calm (adj) disaster sink (v) survivor AWL
A conversation about the changes in a small town ■ Can distinguish present events from past events in a conversation on familiar topics	■ Can describe one's past and present physical appearance and habits	■ Can write a description of a place and how it has changed	destination major (adj) AWL popular revenue AWL traditional AWL transformation AWL
A conversation about a court trial ■ Can identify the main point of a conversation	■ Can ask and answer basic interview questions	■ Can write a series of interview questions that elicit information about a past event	defendant frightened in a hurry indicate AWL record (n)
Conversations about current situations and future plans ■ Can recognize main points of conversations on familiar topics ■ Can distinguish between actions happening now and future plans	■ Can ask and answer questions about plans and intentions ■ Can make future arrangements and plans with reference to a diary or schedule	■ Can write a paragraph about a prediction	edge (n) experience (v) incredible purchase (v) AWL sold out takeoff (n)

AWL = Academic Word List item

LISTENING	SPEAKING	WRITING	VOCABULARY
A conversation about future plans ■ Can follow chronological sequences in extended informal speech at natural speed	■ Can describe future plans and intentions ■ Can discuss the order of future events using future time clauses	■ Can write a description of future plans and goals ■ Can show the time order of future events	achieve AWL catalog (n) goal AWL interview (n) path
A job interview ■ Can determine the length of time of events mentioned in an interview	■ Can carry out a prepared, structured interview with some spontaneous follow-up questions	■ Can write a paragraph about a person's experience and accomplishments	consider oneself dramatically AWL opportunity positive AWL residence AWL support oneself
A conversation about plans for a party ■ Can recognize and discuss tasks on a to-do list or plan	■ Can discuss what has or hasn't happened in everyday plans	■ Can write a paragraph about a goal and the steps needed to reach it	available AWL organized (adj) professional (adj) AWL specific AWL successful
A conversation with a travel agent ■ Can identify the main points of a conversation about travel plans	■ Can briefly give explanations and reasons for opinions ■ Can ask and answer questions about past activities	■ Can write a paragraph in response to a quote from literature	adventure affordable ancient annual AWL survey (n) AWL transportation AWL
An interview with two college professors ■ Can establish the time frame of important details in an interview	■ Can discuss past events and experiences and provide necessary details about them	■ Can write a paragraph about a personal experience of failure and success	attitude AWL award (n) create AWL discouraged (adj) reject (v) AWL
Conversations about recent finished and unfinished activities ■ Can determine the time frame of main events in short conversations	■ Can express opinions and attitudes and give reasons and explanations for them	■ Can write an email or letter that describes one's recent activities, both finished and unfinished	climate design (v) AWL develop energy AWL expert AWL trend AWL

AWL = Academic Word List item

LISTENING	SPEAKING	WRITING	VOCABULARY
A job interview ■ Can identify important details in a job interview	■ Can compare and contrast alternatives about plans and activities ■ Can effectively participate in a classroom discussion about an academic topic	■ Can write a paragraph in response to a question about progress and aspirations	adult AWL advantage field (n) majority AWL research (n) AWL retired
Short conversations asking and giving permission ■ Can distinguish between whether permission was granted or refused in a short conversation	■ Can come to a resolution with others by asking for permission to do something	■ Can write a short note or email that explains a day-to-day situation and asks or responds to a request for permission to do something	annoyed assume AWL establish AWL gain (v) guidelines AWL presentation
Short conversations making and answering requests ■ Can identify details related to a schedule in a short conversation	■ Can create and discuss a daily schedule that involves making requests of others	■ Can write and respond to a request in a text or email message	appreciate AWL deliver distribute AWL respond AWL urgent
An excerpt from a radio call-in show ■ Can evaluate statements of advice from radio and television shows	■ Can express opinions in regard to possible solutions and provide brief reasons and explanations for them	■ Can write a basic email or letter of complaint and request the recipient to take action	avoid behavior communication AWL identity AWL normal AWL protect
A discussion about a list of items ■ Can identify details in a conversation about day-to-day topics	■ Can use turn-taking to maintain a discussion, while emphasizing one's own points	■ Can write a note or letter that lists and describes quantities of items	civilization impressed intentional interpret AWL occasion (n) purpose
Short conversations about books and video games ■ Can understand and interpret important details in basic conversations about day-to-day activities	■ Can summarize and give opinions on the moral of a fable	■ Can write a paragraph about a personal experience that illustrates the meaning of a moral	enormous AWL famous honest immediately wonderful

AWL = Academic Word List item

LISTENING	SPEAKING	WRITING	VOCABULARY
A conversation about online apartment ads ■ Can identify speakers' opinions in a short conversation about day-to-day topics	■ Can use a range of adjectives and adverbs to compare and describe different options for an ideal home	■ Can write a description of one's ideal home	absolutely convenient ideal located in AWL peaceful satisfied
A conversation about opinions on food ■ Can recognize speakers' preferences and opinions in a short conversation	■ Can make simple, direct comparisons between two things using common adjectives ■ Can briefly give reasons and explanations for opinions	■ Can write a paragraph that compares and contrasts foods from different cities or countries	crowded delicious evident AWL relaxed AWL varied AWL
A conversation about travel plans ■ Can identify places and locations by their descriptions	■ Can give opinions and answer questions about cities	■ Can write a detailed description of one's hometown or city	continent (n) dynamic AWL feature (n) AWL financial AWL multicultural public (adj)
A debate ■ Can recognize the main ideas of and opinions in a debate about familiar topics	■ Can express and respond to opinions about controversial topics	■ Can write arguments for and against a statement about an everyday topic	compete debate (n) AWL insult (n) require AWL source (n) AWL value (n)
A conversation about health advice ■ Can determine whether an action is recommended or not recommended	■ Can discuss one's health and exercise habits ■ Can conduct a survey and discuss results ■ Can discuss and give one's opinion on a controversial topic	■ Can write a short opinion essay about a controversial topic	approve of ban (v) illegal AWL in favor of permit (v) prohibit AWL

AWL = Academic Word List item

LISTENING	SPEAKING	WRITING	VOCABULARY
A casual conversation between two friends ■ Can recognize who is being asked to do an action in a conversation on an everyday topic	■ Can give an opinion in response to a literary quote ■ Can start and maintain a discussion about an abstract topic	■ Can write a paragraph on a personal topic using transition words to establish a time frame	appropriate (adj) AWL focus (v) AWL interact AWL participate in AWL significant (adj) AWL tend to
A TV ad ■ Can identify key details about products and recognize whether they are important or not	■ Can express and comment on ideas and suggestions in informal discussions about everyday objects	■ Can write a paragraph that weighs the pros and cons of a smart device	benefit (n) AWL combine (v) device AWL function (n) AWL multipurpose old-fashioned
An interview with a student about her study habits ■ Can identify key details in a recorded interview	■ Can give an opinion in response to a literary quote ■ Can express and comment on how to solve problems in an informal discussion	■ Can write several paragraphs that outline how to achieve one's goals	anxious discouraging (adj) project (n) AWL tactic task AWL universal

LISTENING	SPEAKING	WRITING	VOCABULARY
Workplace conversations ■ Can identify important information in everyday conversations	■ Can complete a questionnaire and discuss results ■ Can discuss illustrations using phrasal verbs	■ Can write an email or letter giving advice	fault (n) impact (v) AWL maintain AWL reaction AWL realize temporary AWL
Classroom conversations about a science class ■ Can recognize the main points of conversations and confirm their validity	■ Can express and comment on ideas and suggestions in informal discussions ■ Can discuss illustrations using phrasal verbs	■ Can write a paragraph in response to a specific question and support opinions with examples and observations	get by go on grow up pick out pick up take off

AWL = Academic Word List item

LISTENING	SPEAKING	WRITING	VOCABULARY
Conversations about driving ■ Can identify the main points of conversations about a familiar topic spoken in standard speech	■ Can recognize common signs and discuss their meaning ■ Can express personal obligations ■ Can discuss the rules and regulations of a public or private institution	■ Can write a paragraph describing rules or procedures for obtaining an official document	equipment AWL hassle (n) inspect AWL regulation AWL strict valid AWL
A radio show about etiquette and manners ■ Can identify details in recorded conversations	■ Can initiate and maintain a discussion about cultural customs	■ Can write a paragraph about a life event in a specific culture	definite AWL familiar issue (n) AWL norm AWL rude sense (v)
A weather forecast ■ Can understand the probability of a situation in a report about a familiar topic	■ Can give a short, rehearsed talk or presentation on a familiar topic ■ Can describe future plans and intentions in detail and give degrees of probability that something will happen	■ Can write short emails or letters that express the probability of future plans	affect (v) AWL exceed AWL forecast (n) local (adj) region AWL
A conversation about a mystery ■ Can recognize the key events in a short conversation and identify the certainty of each speaker about the events	■ Can draw conclusions about everyday objects and situations	■ Can write a paragraph about a short story and draw possible conclusions	advertisement amazed method AWL position (n) salary

AWL = Academic Word List item

About the Authors

Marjorie Fuchs has taught ESL at New York City Technical College and LaGuardia Community College of the City University of New York and EFL at Sprachstudio Lingua Nova in Munich, Germany. She has a master's degree in Applied English Linguistics and a certificate in TESOL from the University of Wisconsin-Madison. She has authored and co-authored many widely used books and multimedia materials, notably *Crossroads 4*; *Top Twenty ESL Word Games: Beginning Vocabulary Development*; *Families: Ten Card Games for Language Learners*; *Focus on Grammar 3* and *4* (editions 1–5); *Focus on Grammar 3* and *4, CD-ROM*; *Longman English Interactive 3* and *4*; *Grammar Express Basic*; *Grammar Express Basic CD-ROM*; *Grammar Express Intermediate*; *Future 1: English for Results*; *OPD Workplace Skills Builder*; workbooks for *Crossroads 1–4*; *The Oxford Picture Dictionary High Beginning* and *Low Intermediate*, (editions 1–3); *Focus on Grammar 3* and *4* (editions 1–5); and *Grammar Express Basic*.

Margaret Bonner has taught ESL at Hunter College and the Borough of Manhattan Community College of the City University of New York, at Taiwan National University in Taipei, and at Virginia Commonwealth University in Richmond. She holds a master's degree in library science from Columbia University, and she has done work toward a PhD in English literature at the Graduate Center of the City University of New York. She has authored and co-authored numerous ESL and EFL print and multimedia materials, including textbooks for the national school system of Oman; *Step into Writing: A Basic Writing Text*; *Focus on Grammar 3* and *4* (editions 1–5); *Focus on Grammar 4 Workbook* (editions 1–5); *Grammar Express Basic*; *Grammar Express Basic CD-ROM*; *Grammar Express Basic Workbook*; *Grammar Express Intermediate*; *Focus on Grammar 3* and *4, CD-ROM*; *Longman English Interactive 4*; and *The Oxford Picture Dictionary Low Intermediate Workbook* (editions 1–3).

Miriam Westheimer taught EFL at all levels of instruction in Haifa, Israel, for a period of six years. She has also taught ESL at Queens College, at LaGuardia Community College, and in the American Language Program of Columbia University. She holds a master's degree in TESOL and a doctorate in Curriculum and Teaching from Teachers College of Columbia University. She is the co-author of a communicative grammar program developed and widely used in Israel.

Acknowledgments

Before acknowledging the many people who have contributed to the fifth edition of *Focus on Grammar*, we wish to express our gratitude to the following people who worked on the previous editions and whose influence is still present in the new work: **Joanne Dresner**, who initiated the project and helped conceptualize the general approach of *Focus on Grammar*; our editors for the first four editions: **Nancy Perry**, **Penny Laporte**, **Louisa Hellegers**, **Joan Saslow**, **Laura LeDrean**, **Debbie Sistino**, and **Françoise Leffler**; and **Sharon Hilles**, our grammar consultant for the first edition.

In the fifth edition, *Focus on Grammar* has continued to evolve as we update materials and respond to valuable feedback from teachers and students who use the series. We are grateful to the following editors and colleagues:

- **Gosia Jaros-White** for overseeing with skill and sensitivity a complex series while never losing sight of the individual components or people involved in the project. She offered concrete and practical advice and was always mindful of learners' needs.

- **Bernard Seal**, of Page Designs International, who joined the *Focus on Grammar* team with a great deal of experience, expertise, energy, and enthusiasm. With his hands-on approach, he was involved in every aspect of the project. He read all manuscript, raising pertinent questions and offering sage advice.

- **Don Williams**, also of Page Designs International, for creating a fresh, new look, which is as user-friendly as it is attractive.

- **Françoise Leffler**, our editor *extraordinaire*, with whom we had the great fortune and pleasure of being able to continue our long collaboration. She provided both continuity and a fresh eye as she delved into another edition of the series, advising us on all things—from the small details to the big picture.

- Series co-authors **Irene Schoenberg** and **Jay Maurer** for their suggestions and support, and Irene for sharing her experience in teaching with earlier editions of this book.

- **Jane Curtis** for her advice founded in many years of teaching with the series.

- **Julie Schmidt** for her helpful presentation of information that was easy to understand and use.

- **Sharon Goldstein** for her insightful and practical suggestions, delivered with wisdom and wit.

- **Cindy Davis** for her classroom-based recommendations at the very beginning of this edition.

Special thanks to **Dr. Eloy Rodriguez** of Cornell University for generously providing us with photos to accompany the unit which features his research on zoopharmacognosy.

Finally, as always, Marjorie thanks **Rick Smith** for his unswerving support and excellent suggestions. He was a steadfast beacon of light as we navigated our way through our fifth *FOG*.

MF and MB

To the memory of my parents, Edith and Joseph Fuchs—MF

To my parents, Marie and Joseph Maus, and to my son, Luke Frances—MB

Reviewers

We are grateful to the following reviewers for their many helpful comments:

Susanna Aramyan, Glendale Community College, Glendale, CA; **Homeretta Ayala**, Baltimore Co. Schools, Baltimore, MD; **Barbara Barrett**, University of Miami, Miami, FL; **Rebecca Beck**, Irvine Valley College, Irvine, CA; **Crystal Bock Thiessen**, University of Nebraska-PIESL, Lincoln, NE; **Janna Brink**, Mt. San Antonio College, Walnut, CA; **Erin Butler**, University of California, Riverside, CA; **Joice Cain**, Fullerton College, Fullerton, CA; **Shannonine M. Caruana**, Hudson County Community College, Jersey City, NJ; **Tonya Cobb**, Cypress College, Cypress, CA; **David Cooke**, Mt. San Antonio College, Walnut, CA; **Lindsay Donigan**, Fullerton College, Fullerton, CA; **Mila Dragushanskya**, ASA College, New York, NY; **Jill Fox**, University of Nebraska, Lincoln, NE; **Katalin Gyurindak**, Mt. San Antonio College, Walnut, CA; **Karen Hamilton**, Glendale Community College, Glendale, CA; **Electra Jablons**, International English Language Institute, Hunter College, New York, NY; **Eva Kozlenko**, Hudson County Community College, Jersey City, NJ; **Esther Lee**, American Language Program, California State University, Fullerton, CA; **Yenlan Li**, American Language Program, California State University, Fullerton, CA; **Shirley Lundblade**, Mt. San Antonio College, Walnut, CA; **Thi Thi Ma**, Los Angeles City College, Los Angeles, CA; **Marilyn Martin**, Mt. San Antonio College, Walnut, CA; **Eve Mazereeuw**, University of Guelph English Language Programs, Guelph, Ontario, Canada; **Robert Mott**, Glendale Community College, Glendale, CA; **Wanda Murtha**, Glendale Community College, Glendale, CA; **Susan Niemeyer**, Los Angeles City College, Los Angeles, CA; **Wayne Pate**, Tarrant County College, Fort Worth, TX; **Genevieve Patthey-Chavez**, Los Angeles City College, Los Angeles, CA; **Robin Persiani**, Sierra College, Rocklin, CA; **Denise Phillips**, Hudson County Community College, Jersey City, NJ; **Anna Powell**, American Language Program, California State University, Fullerton, CA; **JoAnna Prado**, Sacramento City Community College, Sacramento, CA; **Mark Rau**, American River College, Sacramento, CA; **Madeleine Schamehorn**, University of California, Riverside, CA; **Richard Skinner**, Hudson County Community College, Jersey City, NJ; **Heather Snavely**, American Language Program, California State University, Fullerton, CA; **Gordana Sokic**, Douglas College, Westminster, British Columbia, Canada; **Lee Spencer**, International English Language Institute, Hunter College, New York, NY; **Heather Stern**, Irvine Valley College, Irvine, CA; **Susan Stern**, Irvine Valley College, Irvine, CA; **Andrea Sunnaa**, Mt. San Antonio College, Walnut, CA; **Margaret Teske**, Mt. San Antonio College, Walnut, CA; **Johanna Van Gendt**, Hudson County Community College, Jersey City, NJ; **Daniela C. Wagner-Loera**, University of Maryland, College Park, MD; **Tamara Williams**, University of Guelph, English Language Programs, Guelph, Ontario, Canada; **Saliha Yagoubi**, Hudson County Community College, Jersey City, NJ; **Pat Zayas**, Glendale Community College, Glendale, CA

Credits

Present and Past

PART 1

OUTCOMES
- Describe actions that are happening now
- Describe actions, states, and situations that happen regularly, and unchanging facts
- Recognize the use of the present progressive and the simple present in reading and listening
- Express opinions about topics related to cross-cultural differences
- Write a description of a new experience

OUTCOMES
- Use the simple past with regular and irregular verbs
- Describe events, states, and situations in the past
- Identify the order of events in a reading and listening
- Discuss past events and situations
- Write about some important life events

OUTCOMES
- Describe past events or situations
- Use *when* or *while* to link clauses in the simple past and the past progressive
- Identify the order of events in a description of an accident
- Report on events that were interrupted by other events
- Write a description of a past event

OUTCOMES
- Describe past habits and situations, using *used to* and *would*
- Evaluate events and situations described in a reading and a listening
- Describe and discuss one's past and present physical appearance and habits
- Write a description of a place and how it has changed

OUTCOMES
- Ask questions about the past, using *wh-* words
- Identify important information in an interview transcript
- Identify the main point of a conversation
- Write a series of interview questions to get information about a past event

UNIT 1

Present Progressive and Simple Present
DIFFERENT CULTURES

OUTCOMES
- Describe actions that are happening now
- Describe actions, states, and situations that happen regularly, and unchanging facts
- Recognize the use of the present progressive and the simple present in reading and listening
- Express opinions about topics related to cross-cultural differences
- Write a description of a new experience

STEP 1   GRAMMAR IN CONTEXT

BEFORE YOU READ

Look at the cartoons. Discuss the questions.

1. What are the people doing?
2. How do they feel?

READ

01|01   Read this article about cross-cultural communication.

What's Your Cross-Cultural IQ?[1]

Are you living in your native country or in another country? Do you ever travel abroad? Do you understand the misunderstandings in these two situations?

Situation 1

Jason is standing at Dan's door. He thinks he's on time for the party, but he doesn't see any guests, and Dan is wearing shorts and a T-shirt! Dan looks surprised. In his culture, people never arrive at the exact start of a social event. They often come at least 30 minutes later.

> It's 8:00. Why is he wearing shorts and a T-shirt? Is this the wrong day? I don't understand!

PARTY Friday
8:00–Midnight
63 Oak Street

> What is he doing here now? It's only 8:00!

---

1 *What's your cross-cultural IQ?:* How much do you know about other people's cultures?

4   Unit 1

Why is she
standing so close
to me? I feel like
I have no room
to breathe!

What's the matter?[2]
Why is Ina moving
away from me?
Maybe she doesn't
like my perfume![3]

Situation 2

Ina and Marty are talking.
They are both feeling very
uncomfortable. In Marty's
culture, people usually
stand quite close. This
seems friendly to them.
In Ina's culture, people
prefer to have more
distance between them.
This doesn't mean they
are unfriendly.

2 *What's the matter?*: What's wrong?
3 *perfume:* a liquid with a strong pleasant smell that you put on your skin

AFTER YOU READ

A VOCABULARY Choose the word or phrase that is closest in meaning to the word in **bold**.

1. Are you living in your **native** country?
   a. first   **b.** new   **c.** favorite

2. Do you ever travel **abroad**?
   a. by boat   **b.** to foreign countries   **c.** on expensive trips

3. What was the **misunderstanding** about?
   a. fight   **b.** argument   **c.** confusion

4. They come from different **cultures**.
   a. schools   **b.** climates   **c.** ways of life

5. They prefer to have more **distance** between them.
   a. streets   **b.** space   **c.** time

6. There are a lot of parties and other **events** at the Students' Club.
   a. members   **b.** languages   **c.** activities

B COMPREHENSION Complete each statement with the correct name.

1. _____ doesn't have shoes on.

2. _____ isn't expecting people to arrive at 8:00.

3. _____ thinks he's on time.

4. _____ is wearing perfume.

5. _____ wants to stand farther away.

6. _____ probably thinks the other person is a little unfriendly.

C DISCUSSION Work with a partner. Compare your answers in B. Why did you choose
each answer?

PRESENT PROGRESSIVE

Affirmative Statements

Subject	Be	Base Form of Verb + -ing	
I	am		
You	are		
He She It	is	traveling	now.
We You They	are		

Negative Statements

Subject	Be	Not	Base Form of Verb + -ing	
I	am			
He	is	not	traveling	now.
We	are			

Yes/No Questions

Be	Subject	Base Form of Verb + -ing	
Is	he	traveling	now?

Short Answers

Yes,	he	is.
No,		isn't.

Wh- Questions

Wh-Word	Be	Subject	Base Form of Verb + -ing	
Where	are	you	traveling	now?

SIMPLE PRESENT

Affirmative Statements

Subject		Verb
I You		travel.
He She It	often	travels.
We You They		travel.

Negative Statements

Subject	Do	Not	Base Form of Verb	
I	do			
He	does	not	travel	often.
We	do			

Yes/No Questions

Do	Subject	Base Form of Verb	
Does	he	travel	often?

Short Answers

Yes,	he	does.
No,		doesn't.

Wh- Questions

Wh-Word	Do	Subject		Base Form of Verb
Where	do	you	usually	travel?

GRAMMAR NOTES

1 Present Progressive

Use the present progressive to show that something is **happening now** or **in a longer present time**.

• **happening now** (right now, at the moment) 	Diego **is speaking** English *now*. He**'s wearing** shorts *at the moment*.
• **happening in a longer present time** (this month, this year, these days, nowadays), even if it's not happening now 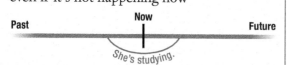	We**'re studying** U.S. history *this month*. *(But we aren't studying it now.)* Laura**'s studying** in France *this year*. **Are** you **studying** hard *these days*?

2 Simple Present

Use the simple present to show that something **happens regularly** or for **unchanging facts**.

• **happens regularly** (usually, often, every day, always) 	Diego *usually* **speaks** Spanish. He **wears** jeans *every day*.
• **unchanging facts**	Miguel **comes** from Oaxaca. Oaxaca **is** in Mexico.
BE CAREFUL! Remember to add *-s* or *-es* to third-person-singular (*he, she, it*) verbs. Also, remember to use *does* in questions and *doesn't* in negatives for third-person-singular verbs.	He **wears** jeans. He **doesn't wear** shorts. NOT He ~~wear~~ jeans. He ~~don't~~ wear shorts.

3 Simple Present + Adverbs of Frequency

Use the simple present with adverbs of frequency to show **how often something happens**.

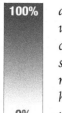 100% *always* *usually* *often / frequently* *sometimes* *rarely / seldom* *hardly ever* 0% *never*	In Spain, women *always* **kiss** on both cheeks. In France, women *often* **kiss** on both cheeks. We *rarely* **stand** very close to each other. In China, children *never* **call** adults by their first names.
Adverbs of frequency usually go **before the verb**. However, *sometimes* and *usually* can also go at the **beginning of the sentence**.	I *sometimes* **wear** shorts at home. or *Sometimes* I **wear** shorts at home.
BE CAREFUL! Adverbs of frequency usually go **after** the verb *be*.	They **are** *never* late. NOT They ~~never are~~ late.

4 Non-Action Verbs

Use non-action verbs to describe **states** or **situations**, but not actions.

Non-action verbs describe:

• **emotions** (like, love, hate, want, feel, fear, trust)	We **like** Claude a lot. We **love** the stories he tells.
• **mental states** (know, remember, believe, think, mean, understand, wonder)	I **know** a lot of U.S. customs now. We **think** they're from Spain. What **do** you **mean**? I **don't understand**.
• **possession** (have, own, possess, belong)	Cesar **has** two brothers. Some students **own** cars.
• **senses** and **perceptions** (hear, see, smell, taste, feel, notice, seem, look, be, appear, sound)	I **hear** the telephone. Dina **looks** tired. They both **sound** sick.

BE CAREFUL! Use the **simple present** with most **non-action verbs**. Do not use the present progressive—even when the verb describes a situation that exists at the moment of speaking.	Jane **wants** to go home now. NOT Jane is wanting to go home now.
USAGE NOTE In **informal conversation**, some people use the **present progressive** with verbs of emotion (especially with *like* and *love*) and with verbs of mental state. This often describes a **temporary feeling** or a change of feelings.	I**'m loving** this book! She**'s liking** him more and more. He**'s understanding** a lot better these days.

5 Non-Action and Action Verbs

Some verbs can have both a **non-action** and an **action** meaning.

	NON-ACTION	ACTION
• **sense and perception verbs** (taste, smell, feel, and look)	The soup **tastes** good. (It's good.)	He**'s tasting** the soup. (He's trying it.)
	His car **looks** great. (It's beautiful.)	I**'m looking** at his car. (I'm examining it.)
• *have* and *think*	I **have** a new watch. (I own a new watch.)	I**'m having** fun. (I'm experiencing fun.)
	I **think** he's right. (My opinion: He's right.)	I**'m thinking** of going. (I'm considering going.)

USAGE NOTE We often use *feel* in the progressive form when it expresses an **emotion**. The **meaning is the same** as when we use the simple present form.	I **feel** very happy about this. or I**'m feeling** very happy about this.

PRONUNCIATION NOTE

01|02

Pronunciation of *What do you* and *What are you*

In informal American English conversation, people often pronounce *What do you . . . ?* and *What are you . . . ?* the same way: "whaddaya."	A: **What do you** do? *(whaddaya)* B: **What are you** doing? *(whaddaya)*

REFERENCE NOTES

For **spelling rules** on forming the **present progressive**, see Appendix 21 on page 330.

For **spelling rules** on forming the third-person singular of the **simple present**, see Appendix 20 on page 329.

For **pronunciation rules** for the **simple present**, see Appendix 29 on page 334.

For **contractions** of *I am, you are,* etc., see Appendix 26 on page 332.

For a list of **non-action verbs**, see Appendix 2 on page 322.

For the **present progressive** and the **simple present** to talk about the **future**, see Unit 6 on page 54.

STEP 3   FOCUSED PRACTICE

EXERCISE 1 DISCOVER THE GRAMMAR

GRAMMAR NOTES 1–5 Read the postings by Brian, a Canadian student studying in Argentina. Underline all the verbs that describe what is happening now. Circle the verbs that describe what regularly happens.

JUNE 30: 7:30 p.m. My host parents are still working. Carlos, my "father," works at home. My "little brother," Ricardo, is cute. He looks (and acts) a lot like Bobby. Right now, he's looking over my shoulder and trying to read my journal.

JULY 4: The weather is cold here in the summer. I usually spend the first weekend of July at the beach. Today, I'm walking around in a heavy sweater.

JULY 10: I'm sitting in the school cafeteria with some of my classmates. In Canada, I only drink tea, but at the moment I'm having a cup of strong coffee. It tastes great! The students here come from all over the world. Most of them don't speak English, so we're all speaking Spanish. It's a great way to learn!

AUGUST 6: I usually feel great in the evening, but tonight I feel really tired.

AUGUST 25: I'm feeling very comfortable here now—but it's almost time to go home! My host parents usually cook a light dinner, but tonight is a special event. They're preparing a big party for me to say goodbye. I miss them already!

EXERCISE 2 PRESENT PROGRESSIVE OR SIMPLE PRESENT

A GRAMMAR NOTES 1–5 Some students are talking outside of a classroom. Circle the correct words to complete their conversations.

Conversation 1

TARO: There's Miguel. He talks /(He's talking)to Luisa.
1.

MARISA: Yes. They take / They're taking a class together this semester.
2.

TARO: They stand / They're standing very close to each other.
3.

Do you think / Are you thinking that they date / they're dating?
4.   5.

MARISA: No. I don't think / I'm not thinking that it means / it's meaning
6.   7.

anything special. I come / I'm coming from Costa Rica, and people
8.

usually stand / are standing that close to each other there.
9.

Conversation 2

LI-WU: Hi, Paulo. What do you do / are you doing?
1.

PAULO: Oh, I wait / I'm waiting for class to begin.
2.

LI-WU: What's the matter? You seem / You're seeming a little down.
3.

PAULO: I'm just tired. I work / I'm working evenings this semester. Hey, is
4.

that your teacher over there?

LI-WU: Yes. She talks / She's talking to a classmate.
5.

PAULO: What's wrong? He doesn't look / He's not looking at her.
6.

He seems / He's seeming uncomfortable.
7.

LI-WU: Oh. That doesn't mean / isn't meaning anything. In some countries,
8.

it's not polite to look directly at your teacher.

01|03 **B** LISTEN AND CHECK Listen to the conversations and check your answers in A.

EXERCISE 3 QUESTIONS AND STATEMENTS

A GRAMMAR NOTES 1–5 Other students are talking outside of a classroom. Complete the conversations. Use the present progressive or the simple present form of the verbs in parentheses.

Conversation 1

RASHA: There's Hans. Why _____*is*_____ he _____*walking*_____ so fast?
1. (walk)

Class _____ at 9:00. He still _____ 10 minutes!
2. (start)   3. (have)

CLAUDE: He always _____ fast. I _____ Swiss people
4. (walk)   5. (think)

often _____ to be in a hurry.
6. (appear)

Conversation 2

IZUMI: Isn't that Sergio and Luis? Why

_____ they _____
                                 1. (shake)

hands? They already _____ each other!
                           2. (know)

LI-JING: In Brazil, men _____ hands every time they
                           3. (shake)

_____ . It's normal in their culture.
          4. (meet)

IZUMI: _____ women _____ hands, too?
                                  5. (shake)

▷01|04   **B** **LISTEN AND CHECK** Listen to the conversations and check your answers in A.

EXERCISE 4 AFFIRMATIVE AND NEGATIVE STATEMENTS

GRAMMAR NOTES 1–2, 5 Look at Brian's schedule in Argentina. He usually has a regular schedule, but today some things are different. Complete the sentences. Use the present progressive or the simple present. Choose between affirmative and negative.

7:00–8:00	~~run in the park~~	_get ready for a field trip_
8:30–12:30	~~attend class~~	_go on a field trip to the museum_
1:00–2:00	eat lunch	
2:00–3:00	~~study with my classmates~~	_work on the family web page_
3:00–5:00	work in the cafeteria	
5:00–6:30	~~do homework~~	_play tennis_
6:30–8:30	~~play tennis~~	_watch a DVD with Eva_
8:30–9:30	have dinner	
9:30–10:00	~~send emails~~	_take a walk with the family_
10:00–10:30	~~take a shower~~	_do homework_

1. Brian always _runs in the park_ _____ early in the morning,

but today he _is getting ready for a field trip_ _____ .

2. Brian usually _____ between 8:30 and 12:30,

but today he _____ .

3. He always _____ between 1:00 and 2:00.

4. It's 1:30. He _____ .

5. He normally _____ after lunch,

but today he _____ .

6. Every day from 3:00 to 5:00, he _____ .

7. It's 5:15, but he _____ now.

He _____ instead.

8. It's 6:45, but he _____ .

He _____ .

9. It's 8:30. Brian _____ .

10. He always _____ at 8:30.

11. After dinner, Brian usually _____ ,

but tonight he _____ .

12. It's 10:15, but he _____ .

He _____ .

EXERCISE 5 EDITING

GRAMMAR NOTES 1–5 **Read this student's blog entry. There are eleven mistakes in the use of the present progressive or simple present. The first mistake is already corrected. Find and correct ten more.**

I'm sitting
It's 12:30 and ~~I sit~~ in the library right now. My

classmates are eating lunch together, but I don't

feel hungry yet. At home, we eat never this

early. Today, our journal topic is culture shock

(the strange feelings you have when you visit a

foreign country for the first time). It's a good

topic for me right now because I'm being pretty

homesick. I miss speaking my native language

with my friends. And I miss my old routine. At

home, we always are eating a big meal at 2:00

in the afternoon. Then we rest. But here in Toronto, I'm having a 3:00 conversation class. Every day, I

almost fall asleep in class, and my teacher ask me, "Are you bored?" Of course I'm not bored. I just need my afternoon nap! This class always is fun. This semester, we work on a project with videos. My team is filming groups of people from different cultures at social events. We are analyze "personal space." That is meaning how close to each other these people stand. According to my new watch, it's 12:55, and I have a 1:00 class. That's all for now. Teachers here really aren't liking lateness!

Simple Past
POETS

OUTCOMES
• Use the simple past with regular and
  irregular verbs
• Describe events, states, and situations in the past
• Identify the order of events in a reading
  and listening
• Discuss past events and situations
• Write about some important life events

| STEP 1 | GRAMMAR IN CONTEXT |

BEFORE YOU READ

Look at the title of the reading and the handwritten
text. Discuss the questions.

1. How long did Matsuo Basho live?

2. What did he do?

READ

▶02|01 Read this short biography of Basho.

Matsuo Basho, 1644–1694

Matsuo Basho wrote more than 1,000 *haiku*
(three-line poems). He chose topics from nature,
daily life, and human emotions. He became one of
Japan's most famous poets, and his work established
haiku as an important
art form.

> The old pond
> A frog jumped in—
> The sound of water
>
> ~Matsuo Basho

Basho was born Matsuo
Munefusa near Kyoto in
1644. ("Basho" is the name
he later used as a poet.) He
did not want to become
a samurai[1] like his father.
Instead, he moved to Edo (present-day Tokyo) and
studied poetry. Then he became a teacher, and by
1681 he had many students and admirers.

Basho, however, was restless. Starting in 1684,
he traveled on foot and on horseback all over
Japan. Sometimes his friends joined him, and they
wrote poetry together. Travel was difficult in the
seventeenth century, and Basho often got sick. He
died in 1694 during a journey to Osaka. At that time,
he had 2,000 students.

---

1 *samurai:* a member of the soldier class in Japan in past times

AFTER YOU READ

A VOCABULARY **Complete the sentences with the words from the box.**

admirers	emotions	journey	restless	topic

1. Basho wrote about everyday things. A frog is the _____ of one of his most famous poems.

2. Basho's students and _____ loved him and called him a great poet.

3. On his first _____, Basho traveled a long way and visited his native village.

4. Basho became _____ and did not want to stay in one place for very long.

5. Basho felt all kinds of strong _____ in his travels, such as fear and happiness.

B COMPREHENSION **Check (✓) the boxes to complete the statements. Each statement has two correct answers.**

1. Basho lived _____.
   - ☐ from 1644 to 1694
   - ☐ in the sixteenth century
   - ☐ in the seventeenth century

2. Basho became a _____.
   - ☐ samurai
   - ☐ poet
   - ☐ traveler

3. In Edo, Basho _____.
   - ☐ studied poetry
   - ☐ became a teacher
   - ☐ became a samurai

4. On his journeys, he _____.
   - ☐ traveled in boats
   - ☐ walked
   - ☐ rode horses

5. At the end of his life, Basho _____.
   - ☐ had only a few students
   - ☐ traveled to Osaka
   - ☐ was famous

C DISCUSSION **Work with a partner. Compare your answers in B. Why did or didn't you check each answer?**

STEP 2   GRAMMAR PRESENTATION

SIMPLE PAST: *BE*

Affirmative Statements

Subject	*Be*	
I	**was**	
You	**were**	
He She It	**was**	famous.
We You They	**were**	

Negative Statements

Subject	*Be + Not*	
I	**wasn't**	
You	**weren't**	
He She It	**wasn't**	famous.
We You They	**weren't**	

Yes/No Questions

Be	Subject	
Was	I	
Were	you	
Was	he she it	famous?
Were	we you they	

Short Answers

Affirmative			
Yes,	you	**were.**	
	I	**was.**	
	he she it	**was.**	
	you we they	**were.**	

Negative			
No,	you	**weren't.**	
	I	**wasn't.**	
	he she it	**wasn't.**	
	you we they	**weren't.**	

Wh- Questions

Wh- Word	*Be*	Subject	
Where When Why	**was**	I	
	were	you	
	was	he she it	famous?
	were	we you they	

SIMPLE PAST: REGULAR AND IRREGULAR VERBS

Affirmative Statements

Subject	Verb	
I You He She	**moved** **traveled**	to Japan.
It We You They	**came** **left**	in 2012.

Negative Statements

Subject	*Did not*	Base Form of Verb	
I You He She It We You They	**didn't**	**move** **travel**	to Japan.
		come **leave**	in 2012.

Yes/No Questions

Did	Subject	Base Form of Verb	
Did	I you he she it we you they	**move** **travel**	to Japan?
		come **leave**	in 2012?

Short Answers

Affirmative		
Yes,	you I he she it you we they	**did**.

Negative		
No,	you I he she it you we they	**didn't**.

Wh- Questions

Wh- Word	*Did*	Subject	Base Form of Verb	
When Why	**did**	I you he she it we you they	**move** **travel**	to Japan?
			come? **leave?**	

GRAMMAR NOTES

1 Simple Past

Use the simple past to show that an action, state, or situation is **finished**.

Past — ✕ — Now ┃ — Future He was a poet.	Basho **lived** in the 17th century. He **was** a poet. He **wrote** haiku. He **didn't stay** in one place. Where **did** he **travel**?

2 Simple Past + Past Time Expressions

We often use the simple past with past time expressions.

Some examples of **past time expressions** are:

• *yesterday*	**Yesterday**, I **wrote** my first poem.
• *last week*	**Last week**, I **read** a poem by Basho.
• *300 years ago*	He **died** more than **300 years ago**.
• *in the 17th century*	He **lived** *in the 17th century*.
• *by 1681*	**By 1681**, he **had** many students.

3 Regular Verbs

Form the simple past of regular verbs by **adding -*d*** or **-*ed*** to the base form of the verb.

	BASE FORM		SIMPLE PAST
• adding -*d*	live	→	liv**ed**
• adding -*ed*	want	→	want**ed**
IN WRITING There are often **spelling changes** when you add -*ed* to the verb.	study	→	stud**ied**
	plan	→	plan**ned**

4 Irregular Verbs

Many common verbs are irregular. Do not form their simple past by adding -*d* or -*ed* to the base form of the verb.

	BASE FORM	SIMPLE PAST	BASE FORM	SIMPLE PAST
The list to the right includes the **most common irregular verbs**. They are especially common in conversation.	be →	**was/were**	know →	**knew**
	come →	**came**	make →	**made**
	get →	**got**	mean →	**meant**
	give →	**gave**	say →	**said**
	go →	**went**	see →	**saw**
	have →	**had**	think →	**thought**

	BASE FORM	SIMPLE PAST
USAGE NOTE Some verbs have **two simple past forms**—one **regular** and one **irregular**. In conversation, the irregular past form is more common. There is one exception: for *dream*, the regular form is more common.	kneel →	kneel**ed**/**knelt**
	light →	light**ed**/**lit**
	dream →	dream**ed**/**dreamt**
USAGE NOTE A few verbs have **two irregular simple past forms**.	forbid →	**forbade/forbid**
	sink →	**sank/sunk**

REFERENCE NOTES

For **spelling rules** for the **simple past of regular verbs**, see Appendix 22 on page 330.
For **pronunciation rules** for the **simple past of regular verbs**, see Appendix 30 on page 335.
For a list of **irregular verbs**, see Appendix 1 on page 321.

STEP 3 FOCUSED PRACTICE

EXERCISE 1 DISCOVER THE GRAMMAR

GRAMMAR NOTES 1–4 Read more about Basho. Underline all the regular simple past verbs. Circle all the irregular simple past verbs. Then complete the timeline on the right.

As the son of a samurai, Basho (grew up) in the household of Todo Yoshitada, a young lord. After his father's death in 1656, Basho stayed in the Yoshitada household. He and Todo wrote poetry together, and in 1664, they published some poems. Two years later, Todo died suddenly. Basho left the area.

Basho was a restless young man, and he moved around for several years. In the 1670s, he went to Edo and stayed there. He found friendship and success once again. Basho judged poetry contests, published his own poetry, and taught students. His students built him a home outside the city in 1681. They planted a banana tree (*basho* in Japanese) in front and called his home "Basho Hut." That is how the poet got his name: Basho.

In spite of this success, Basho became unhappy. He often wrote about loneliness. He dreamed of traveling. His mother died in 1683, and he began his travels a year later. His trip to the northern part of Honshu in 1689 was difficult, but his travel diary about this journey, *Narrow Road to the Deep North*, became one of Japan's greatest works of literature.

As a famous poet, Basho had many visitors—too many, in fact. In 1693 he locked his gate for a month, stayed alone, and wrote. The following year, he took his final journey, to Osaka. He died there among his friends and admirers.

1644	Basho was born.
_1656_	Basho's father died.
1664	_Basho (and Todo) published some poems._
1666	_____
_____	Students built the Basho Hut.
1683	_____
1684	_____
_____	Basho traveled to northern Honshu.
_____	Basho locked his gate to visitors.
1694	_____

EXERCISE 2 AFFIRMATIVE STATEMENTS

GRAMMAR NOTES 1–4 Complete this biography of American poet Emily Dickinson. Use the simple past form of the verbs in parentheses. See Appendix 1 on page 453 for help with the irregular verbs.

Emily Dickinson, one of the most famous American poets,

_____lived_____ from 1830 to 1886. Her favorite topics
  1. (live)

_____ nature, time, and human emotions.
  2. (be)

Dickinson _____ an unusual life. During the
              3. (lead)

1860s, she _____ a recluse[1]—she almost never
              4. (become)

_____ her house in Amherst, Massachusetts, and she
  5. (leave)

only _____ white. Dickinson _____
       6. (wear)   7. (allow)

very few people to visit her, but she _____ a lot of
                                         8. (have)

friends, and she _____ them many letters.
                   9. (write)

1 *recluse:* someone who stays away from other people

EXERCISE 3 AFFIRMATIVE AND NEGATIVE STATEMENTS

GRAMMAR NOTES 1–4 Complete this list of facts about Emily Dickinson. Use the simple past form of the verbs in parentheses. See Appendix 1 on page 453 for help with the irregular verbs.

1. Dickinson _____wasn't_____ only interested in poetry.
                     (not be)

2. She also _____ science.
               (like)

3. She _____ topics from science in many of her poems.
         (use)

4. She never _____ far from home, but she _____ many people.
               (go)   (know)

5. Dickinson _____ only poetry.
               (not write)

6. She _____ her friends and admirers hundreds of letters.
         (send)

7. Her letters _____ full of jokes, recipes, cartoons, and poems.
                 (be)

8. But she _____ the envelopes—other people _____ that for her.
             (not address)   (do)

9. Dickinson _____ a typewriter.
               (not own)

10. She _____ the first drafts[1] of her poems on the back of old grocery lists.
          (write)

11. During her lifetime, 7 of her 1,700 poems _____ in print.
                                                 (appear)

12. She _____ about this, and no one _____ her permission.
          (not know)   (ask)

1 *first drafts:* first copies of a piece of writing, with no corrections

EXERCISE 4 REGULAR AND IRREGULAR VERBS

Ⓐ GRAMMAR NOTES 1–4 Complete the lines from a poem by Emily Dickinson. Use the simple past form of the verbs from the box. See Appendix 1 on page 453 for help with the irregular verbs.

bite	~~come~~	drink	eat	hop	not know

A bird _____came_____ down the walk:
           1.
He _____ I saw;
    2.
He _____ an angle-worm in halves
    3.
And _____ the fellow raw.
    4.

And then he _____ a dew
           5.
from a convenient grass,
And then _____ sidewise to the wall
        6.
To let a beetle pass.

▶02|02 Ⓑ LISTEN AND CHECK Listen to the poem and check your answers in A.

EXERCISE 5 QUESTIONS AND ANSWERS

Ⓐ GRAMMAR NOTES 1–4 Read the statements about Basho. Write questions about Emily Dickinson using the words in parentheses. Then answer your questions using the information from Exercises 2 and 3. Use short answers for yes/no questions and long answers for wh- questions.

1. Basho was a poet. (Dickinson / a poet)

   Q: _Was Dickinson a poet?_

   A: _Yes, she was._

2. He was born in 1644. (when / she / born)

   Q: _When was she born?_

   A: _She was born in 1830._

3. He lived in Japan. (where / she / live)

   Q: _____

   A: _____

4. He became famous during his lifetime. (she / become / famous during her lifetime)

   Q: _____

   A: _____

5. Basho's admirers often visited him. (Dickinson's admirers / often / visit her)

Q: _____

A: _____

6. He traveled a lot. (she / travel / a lot)

Q: _____

A: _____

7. Basho wrote more than 1,000 poems. (how many poems / Dickinson / write)

Q: _____

A: _____

8. He wrote about nature. (what / she / write about)

Q: _____

A: _____

9. He died in 1694. (when / she / die)

Q: _____

A: _____

02|03 **B** LISTEN AND CHECK **Listen to the Questions and Answers about Emily Dickinson and check your answers in A.**

EXERCISE 6 AFFIRMATIVE AND NEGATIVE STATEMENTS

A GRAMMAR NOTES 2–4 **Read this article about a modern writer.**

ANA CASTILLO is a modern poet, novelist, short story writer, and teacher. She was born in Chicago in 1953, and she lived there for 32 years. *Otro Canto*, her first book of poetry, appeared in 1977.

In her work, Castillo uses humor and a lively mixture of Spanish and English (Spanglish). She got her special writer's "voice" by living in a neighborhood with many different ethnic groups. She also thanks her father for her writing style. "He had an outgoing and easy personality, and this...sense of humor. I got a lot from him."

Castillo attended high school, college, and graduate school in Chicago. In the 1970s, she taught English and Mexican history. She received a PhD in American Studies from Bremen University in Germany in 1992. Her latest novel, *Give It to Me*, appeared in 2014.

B Read the statements. Write *That's right* or *That's wrong*. Correct the incorrect statements.

1. Ana Castillo was born in Mexico City.

   That's wrong. She wasn't born in Mexico City. She was born in Chicago.

2. She lived in Chicago until 1977.

   _____

3. Her father was very shy.

   _____

4. She grew up among people of different cultures.

   _____

5. Castillo got most of her education in Chicago.

   _____

6. She taught Spanish in the 1970s.

   _____

7. She went to France for her PhD.

   _____

8. Her latest novel appeared in 2004.

   _____

EXERCISE 7 EDITING

GRAMMAR NOTES 1–4 Read this student's journal. There are ten mistakes in the use of the simple past. The first mistake is already corrected. Find and correct nine more.

> Today in class, we read a poem by the American poet Robert Frost.
> enjoyed
> I really ~~enjoy~~ it. It was about a person who choosed between two roads in
> a forest. Many people believed the person were Frost. He thinked about his
> choice for a long time. The two roads didn't looked very different. Finally,
> he didn't took the road most people take. He took the one less traveled
> on. At that time, he didn't thought it was an important decision, but his
> choice change his life.
>
>   Sometimes I feel a little like Frost. As a child, I dreamed of traveling.
> Two years ago, I decide to move to a new country. It was a long journey
> and a big change. Did I made the right decision? I hope so.

Simple Past **23**

Past Progressive and Simple Past

REPORTING EVENTS

STEP 1   GRAMMAR IN CONTEXT

BEFORE YOU READ

Look at the picture. Discuss the questions.

1. What do you know about the *Titanic*?

2. What happened to the ship?

READ

03|01   Read this newspaper article about a terrible event.

| VOL CCXII, NO 875 | Monday, April 15, 1912 | Price One Cent |

DISASTER AT SEA

NEW YORK, April 15—It was a clear night. The sea was calm. The *Titanic*, the largest luxury ship[1] in the world, was sailing from Southhampton, England, to New York City. This was its first voyage,[2] and it was carrying more than 2,200 passengers and crew.[3] At around 11:30 p.m. crew member Frederick Fleet was looking at the sea when, suddenly, he saw a huge white

---

1 *luxury ship:* a boat that has many great things (beautiful rooms, swimming pools, restaurants, etc.)
2 *voyage:* a long trip, usually on a ship
3 *crew:* the people who work on a ship or airplane

form in front of the ship. When he saw it, Fleet immediately rang the ship's bell three times and shouted, "Iceberg ahead!" But it was too late. The great ship crashed into the mountain of ice.

When the *Titanic* hit the iceberg, people were sleeping, reading, and playing cards. Some passengers heard a loud noise, but they were not alarmed. They believed the ship was unsinkable.[4] But soon it became clear that the *Titanic* was in danger. There was a hole in the side of the ship. Water was entering fast, and it was starting to sink. There were lifeboats, but only 1,178 spaces for 2,224 people. In an attempt to keep everyone calm, the ship's band played a lively tune while people were getting into the boats.

The *Titanic* was not the only ship on the sea that night. There were several other ships in the area. The *Californian* was nearby, but it did not hear the *Titanic's* calls for help. And then there was the *Carpathia*. While the *Titanic* was sailing toward New York, the *Carpathia* was traveling from New York to the Mediterranean.

When it heard the *Titanic's* distress signals,[5] the *Carpathia* turned around and headed back toward the sinking ship. By the time the *Carpathia* arrived, the *Titanic* was already at the bottom of the sea, but there were 18 lifeboats full of cold and frightened survivors. Thanks to the *Carpathia*, more than 700 people lived to tell the story of that terrible night.

---

4 *unsinkable:* cannot go underwater
5 *distress signals:* calls for help

AFTER YOU READ

Ⓐ VOCABULARY **Match the words with their definitions.**

_____ **1. disaster**   **a.** afraid

_____ **2. calm**   **b.** someone who continues to live after an accident

_____ **3. area**   **c.** to go underwater

_____ **4. survivor**   **d.** one part of a larger place

_____ **5. alarmed**   **e.** a terrible event

_____ **6. sink**   **f.** quiet

Ⓑ COMPREHENSION **Number the events in order (1–7).**

_____ Water entered the *Titanic*.

_____ Frederick Fleet rang the ship's bell.

_____ The *Titanic* hit an iceberg.

_____ The *Carpathia* arrived and saved the survivors.

_____ The *Titanic* was sailing to New York.

_____ The *Titanic* sank.

_____ Frederick Fleet saw an iceberg.

Ⓒ DISCUSSION **Work with a partner. Compare your answers in B. Are they the same? Explain your choices.**

PAST PROGRESSIVE

Statements

Subject	Was/ Were	(Not)	Base Form of Verb + -ing	
I	was			
You	were			
He She	was	(not)	reading eating sleeping	yesterday at 11:30 p.m. when Anton called. while Mia was talking.
We You They	were			

Yes/No Questions

Was/ Were	Subject	Base Form of Verb + -ing	
Was	I		
Were	you		
Was	he she	reading eating sleeping	yesterday at 11:30 p.m.? when Anton called? while Mia was talking?
Were	we you they		

Short Answers

Affirmative				Negative			
		you	were.			you	weren't.
		I	was.			I	wasn't.
Yes,		he she	was.	No,		he she	wasn't.
		you we they	were.			you we they	weren't.

Wh- Questions

Wh- Word	Was/ Were	Subject	Base Form of Verb + -ing	
	was	I		
	were	you		
Why	was	he she	reading eating sleeping	yesterday at 11:30 p.m.? when Anton called? while Mia was talking?
	were	we you they		

GRAMMAR NOTES

1 Past Progressive

Use the past progressive to focus on the **duration of a past action**, not its completion.

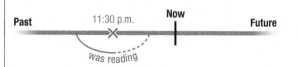

	Paul **was reading** a book last night.
	(We don't know if he finished it.)

| USAGE NOTE We often use the past progressive with a **specific time in the past**. | He **was reading** a book *at 11:30 p.m.* |

2 Simple Past

Use the simple past to focus on the **completion of a past action**.

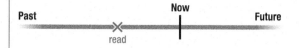

	Paul **read** a book last night.
	(He finished it.)

| BE CAREFUL! Use the **simple past** with most **non-action verbs**. Do not use the past progressive. | She **heard** about the disaster. |
| | NOT She ~~was hearing~~ about the disaster. |

3 Past Progressive + Simple Past

Use the past progressive with the simple past to show that **one action interrupted another action in progress in the past**. Use the simple past for the interrupting action.

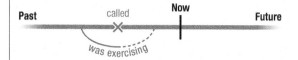

	I **was exercising** when he **called**.
	(I was exercising. The phone rang and interrupted my exercises.)

Use **when** or **while** to introduce one of the actions:

- **when** for the action in the **simple past**
- **while** for the action in the **past progressive**

| | He was running **when** he **fell**. |
| | **While** he **was running**, he fell. |

| USAGE NOTE We can also use **when** to introduce the action in the past progressive. | **When** he **was running**, he fell. |

4 Past Progressive + *While* or *When*

Use the past progressive with *while* or *when* to show **two actions in progress at the same time in the past**. Use the past progressive in both clauses.

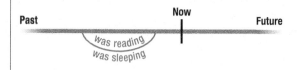

	While I **was reading**, Amy **was sleeping**.
	When I **was reading**, Amy **was sleeping**.
	(I was reading. At the same time, Amy was sleeping.)

5 Simple Past + Simple Past or Simple Past + Past Progressive

A sentence with both clauses in the simple past has a very **different meaning** from a sentence with one clause in the simple past and one clause in the past progressive.

• both clauses in the **simple past** 	When she **heard** the news, she **drove** home. *(First she heard the news; then she drove home.)*
• one clause is in the **simple past**, the other clause in the **past progressive** 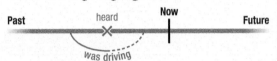	When she **heard** the news, she **was driving** home. *(First she was driving home; then she heard the news.)*

6 Position of the Time Clause

The **time clause** (the part of the sentence with *when* or *while*) can come at **the beginning or the end** of the sentence. The meaning is the same.

• at the **beginning** • at the **end**	***When** you called,* I was eating. I was eating ***when** you called*.
IN WRITING Use a **comma after the time clause** when it comes at the **beginning** of the sentence. Do not use a comma after the main clause when the main clause comes first.	***While** she was sleeping,* I was reading. I was reading ***while** she was sleeping*. NOT I was reading, while she was sleeping.

REFERENCE NOTES

For **spelling rules** on forming the **past progressive**, see Appendix 21 on page 330.
For a list of **non-action verbs**, see Appendix 2 on page 322.

STEP 3   FOCUSED PRACTICE

EXERCISE 1 DISCOVER THE GRAMMAR

GRAMMAR NOTES 1–6 Read each question. Then choose the correct sentence (*a* or *b*). In one item, both answers are correct.

1. In which sentence did the passengers arrive before the ship left?
   a. When the passengers arrived, the ship was leaving.
   b. When the passengers arrived, the ship left.

2. Which sentence tells us that the ship reached New York?
   a. It was sailing to New York.
   b. It sailed to New York.

3. In which sentence do we know that the ship went completely underwater?

   a. It was sinking.

   b. It sank.

4. In which sentence did the man fall asleep during the movie *Titanic*?

   a. He fell asleep while he was watching *Titanic*.

   b. While he was watching *Titanic*, he fell asleep.

5. Which sentence talks about two actions that were in progress at the same time?

   a. While the ship was sinking, passengers were getting into lifeboats.

   b. When the ship sank, passengers got into lifeboats.

6. In which sentence was the phone call interrupted?

   a. When he heard the news, he called me.

   b. When he heard the news, he was calling me.

7. In which sentence did the woman leave after the phone call?

   a. When he called her, she left the house.

   b. When he called her, she was leaving the house.

EXERCISE 2
PAST PROGRESSIVE STATEMENTS

GRAMMAR NOTE 1 Douglas is sailing to Europe on the SS *Atlantic*. Look at his schedule for yesterday. Complete the sentences. Use the past progressive form of the verbs in parentheses. Choose between affirmative and negative.

SS ATLANTIC

10:00 breakfast – Sea Breezes – Donna
11:00 exercise – gym – Michel
12:00 swimming contest – Olympic pool
1:00 lunch – Oceania – Raul
2:30 lecture on Italian art – library
4:00 coffee – Café Rose – Natasha
5:00 haircut – Suave Salon – Alain
7:00 dinner – Thalassa – Kim and Jason
9:00 card game – Casino Royal – Massimo

1. At 10:15, Douglas _____*wasn't sleeping*_____ in his cabin.
   a. (sleep)

   He _____*was having*_____ breakfast at Sea Breezes with Donna.
   b. (have)

2. At 11:05, he _____ in the ship's gym with Michel.
   a. (exercise)

   He _____ in the pool.
   b. (swim)

3. At 1:10, he _____ coffee at Café Rose.
   a. (drink)

   He _____ lunch at Oceania with Raul.
   b. (eat)

4. At 2:40, he _____ for a book in the ship's library.
   a. (look)

   He _____ to a lecture on Italian art.
   b. (listen)

5. At 4:05, he _____ a haircut at the Suave Salon.
a. (get)

He _____ coffee at Café Rose with Natasha.
b. (have)

6. At 7:10, he _____ in his room.
a. (rest)

He _____ dinner at Thalassa with Kim and Jason.
b. (enjoy)

7. At 9:15, he _____ cards at the Casino Royal with Massimo.
a. (play)

He _____ with Donna at the Discothèque.
b. (dance)

EXERCISE 3 PAST PROGRESSIVE OR SIMPLE PAST

GRAMMAR NOTES 1–5 Complete the information about the *Titanic* disaster. Use the past progressive or simple past form of the verbs in parentheses. See Appendix 1 on page 321 for help with irregular verbs.

Eyewitness Accounts[1]

According to eyewitness Lawrence Beesley, when the ship _____*hit*_____ the iceberg, the
1. (hit)

engines _____. Minutes later, when Professor Beesley _____ on deck,
2. (stop)   3. (go)

he _____ only a few other passengers there. Everyone was calm. A few people
4. (find)

_____ cards in the smoking room. When he _____ out the window,
5. (play)   6. (look)

he _____ an iceberg at the side of the ship.
7. (see)

Another survivor, Washington Dodge, said that it _____ 11:30 p.m. when the
8. (be)

crash _____. He _____ to go on deck. While the ship
9. (happen)   10. (decide)

_____, the band _____ a lively tune. At 1:55 a.m., the ship
11. (sink)   12. (play)

_____ completely into the sea.
13. (sink)

While passenger Elizabeth Shutes _____ a chicken sandwich in her cabin, she
14. (eat)

"_____ a shudder[2] travel through the ship." Shortly after, she _____ in
15. (feel)   16. (sit)

a lifeboat in the middle of the ocean with thirty-four other people. Hours later, someone shouted

"A light, a ship!" When Shutes _____, she _____ a ship with bright
17. (look)   18. (see)

lights coming toward them. It was the *Carpathia*—the only ship in the area that came to help.

When Harold Bride, one of the ship's two radio operators, _____ some lights in
19. (notice)

the distance, he _____ it was a steamship. It _____ to rescue them.
20. (know)   21. (come)

When the *Carpathia* _____, it _____ all of the survivors—including
22. (arrive)   23. (pick up)

Mr. Bride.

---
1 *eyewitness accounts:* reports by people who saw an accident or crime
2 *shudder:* a quick shaking movement

EXERCISE 4 *YES/NO* AND *WH-* QUESTIONS

A GRAMMAR NOTES 1–5 A newspaper is interviewing a *Titanic* passenger. Read the passenger's answers. Write the interviewer's questions. Use the words in parentheses and the past progressive or simple past.

1. INTERVIEWER: _What were you doing Sunday night?_
   (what / you / do / Sunday night)

   PASSENGER: As I was saying, I was playing cards with some other passengers.

2. INTERVIEWER: _____
   (your wife / play / with you)

   PASSENGER: No, she wasn't. My wife wasn't with me at the time.

3. INTERVIEWER: _____
   (what / she / do / while you / play cards)

   PASSENGER: She was reading in our room.

4. INTERVIEWER: _____
   (you / feel / the crash)

   PASSENGER: Not really. But I heard a very loud noise.

5. INTERVIEWER: _____
   (what / you / do / when you / hear the noise)

   PASSENGER: At first, we all continued to play. We weren't alarmed. Everyone stayed calm.

6. INTERVIEWER: _____
   (what / you / do / when the lights / go out)

   PASSENGER: I tried to find my wife.

7. INTERVIEWER: _____
   (what / she / do / while you / look for her)

   PASSENGER: She was looking for *me*. Thank goodness we found each other!

8. INTERVIEWER: _____
   (what / you / do / when you / find her)

   PASSENGER: We tried to get into a lifeboat.

03|02 **B** LISTEN AND CHECK Listen to the interview and check your answers in A.

EXERCISE 5 STATEMENTS WITH *WHEN* AND *WHILE*

GRAMMAR NOTES 1–6 Combine the pairs of sentences. Use the past progressive or the simple past form of the verb. Keep the order of the two sentences. Remember to use commas when necessary.

1. The storm started. Mr. Taylor attended a party.

   When _the storm started, Mr. Taylor was attending a party._

2. The electricity went out. The wind began to blow.

   _____ when _____

3. He drove home. He listened to his car radio.

   While _____

4. He pulled over to the side of the road. He couldn't see anything.

_____ when _____

5. He listened to the news. He heard about a car crash near his home.

While _____

6. It stopped raining. Mr. Taylor drove home in a hurry.

When _____

EXERCISE 6 EDITING

GRAMMAR NOTES 1–6 **Read this blog post. There are ten mistakes in the use of the past progressive and the simple past. The first mistake is already corrected. Find and correct nine more. Remember to look at punctuation!**

Julio Delgado   6:15 p.m.   April 15

                         went

This afternoon I ~~was going~~ to a movie at school. It was _Titanic_. They were showing it

because it was the anniversary of the 1912 disaster. What a beautiful and sad film! Jack

(Leonardo DiCaprio) was meeting Rose (Kate Winslet) while they both sailed on the huge

ship. It was the _Titanic_'s first voyage.

Rose was from a very rich family; Jack was from a poor family. They fell in love, but

Rose's mother wasn't happy about it. When the ship was hitting the iceberg, the two

lovers were together, but then they got separated. Rose was finding Jack while the ship

was sinking. Seconds before the ship went under, they held hands and were jumping into

the water. Rose survived, but Jack didn't. It was so sad. When I left the theater, I still was

having tears in my eyes.

That wasn't my only adventure of the day. When the movie was over I left the school

auditorium. While I walked home, I saw an accident between two pedestrians and a

car. I was the only one in the area, so while I saw the accident, I immediately called the

police. When the police got there, they asked me a lot of questions—there were no other

witnesses. I'm glad to say that the accident had a happier ending than the movie!

OUTCOMES
• Describe past habits and situations, using *used to* and *would*
• Evaluate events and situations described in a reading and a listening
• Describe and discuss one's past and present physical appearance and habits
• Write a description of a place and how it has changed

STEP 1	GRAMMAR IN CONTEXT

BEFORE YOU READ

Look at the photos. Discuss the questions.

1. What part of the world is Dubai in?

2. What was Dubai like before 1966? What is it like now?

READ

04|01   Read this article about an amazing change.

Dubai: Then and Now

Cities change, but usually not as much or as fast as Dubai. This exciting city in the United Arab Emirates used to be a small town in the desert. Today, it is a large international center with towering[1] skyscrapers. Not very long ago, people used to ride camels to get from place to place, and they would do most of their shopping at outdoor markets. Today, they drive expensive foreign sports cars and shop at huge indoor malls filled with luxury stores.[2]

How did this amazing transformation happen? The answer is oil. After its discovery in 1966, oil provided 60 percent of the city's revenue. The government used the money to build roads, ports,[3] and

Before 1966

Now

1 *towering:* very tall
2 *luxury stores:* stores selling expensive, high-quality items
3 *ports:* places where ships can load and unload people or things

skyscrapers. Today, a large part of the city's money comes from tourism. Tourism? People never used to think of Dubai as a popular vacation destination. But today, tourists come from around the world to view the sights from the Burj Khalifa, the tallest building in the world. They also come to ski indoors when it's 120°F (49°C) outside and to dance under the stars on artificial⁴ islands in the shape of palm trees.

The city planners did an amazing job in changing Dubai from a sleepy town to a major international city. Not everyone, however, believes that all the changes are good. For example, because of heavy traffic, a trip that used to take only 10 minutes now takes much longer. And some people believe that Dubai lost a lot of its charm⁵ when the skyscrapers went up. They miss the small, traditional houses and markets. But love the changes or not, one thing everyone agrees on: Dubai is not the same city it used to be.

---

4 *artificial:* not natural, made by people
5 *charm:* the special quality that makes people like something or someone

AFTER YOU READ

Ⓐ VOCABULARY Choose the word or phrase that best completes each sentence.

1. If a city is **popular**, _____ .
   a. it's very large
   b. it's poor
   c. many people like it

2. A **destination** is a place people _____ .
   a. live in
   b. travel to
   c. don't like

3. A **transformation** is a _____ .
   a. way to travel
   b. city
   c. change

4. A **traditional** house has a(n) _____ style.
   a. old
   b. modern
   c. amazing

5. A **major** city is usually _____ .
   a. important
   b. small
   c. not very big

6. **Revenue** is _____ that a government gets.
   a. a review
   b. information
   c. money

Ⓑ COMPREHENSION Read the statements. Check (✓) *True* or *False*.

	True	False
1. Dubai is a small town in the desert.	☐	☐
2. In the past, camels were a common form of transportation.	☐	☐
3. Today, most people shop at outdoor markets.	☐	☐
4. In the past, Dubai was a popular tourist destination.	☐	☐
5. Today, traffic is a problem in Dubai.	☐	☐
6. Dubai today is very different from Dubai in the past.	☐	☐

Ⓒ DISCUSSION Work with a partner. Compare your answers in B. Why did you check *True* or *False*?

USED TO

Statements

Subject	Used to / Did not use to	Base Form of Verb	
I You He She It We You They	used to didn't use to	be	popular.

Yes/No Questions

Did	Subject	Use to	Base Form of Verb	
Did	you it they	use to	be	popular?

Short Answers

Affirmative			Negative		
Yes,	I it they	did.	No,	I it they	didn't.

Wh- Questions

Wh- Word	Did	Subject	Use to	Base Form of Verb	
When	did	you it they	use to	be	popular?

WOULD

Statements

Subject	Would	Base Form of Verb	
I He They	would	shop	all day.

Contractions*

I would	=	I'd
He would	=	He'd
They would	=	They'd

*The contraction for would is the same for all subjects.

GRAMMAR NOTES

1 *Used to* for Past Habits and Situations

Use *used to* + **base form** of the verb for past habits (repeated activities) and situations that are no longer happening or true in the present.

• **past habits** 	When my father was a teenager, he **used to ride** a camel. *(He rode a camel many times in the past, but he doesn't ride one now.)*
• **past situations** 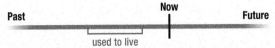	We **used to live** in Dubai. *(We lived in Dubai for a period of time, but we don't live there any longer.)*

USAGE NOTE We often use *used to* in order to contrast the past and the present. **Time expressions** such as *now*, *no longer*, and *not anymore* emphasize the contrast.	He **used to ride** his camel every day, but *now* he drives a car. They **used to shop** at an outdoor market, but they do*n't* shop there **anymore**.
BE CAREFUL! Use the **simple past** for a one-time past activity. Do not use *used to*.	He **drove** to the mall *yesterday*. NOT He ~~used to drive~~ to the mall yesterday.
BE CAREFUL! Use the **simple past** in a time clause with *when*. Do not use *used to*.	*When* I **lived** in Dubai, I used to ride a camel. NOT When I ~~used to live~~ in Dubai, . . .

2 Forms of *Used to*

Used to always refers to the **past**. There is no present or future forms.	She **used to** ski when she was younger. NOT She ~~uses~~ to ski every winter. NOT She ~~will use~~ to ski next month.
IN WRITING The form *use to* often comes after *did* in **negative statements** or **questions**, but people sometimes write *used to*. Some people, including many English teachers, think this is not correct in American English. However, other people think it is correct. In conversation, *use to* and *used to* sound the same: /'yustə/	He *didn't* **use to** live there. or He *didn't* **used to** live there. *Did* you **use to** have long hair? or *Did* you **used to** have long hair?
USAGE NOTE In **negative statements**, *never* + *used to* is much more common than *didn't use(d) to*.	He *never* **used to** study. *(more common)* He *didn't* **use(d) to** study. *(less common)*
USAGE NOTE In **questions**, the **simple past** is more common than *did* + *use(d) to*.	*Did* you **have** long hair then? *(more common)* *Did* you **use(d) to** have long hair then? *(less common)*

3 *Would* **for Past Habits**

You can also use *would* + **base form** of the verb for past habits (repeated activities) that no longer happen in the present.

• **past habits**
 	
 Past ——×—×—×———│——— Future
             Now
        would go
	When I was a teenager, I **would go** to the mall every Saturday afternoon.
	 (I went to the mall every Saturday afternoon, but I no longer do that.)

BE CAREFUL! Do not use *would* for past situations. Use *used to*.	I **used to live** in Dubai. NOT I ~~would live~~ in Dubai.
USAGE NOTE When we reminisce (tell stories) about the past, we often begin with *used to* and then continue with *would* to give more details or examples.	When I was a kid, I **used to ride** my bike everywhere. I **would ride** it to school during the week, and I **would take** it to the park on weekends.
BE CAREFUL! When we use *would*, it must already be clear that we are talking about the past. Do not begin a story with *would*.	I hear you got a new bike! I **used to** ride my bike everywhere. I would ride it to school . . . NOT I hear you got a new bike! I ~~would~~ ride my bike everywhere. I would ride it to school . . .

STEP 3 FOCUSED PRACTICE

EXERCISE 1 DISCOVER THE GRAMMAR

GRAMMAR NOTES 1–3 Read this tourist's email. Underline the expressions that refer to past habits and situations that are no longer true.

Greetings from Dubai!

Every time I return here, I'm absolutely amazed at all the changes! Today, I did some typical tourist things. First, I went to the top of the Burj Khalifa—the tallest building in the world. (As I'm

sure you know, our CN Tower back home in Canada <u>used to be</u> the tallest. Oh, well. Things change.) Today, from the observation deck, I had a bird's-eye view of the city. It's hard to believe that Dubai used to be just a small town! The transformation is really amazing.

This afternoon, I walked around for hours. I also visited one of the Palm Islands. They're

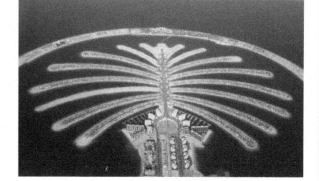

islands built in the early 2000s in the Persian Gulf. They are artificial, but the builders used only natural sand and rock. Amazing—as you can see from the photo. By the way, I used that new travel app on my smartphone. Thanks for telling me about it! It was really helpful—especially the maps. I used to get lost a lot!

After all my sightseeing, I was tired, so right now I'm sitting in an Internet café. There used to be a small hotel right across the street on the corner. I would sometimes stay there when I came here on business. Now there's another huge skyscraper in its place. So many changes! Prices have changed, too. This cup of tea didn't use to cost so much!

Wish you were here. I think you would like it.

Dania

EXERCISE 2 FORMS OF *USED TO*

GRAMMAR NOTE 2 Complete the Questions and Answers (Q & A) about Dubai. Use the correct form of *used to* and the words in parentheses.

Q: What are some of the major tourist attractions in Dubai?

A: Well, there are many, of course, but the Burj Khalifa is probably the most famous one. It's the tallest building in the world. That title _____*used to belong*_____ to the CN Tower in Canada.
   1. (belong)

Q: What's the population of Dubai?

A: It _____ just about 60,000. And that was only fifty years ago! Today, it's over
   2. (be)
   two million.

Q: Do many foreigners live in Dubai?

A: Yes. Very few foreigners _____ here, but now a large percentage of Dubai's
   3. (live)
   population is foreign born. Many of them are workers from other countries.

Q: _____ there always _____ so much traffic?
   4. (be)

A: No, not at all. Traffic is much worse these days. Remember, not too long ago many people
   _____ camels.
   5. (ride)

Q: How are the roads?

A: Dubai _____ many roads. In fact, there was only one major road. Today, of
   6. (not have)
   course, there are many more and they are very good. The famous Sheikh Zayed Road, for
   example, _____ just one lane. Today, it has twelve.
   7. (have)

Q: Where _____ people _____ before all the big malls?
   8. (shop)

A: They _____ to outdoor marketplaces. These traditional *souks* still exist, but
   9. (go)
   there are fewer of them.

Q: Do a lot of tourists visit Dubai?

A: Yes! Dubai never _____ a tourist destination, but today it is very, very popular.
   10. (be)

EXERCISE 3 *USED TO* OR *WOULD*

GRAMMAR NOTES 1–3 Just like cities, people's lives can change a lot. Read this online
newsletter. Circle *used to* or *would* to complete the article. Sometimes only *used to* is
possible. Sometimes both *used to* and *would* are possible.

David Beckham (used to)/ would live in London, England. Today, he owns homes around the world,
1.
including on one of the Palm Islands in Dubai. Born in 1975, Beckham grew up in a family that loved
football,[1] and he used to / would often play in London's Ridgeway Park. His family used to / would
2.   **3.**
frequently travel to see their team, Manchester United, compete. Beckham
used to / would love those trips, and he knew even then that he wanted to play
4.
football professionally. When his teachers used to / would ask the young Beckham the
5.
typical "What do you want to be when you grow up?" question, his answer was
always the same: "I want to be a footballer." Beckham, who is now retired,
went on to become one of the greatest football players in the world.

BECKHAM BIO BYTES ● He used to / would be a famous football
6.
player, but now he's retired. ● When he was a child, Beckham and his
father used to / would play football together for hours. ● They also
7.
used to / would watch Manchester United compete. ● Later, Beckham joined
8.
the team. ● He didn't use to / wouldn't be rich, but he became the richest athlete
9.
in England. ● He used to / would be single, but now he's married to famous
10.
Spice Girls singer Victoria Adams. ● In the past, the couple used to / would
11.
spend most of their time in the United States, but now they live in England
again. ● They used to / would have all boys, but now they also have
12.
a daughter.

_____
1 *football:* the sport called "soccer" in the United States

EXERCISE 4 *USED TO* OR *WOULD*

GRAMMAR NOTES 1–3 Complete the conversation between two travelers at Dubai International airport. Use *used to* or *would* and the correct verb from the box. Use *would* when possible. You will use one verb more than once.

be	buy	eat	live	make	take	watch

A: This is a beautiful airport. And it's huge!

B: Yes. I remember when it _____used to be_____ just a small airport with only a few flights a
   <u>1.</u>
   week and there were often delays. It really _____ a long time to get anywhere.
   <u>2.</u>

A: I remember that, too, of course. And there

   _____ so many stores
   <u>3. (negative)</u>
   or restaurants.

B: That's right. We _____
   <u>4.</u>
   cheese sandwiches at home and then we

   _____ them right here
   <u>5.</u>
   in the terminal.

A: Flying from here _____
   <u>6. (negative)</u>
   much fun. Now, there are more than eighty

   places to get something to eat or drink.

B: Oh, look. Isn't that David and Victoria

   Beckham over there?

A: Yes! I read that they own a house on one of

   the Palm Islands.

B: But don't they live in California?

A: No. They _____ there, but they moved back to England. And now they come
   <u>7.</u>
   here sometimes, too.

B: I'm a big football fan. When I was younger, I _____ all Beckham's games on
   <u>8.</u>
   TV. And I _____ tickets every time he played in England.
   <u>9.</u>

A: Oh, wait. There's an announcement. . . . Our flight is delayed.

B: Well, you know that old saying: "The more things change, the more they remain the same!"

A: But not in Dubai! Things are *always* changing here, and life seems very different from the

   way it _____ .
   <u>10.</u>

EXERCISE 5 EDITING

GRAMMAR NOTES 1–3 Read these online posts from foreigners visiting or living in Dubai. There are seven mistakes in the use of *used to* and *would*. The first mistake is already corrected. Find and correct six more.

Jason Smith, USA: I come here often for business. It's a great city, but driving in Dubai is
difficult. The traffic is really heavy. It used to ~~took~~ ^{take} me just 20 minutes to drive from the airport
to my hotel. Now, it sometimes takes me almost an hour. Also, the police are very strict. I was
only going a little over the speed limit, but I got a ticket last week on the way to my hotel. I
was upset at first, but at least these days you can pay the ticket online. You used to have to pay
in person. It would took forever!

Lynda Davis, Australia: I love Dubai. It's so international. The population never would be
so diverse. Now, more than 85 percent of the people living here are foreign born (including
me)! It's all very exciting. And there is so much to do. Today, I used to visit the Burj Khalifa.
Afterwards, I walked around for hours. I love all the malls and theaters. When I first came here,
there didn't use to be that many things to do in the evening. After work, I would just go home.
Now, I can choose from many different activities and events.

Wolfgang Meyer, Germany: There are still these wonderful traditional *souks* (marketplaces),
but there used to be many more of them. When I lived here twenty years ago, I would stop at
one or more of them on my way home from work. I would buy some fresh fish and vegetables
and maybe some interesting spices. Then I would went home and cook a great meal for
my family.

Graham Scott, UK: This is my first time back in fifteen years. People look really different
from before. For one thing, you used to saw more people wearing traditional clothing. Men
would wearing *kanduras* (long white robes). Women would wear the *abaya* (a full-length black
piece of clothing they wear over other clothes). Today, you see more Western-style clothing.

5

Wh- Questions

IN COURT

OUTCOMES
- Ask questions about the past, using *wh-* words
- Identify important information in an interview transcript
- Identify the main point of a conversation
- Write a series of interview questions to get information about a past event

---

STEP 1   GRAMMAR IN CONTEXT

BEFORE YOU READ

A lawyer is questioning a crime witness in court. Look at the photo. Discuss the questions.

1. Who is the lawyer? The judge? The witness?

2. What do you think the lawyer is asking?

READ

05|01   Read this excerpt from a court transcript.

State of Illinois vs.¹ Harry M. Adams

March 30, 2015

LAWYER: What happened on the night of May 12, 2014? Please tell the court.²

WITNESS: I went to Al's Grill.

LAWYER: Who did you see there?

WITNESS: I saw one of the defendants.

LAWYER: Which one did you see?

WITNESS: It was that man. *[The witness is pointing to Mr. Adams.]*

---

1 *vs.:* against (*vs.* is the written abbreviation of *versus*)
2 *court:* the people (judge, lawyers, jury) who decide if someone is guilty of a crime

LAWYER:	Let the record show that the witness is indicating the defendant, Harry Adams. OK, you saw Mr. Adams. Did he see you?
WITNESS:	No, no, he didn't see me.
LAWYER:	But somebody saw you. Who saw you?
WITNESS:	A woman. He was talking to a woman. She saw me.
LAWYER:	OK. What happened next?
WITNESS:	The woman gave him a box.
LAWYER:	A box! What did it look like?
WITNESS:	It was about this long...
LAWYER:	So, about a foot and a half. What did Mr. Adams do then?
WITNESS:	He took the box. He looked frightened.
LAWYER:	Why did he look frightened? What was in the box?
WITNESS:	I don't know. He didn't open it. He just took it and left in a hurry.
LAWYER:	Where did he go?
WITNESS:	Toward the parking lot.
LAWYER:	When did the woman leave?
WITNESS:	I don't know. She was still there when we heard his car speed away.

AFTER YOU READ

Ⓐ VOCABULARY **Choose the word or phrase that best completes each sentence.**

1. A **defendant** is someone that _____.
   a. saw a crime b. possibly broke a law c. works in the court

2. If something is for the **record**, you can find it in a _____.
   a. music CD b. box c. written report

3. If you are **frightened**, you are _____.
   a. dangerous b. afraid c. unhappy

4. If you leave **in a hurry**, you leave _____.
   a. quickly b. in a storm c. by bus

5. The witness **indicated** Harry Adams by _____ him.
   a. laughing at b. speaking about c. pointing to

Ⓑ COMPREHENSION **Match the questions and answers.**

_____ 1. Where does the reading take place? a. Harry Adams.
_____ 2. When did the events take place? b. In court.
_____ 3. Where did the witness go that night? c. A box.
_____ 4. Who did the witness see there? d. Toward the parking lot.
_____ 5. Who saw the witness? e. May 12, 2014.
_____ 6. What did the woman give Mr. Adams? f. Al's Grill.
_____ 7. Where did Mr. Adams go? g. A woman.

Ⓒ DISCUSSION **Work with a partner. Compare your answers in B. Why did you choose each answer?**

WH- QUESTIONS: *WHO, WHAT*

Questions About the Subject			Answers		
Wh- Word Subject	**Verb**	**Object**	**Subject**	**Verb**	**Object**
Who	saw	Harry?	Marta	saw	him.
		the box?			it.

Questions About the Object				Answers		
Wh- Word Object	**Auxiliary Verb**	**Subject**	**Main Verb**	**Subject**	**Verb**	**Object**
Who	did	Marta	see?	She	saw	Harry.
What						the box.

WH- QUESTIONS: *WHICH, WHOSE, HOW MANY*

Questions About the Subject			Answers		
Wh- Word + Noun	**Verb**	**Object**	**Subject**	**Verb**	**Object**
Which witness			Mr. Ho		
Whose lawyer	saw	you?	Harry's lawyer	saw	me.
How many people			Five people		

Questions About the Object				Answers		
Wh- Word + Noun	**Auxiliary Verb**	**Subject**	**Main Verb**	**Subject**	**Verb**	**Object**
Which witness						the first witness.
Whose lawyer	did	you	see?	I	saw	Harry's lawyer.
How many people						five people.

WH- QUESTIONS: *WHEN, WHERE, WHY*

Questions				Answers		
Wh- Word	**Auxiliary Verb**	**Subject**	**Main Verb**	**Subject**	**Verb**	**Time/Place/Reason**
When						yesterday.
Where	did	Marta	go?	She	went	to the police.
Why						because she was frightened.

GRAMMAR NOTES

1 Wh- Questions and Wh- Words

Use **wh- questions** (also called **information questions**) to ask for specific information.

Wh- questions begin with **wh- words** such as: who, what, when, where, why, which, whose, how, how many, how much, and how long.	A: **Who** did you see at Al's Grill? B: Harry Adams. A: **When** did you go there? B: On May 12, 2014. A: **How many** people saw you? B: Two.
USAGE NOTE In conversation, **answers** to wh- questions are usually **short**. They just give the requested information.	A: How long did you stay there? B: **Three hours.** *(more common)* I stayed there three hours. *(less common)*

2 Wh- Questions with Who and What

Use **who** to ask for information about **people**. Use **what** to ask for information about **things**.

For **questions about the subject**, use **who** or **what** in place of the subject, and use statement word order: **wh- word (= subject) + verb**	SUBJECT Someone saw you. **Who** saw you?	SUBJECT Something happened. **What** happened?
For **questions about the object**, use **who** or **what** and question word order: **wh- word + auxiliary + subject + verb**	OBJECT You saw someone. **Who** did you see?	OBJECT He said something. **What** did he say?
Remember that an **auxiliary verb** is a verb such as **do** (does, did), **have** (has, had), **can**, or **will**. *Be* can be an auxiliary too.	What *does* he **do**? Who *will* she **defend**? What *is* he **doing**?	
BE CAREFUL! Do not use an auxiliary verb in questions about the **subject**.	Who **saw** you there? NOT Who ~~did see~~ you there?	
USAGE NOTE In very formal English, we sometimes use **whom** instead of *who* in questions about the **object**.	**Whom** did you see? *(very formal)* **Who** did you see? *(more common)*	

3 Wh- Questions with Which, Whose, and How many

You can also use **which**, **whose**, and **how many** to ask for information about **people** and **things**.

• **which + noun** (to ask about a choice) • **whose + noun** (to ask about possessions) • **how many + noun** (to ask about quantities)	*Which* **witness** told the truth? *Whose* **lawyer** do you believe? *How many* **questions** did the lawyer ask?
For **questions about the subject**, use the word order: **wh- word + noun + verb**	*Which* **defendant answered** best?
For **questions about the object**, use the word order: **wh- word + noun + auxiliary + subject + verb**	*Which* **defendant did you trust** more?

4 Wh- Questions with *Where, Why,* and *When*

Use *where, why,* and *when* to ask about **place**, **reason**, and **time**.

• *where* (to ask about place)	**Where** will she go?
• *why* (to ask about reason)	**Why** does she want to defend him?
• *when* (to ask about time)	**When** did she arrive?

Use the word order: *wh-* **word + auxiliary + subject + verb**	**Where did they travel?**

5 Wh- Questions with *Be*

When the **main verb** is a form of *be* (*am, is, are, was, were*), it goes directly after the *wh-* question word or *wh-* question word + noun combination.

• *wh-* **word +** *be*	**Who is** the witness?
	What was the best answer?
	Where are the lawyers?
• *wh-* **word + noun +** *be*	**Which witnesses are** in court?
	How many people were in the room?

STEP 3   FOCUSED PRACTICE

EXERCISE 1   DISCOVER THE GRAMMAR

GRAMMAR NOTES 1–5 Match the questions and answers.

_*h*_ 1. Where were you?

____ 2. Who did you see?

____ 3. Who saw you?

____ 4. What hit her?

____ 5. Why did he leave?

____ 6. What did she hit?

____ 7. Which man did you give the money to?

____ 8. Which man gave you the money?

____ 9. How many witnesses were there?

a. His wife saw me.

b. She hit a car.

c. I gave the money to Harry.

d. A car hit her.

e. Six.

f. Harry gave me the money.

g. I saw the defendant.

~~h.~~ At Al's Grill.

i. Because he wanted to meet Harry.

EXERCISE 2 WH- QUESTIONS

Ⓐ GRAMMAR NOTES 1–5 Complete the cross-examination. Write the lawyer's questions.
Use the words in parentheses and make any necessary changes.

1. LAWYER: *What time did you return home?*
   (what time / you / return home)
   WITNESS: I returned home just before midnight.

2. LAWYER: _____
   (how / you / get home)
   WITNESS: Someone gave me a ride. I was in a hurry.

3. LAWYER: _____
   (who / give you / a ride)
   WITNESS: A friend from work.

4. LAWYER: _____
   (what / happen / next)
   WITNESS: I opened my door and saw someone on my living room floor.

5. LAWYER: _____
   (who / you / see)
   WITNESS: Deborah Collins.

6. LAWYER: For the record, _____
   (who / be / Deborah Collins)
   WITNESS: She's my wife's boss. I mean, she *was* my wife's boss. She's dead now.

7. LAWYER: _____
   (what / you / do)
   WITNESS: I called the police.

8. LAWYER: _____
   (when / the police / arrive)
   WITNESS: In about 10 minutes.

9. LAWYER: _____
   (what / they / ask you)
   WITNESS: They asked me to describe the crime scene.

10. LAWYER: _____
(how many police officers / come)

WITNESS: I don't remember. Why?

LAWYER: I'm asking the questions here. Please just answer.

05|02 **B** LISTEN AND CHECK **Listen to the cross-examination and check your answers in A.**

EXERCISE 3 *WH-* QUESTIONS

GRAMMAR NOTES 1–5 **Read the answers. Then ask questions about the underlined words or phrases.**

1. Court begins at 9:00 a.m.

   When does court begin?

2. Something horrible happened.

   _____

3. Five witnesses described the crime.

   _____

4. The witness indicated Harry Adams.

   _____

5. The witness indicated Harry Adams.

   _____

6. The lawyer questioned the restaurant manager.

   _____

7. The manager looked frightened.

   _____

8. The judge spoke to the jury.

   _____

9. The verdict was "guilty."

   _____

10. The jury found Adams guilty because he didn't have an alibi.

    _____

11. The trial[1] lasted two weeks.

    _____

12. Adams paid his lawyer $2,000.

    _____

---

1 *trial:* a legal process in a court of law that decides if someone is guilty of a crime

QUESTIONS

did Jones go
Where ~~Jones went~~ on January 15?

Who went with him?

What time he return home?

Who he called?

How much money he had with him?

Whom saw him at the station the next day?

How did he look?

Why he was in a hurry?

How many suitcases did he have?

When the witness call the police?

What did happen next?

What his alibi was?

EXERCISE 4
EDITING

GRAMMAR NOTES 1–5

Read a reporter's notes. There are nine mistakes in the use of *wh-* questions. The first mistake is already corrected. Find and correct eight more.

The Future

OUTCOMES

- Discuss future facts, predictions, plans, and scheduled events
- Express quick decisions, offers, and promises
- Identify important information in an interview transcript
- Identify actions happening now and future plans in a conversation
- Write a paragraph about a prediction

OUTCOMES

- Describe the order between future events, using a future time clause
- Follow the sequence of two future events in a reading
- Follow the time order of events in a conversation
- Discuss future plans and goals
- Write a description of future plans and goals

OUTCOMES
• Discuss future facts, predictions, plans, and scheduled events
• Express quick decisions, offers, and promises
• Identify important information in an interview transcript
• Identify actions happening now and future plans in a conversation
• Write a paragraph about a prediction

STEP 1   GRAMMAR IN CONTEXT

BEFORE YOU READ

Look at the photo. Discuss the questions.

1. Where do you think the first space tourists will travel?

2. Why do people want to travel into space? Would *you* like to?

READ

06|01   Read this transcript of a radio program about space tourism.

Space Tourism: Not Just Science Fiction[1]

ROHAN: Good evening, and welcome to *The Future Today*. I'm Enid Rohan, and tonight Dr. Richard Starr, president of YourSpace, Inc., is going to talk to us about space tourism. Dr. Starr, is space really going to become a popular tourist destination?

STARR: Yes, it is, Enid. We're already building the space planes. And we're selling tickets and planning our first trips now. In fact, our training program for passengers is starting next January.

ROHAN: Where will these tours go? Will they travel to the Moon? Mars?

STARR: No, they won't. The first space tourists aren't going to go that far. They're only going to travel about 110 kilometers, or 68 miles above the Earth. That's the edge of space. A trip will last about two and a half hours.

ROHAN: Tickets cost $250,000. Who's going to pay that much for just a few hours?

STARR: Hundreds of people are purchasing tickets and are waiting for takeoff. It's going to be an incredible trip. And tickets won't always be so expensive. Costs are going to fall a lot.

ROHAN: What will a trip be like?

---

1 *science fiction:* stories about the future, often about space travel and scientific discoveries

STARR: First of all, you'll experience zero gravity.[2] That means you will float freely in the cabin. And you'll get a bird's-eye view[3] of the Earth from space. You won't believe your eyes! You're going to think about the Earth in a whole new way.

ROHAN: Sounds great. I think I'll ask my boss to send me on a trip. When does the next flight leave?

STARR: January 1, two years from now. But you won't be on that one—our next three flights are already sold out!

---

2 *gravity:* the force that makes things fall to the ground. (In zero gravity, things do not stay on the ground.)

3 *bird's-eye view:* a view from a very high place

AFTER YOU READ

A VOCABULARY Complete the sentences with the words from the box.

edge	experience	incredible	purchase	sold out	takeoff

1. I want to go on this trip. How can I _____ a ticket?

2. There are no more tickets for the space tour. It's _____.

3. I was so excited watching *Gravity 3* that I was at the _____ of my seat!

4. I was only scared at _____—when the space plane left the ground.

5. Sy took _____ photos from the spacecraft. He saw some amazing sights.

6. In space, people _____ a lot of feelings—amazement, excitement, fear, and much more.

B COMPREHENSION Read the statements. Which of the statements are true right now? Which will be true only in the future? Check (✓) *Now* or *Future*.

	Now	Future
1. Tourists are buying tickets.	☐	☐
2. A training program for passengers is starting.	☐	☐
3. Space tours travel about 110 km (68 miles) above the Earth.	☐	☐
4. Tickets are very expensive.	☐	☐
5. The next flight is ready to leave.	☐	☐
6. A trip lasts about two and a half hours.	☐	☐

C DISCUSSION Work with a partner. Compare your answers in B. Why did you check *Now* or *Future*?

BE GOING TO FOR THE FUTURE

Statements

Subject	*Be*	*(Not) Going to*	Base Form of Verb	
I	**am**			
You	**are**			
He She It	**is**	**(not) going to**	**leave**	soon.
We You They	**are**			

Yes/No Questions

Be	Subject	*Going to*	Base Form of Verb	
Am	I			
Are	you			
Is	he she it	**going to**	**leave**	soon?
Are	we you they			

Short Answers

Affirmative			Negative		
	you	are.		you're	
	I	am.		I'm	
Yes,	he she it	is.	**No,**	he's she's it's	**not.**
	you we they	are.		you're we're they're	

Wh- Questions

Wh- Word	*Be*	Subject	*Going to*	Base Form of Verb
When Why	**are**	you	**going to**	**leave?**

WILL FOR THE FUTURE

Statements

Subject	*Will (not)*	Base Form of Verb	
I You He She It We You They	**will (not)**	**leave**	soon.

Yes/No Questions

Will	Subject	Base Form of Verb	
Will	I you he she it we you they	**leave**	soon?

Short Answers

Affirmative				Negative		
Yes,	you I he she it you we they	**will**.		**No,**	you I he she it you we they	**won't**.

Wh- Questions

Wh- Word	*Will*	Subject	Base Form of Verb
When	**will**	you	**leave**?

PRESENT PROGRESSIVE FOR THE FUTURE

Statements

Subject + *Be*	*(Not)* + Base Form + *-ing*	
We're	**(not) leaving**	soon.
It's		

SIMPLE PRESENT FOR THE FUTURE

Statements

Subject	Verb	
We	leave	Monday at 6:45 a.m.
It	leaves	

GRAMMAR NOTES

1 Referring to Future Events

There are **several ways to refer to future events**. Sometimes only one form is appropriate, but in many cases more than one form is possible.

• *be going to*	They**'re going to have** a meeting.
• *will*	I think I**'ll go. Will** you **be** there?
• **present progressive**	It**'s taking** place next week.
• **simple present**	It **starts** at 9:00 a.m. on Monday.

Past — Now | meeting ✕ — Future

2 Future Facts

For facts or events that you are **certain will happen in the future**, you can use *be going to* or *will*.

• *be going to*	The sun **is going to rise** at 6:43 tomorrow.
• *will*	The sun **will rise** at 6:43 tomorrow.

3 Predictions

For predictions about things you are **quite sure will happen in the future**, you can also use *be going to* or *will*.

• *be going to*	I think a lot of people **are going to travel** to space.
• *will*	I think a lot of people **will travel** to space.

USAGE NOTE We often use *I think* before a prediction.	*I think* tickets **are going to get** cheaper.
IN WRITING We use *will* more in **formal writing** and *be going to* more in **conversation**.	Prices **will drop** in time. *(formal writing)* Prices **are going to drop** in time. *(conversation)*
BE CAREFUL! Do not use *will* when something you notice right now makes you almost certain that an event is going to happen. Use *be going to*.	A: Look at that car! B: Oh, no. It**'s going to crash**! NOT It'll crash.

4 Future Plans

For plans or things that are **already decided**, use *be going to* or the **present progressive**.

• *be going to*	I**'m going to fly** to Chicago next week.
• **present progressive**	I**'m flying** to Chicago next week. NOT I'll fly to Chicago next week.

USAGE NOTE We often use the **present progressive** for plans that are already arranged.	I**'m flying** to Chicago next week. I already have a ticket.
USAGE NOTE When the main verb is *go*, it is more common to use the **present progressive** (*be going*) than *be going to go*.	I**'m going** to Paris tomorrow. *(more common)* I**'m going to go** to Paris tomorrow. *(less common)*

5 Quick Decisions, Offers, and Promises

For decisions that you make quickly while you are speaking, or to make offers or promises, use *will*.

• **quick decision**	A: The Space Show is opening next week.
	B: Really? Sounds interesting. I think I**'ll go**.
	A: I'd like to go too, but I don't have a ride.
• **offer**	B: I**'ll drive** you. But I'd like to leave by 7:00.
• **promise**	A: No problem. I**'ll be** ready.

6 Future Scheduled Events

For scheduled future events such as **timetables**, **programs**, and **schedules**, you can use the **simple present**.

• **simple present**	The shuttle **leaves** at 9:00 a.m.
	Dr. Starr **speaks** Tuesday afternoon.
USAGE NOTE We often use verbs such as *begin*, *start*, *leave*, *arrive*, *last*, and *end* for scheduled future events.	The conference **begins** May 11. Registration **lasts** until May 10.
USAGE NOTE You can also use *be going to* and *will* for scheduled future events.	Registration **is going to last** until May 10. Registration **will last** until May 10.

PRONUNCIATION NOTE

◗06|02

Pronunciation of *Going to*

In **informal conversation**, we often pronounce *going to* as "gonna."	A: What time are you **going to** be home? *(gonna)*
	B: I'm **going to** get home late. *(gonna)*
IN WRITING Sometimes people use *gonna* in **informal notes**, **text messages**, and **email** to friends.	Hi Lyn, I'm **gonna** be late. *(email)*
BE CAREFUL! Do not use *gonna* when you write to people you have a formal relationship with.	Professor, I'm **going to** be late. *(email)*
	NOT Professor, I'm ~~gonna~~ be late.
Also do not use *gonna* in formal writing.	According to scientists, Mars is **going to** become a tourist destination. *(paper)*
	NOT According to scientists, Mars is ~~gonna~~ become a tourist destination.

REFERENCE NOTES

For **contractions** of *I am*, *you are*, *I will*, *you will*, etc., see Appendix 26, page 332.

For the **present progressive** and **simple present** forms, see Unit 1, page 4.

For *will* for **making a request**, see Unit 15 on page 142.

EXERCISE 1   DISCOVER THE GRAMMAR

Ⓐ GRAMMAR NOTES 1–6 Read this transcript of an interview with a future space tourist. There are thirteen forms of the future. The first form is already underlined. Find and underline twelve more.

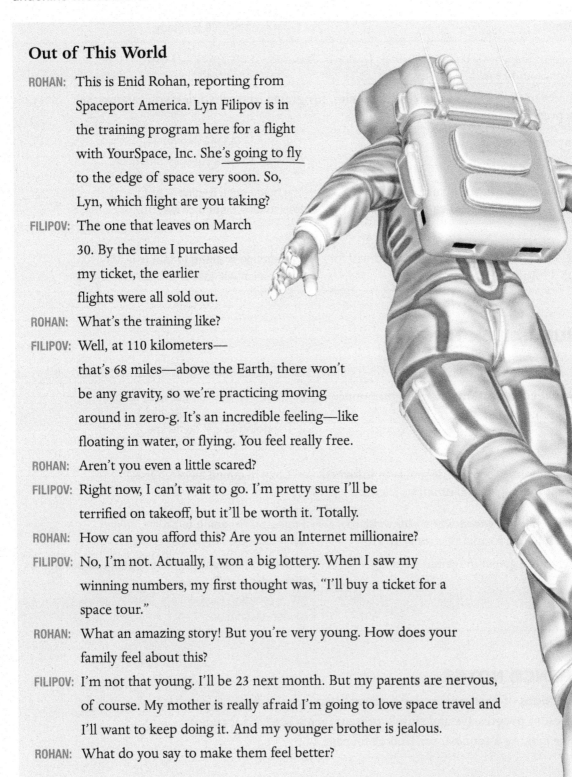

Out of This World

ROHAN: This is Enid Rohan, reporting from Spaceport America. Lyn Filipov is in the training program here for a flight with YourSpace, Inc. She's going to fly to the edge of space very soon. So, Lyn, which flight are you taking?

FILIPOV: The one that leaves on March 30. By the time I purchased my ticket, the earlier flights were all sold out.

ROHAN: What's the training like?

FILIPOV: Well, at 110 kilometers— that's 68 miles—above the Earth, there won't be any gravity, so we're practicing moving around in zero-g. It's an incredible feeling—like floating in water, or flying. You feel really free.

ROHAN: Aren't you even a little scared?

FILIPOV: Right now, I can't wait to go. I'm pretty sure I'll be terrified on takeoff, but it'll be worth it. Totally.

ROHAN: How can you afford this? Are you an Internet millionaire?

FILIPOV: No, I'm not. Actually, I won a big lottery. When I saw my winning numbers, my first thought was, "I'll buy a ticket for a space tour."

ROHAN: What an amazing story! But you're very young. How does your family feel about this?

FILIPOV: I'm not that young. I'll be 23 next month. But my parents are nervous, of course. My mother is really afraid I'm going to love space travel and I'll want to keep doing it. And my younger brother is jealous.

ROHAN: What do you say to make them feel better?

FILIPOV: I tell my mother, "Listen, Mom, this is an incredible once-in-a-lifetime thing. I won't make a habit of space travel, I promise." My brother? He wants a career in space travel, so he's going to study a lot harder from now on. That's what he says, anyway.

ROHAN: Thanks for the interview, Lyn. And good luck!

FILIPOV: Thanks. I'll send you photos.

B Complete the chart. List the thirteen future verb forms. Then check (✓) the correct column for each form.

	Facts	Predictions	Plans	Quick Decisions	Promises	Schedules
1. 's going to fly			✓			
2.						
3.						
4.						
5.						
6.						
7.						
8.						
9.						
10.						
11.						
12.						
13.						

EXERCISE 2 *WILL* FOR FACTS AND PREDICTIONS

A GRAMMAR NOTES 1–2 It is the year 2020, and an international group of space tourists is getting ready for its space flight. Part of the training program includes a Question and Answer (Q & A) session. Complete the questions and answers. Use the verbs in parentheses with *will* or *won't*.

Q: _____*Will*_____ it _____*take*_____ a long time to get used to zero gravity?
               1. (take)

A: No, it _____*won't*_____. Every day you _____ more comfortable, and after
          2.   **3.** (feel)

   three days you _____ used to being in space.
                    4. (become)

Q: _____ I _____ sick?
                    5. (feel)

A: Yes, you might feel sick for a little while. But it _____ long.
                                         6. (last)

Q: I'm a runner. How _____ I _____ in shape in space?
7. (stay)

A: Actually, all space tourists, or "spaceflight participants," as they prefer to be called,

_____ exercises during the flight. There _____ at least one stationary
8. (do)   9. (be)

bike on board, for example.

Q: _____ I _____ the same?
10. (look)

A: Actually, you _____ the same at all. Your face and eyes _____ puffy.
11. (look)   12. (get)

The first time you look in a mirror, you probably _____ yourself.
13. (recognize)

Q: _____ I _____ in my sleep?
14. (float)

A: Yes, if you are not tied down. And then you should be careful because you _____
15. (bump)

into things all night long. Trust me. You can get hurt!

Q: I like salt and pepper on my food. Can I still use them in zero gravity?

A: Yes, you _____ still _____ salt and pepper, but not like you do on
16. (have)

Earth. You _____ small, squeezable bottles with salt water and pepper water so the
17. (use)

grains don't float away. You just squeeze it on your food. Don't worry about it. It

_____ great!
18. (be)

○06|03 ⑧ LISTEN AND CHECK Listen to the Question and Answer session and check your
answers in A.

EXERCISE 3 *BE GOING TO* FOR PREDICTION

GRAMMAR NOTE 3 Look at the pictures. They show future events in the life of Professor
Starr. Write predictions or guesses. Use the words from the box and a form of *be going to*
or *not be going to*. Choose between affirmative and negative.

answer the phone	get out of bed	give a speech	rain	~~take a trip~~
drive	get very wet	have dinner	sleep	watch TV

1. *He's going to take a trip.* _____   2. _____

3. _____

4. _____

5. _____

6. _____

7. _____

8. _____

9. _____

10. _____

EXERCISE 4 PRESENT PROGRESSIVE FOR PLANS

GRAMMAR NOTE 4 Write about Professor Starr's plans for next week. Use the information from his calendar and the present progressive.

	MONDAY	TUESDAY	WEDNESDAY	THURSDAY	FRIDAY	SATURDAY
A.M.	Teach my science class	Take the train to Chicago	Do the interview for *The Space Show*	Work on the Space Future website	Go to an exercise class	Answer emails from the Space Future website
P.M.		Meet friends from England for dinner	Answer questions from the online chat		Fly to New York for the Space Transportation Conference	Write a speech for the next space travel conference

1. On Monday morning, *he's teaching his science class* _____.

2. On Tuesday morning, _____.

3. On Tuesday evening, _____.

4. On Wednesday morning, _____.

5. On Wednesday afternoon, _____.

6. All day Thursday, _____.

7. On Friday morning, _____.

8. On Friday evening, _____.

9. On Saturday morning, _____.

10. On Saturday afternoon, _____.

EXERCISE 5 SIMPLE PRESENT FOR SCHEDULES

GRAMMAR NOTE 6 It is June 2050. You and a friend are planning a trip to the Moon. Your friend just got the schedule, and you are deciding which shuttle to take. Use the words in parentheses to ask questions and look at the schedule to write the answers. Use the simple present.

2050 SHUTTLE SERVICE TO THE MOON					
Fall Schedule • All times given in Earth's Eastern Standard Time					
SEPTEMBER		OCTOBER		NOVEMBER	
Leave Earth	Arrive Moon	Leave Earth	Arrive Moon	Leave Earth	Arrive Moon
9/4 7:00 a.m.	9/7 6:00 a.m.	10/15 4:00 a.m.	10/18 3:00 a.m.	11/4 1:00 a.m.	11/8 12:00 a.m.
9/20 10:00 a.m.	9/23 9:00 a.m.	10/27 11:00 a.m.	10/30 10:00 a.m.	11/19 6:00 a.m.	11/23 5:00 a.m.

1. (when / the shuttle / fly to the Moon this fall)

A: _When does the shuttle fly to the Moon this fall?_

B: _It flies to the Moon in September, October, and November._

2. (how many / shuttle flights / leave this fall)

A: _____

B: _____

3. (how often / the shuttle / depart for the Moon each month)

A: _____

B: _____

4. (when / the October 27 flight / arrive on the Moon)

A: _____

B: _____

5. (how long / the November 19 flight / last)

A: _____

B: _____

EXERCISE 6 FORMS OF THE FUTURE

Ⓐ GRAMMAR NOTES 1–6 Two people are having a cup of coffee and planning their trip to the Space Conference. Circle the correct words to complete their conversation.

JASON: I just heard the weather report. It's raining / (It's going to rain) tomorrow.
_____1._____

ARIEL: Oh no. I hate driving in the rain. And it's a long drive to the conference.

JASON: Wait! I have an idea. We'll take / We're going to take the train instead!
_____2._____

ARIEL: Good idea! Do you have a train schedule?

JASON: Yes. Here's one. There's a train that will leave / leaves at 7:00 a.m.
_____3._____

ARIEL: What about lunch? Oh, I know. I'll make / I'm making some sandwiches for us.
_____4._____

JASON: Good idea! You know, it's a long trip. What are we doing / are we going to do all those hours?
_____5._____

ARIEL: Don't worry. We'll think / We're thinking of something.
_____6._____

JASON: Maybe I'll bring / I'm bringing my laptop, and we can watch a movie.
_____7._____

ARIEL: Great. Hey, Jason, your cup will fall / is going to fall! It's right at the edge of the table.
_____8._____

JASON: Got it! You know, we have to get up really early. I think I'm going / I'll go home now.
_____9._____

ARIEL: OK. In that case, I'm seeing / I'll see you tomorrow. Good night.
_____10._____

▷06|04 **Ⓑ LISTEN AND CHECK** Listen to the conversation and check your answers in A.

EXERCISE 7 EDITING

GRAMMAR NOTES 1–6 Read this student's report on space travel. There are eleven mistakes in the use of the future. The first mistake is already corrected. Find and correct ten more.

travel
Both astronauts and space tourists will ~~traveling~~ in space, but tourists are gonna have a much different experience. Space tourists is going to travel for fun, not for work. So, they will no have to worry about many of the technical problems that astronauts worry about. For example, space tourists will need not to figure out how to use tools without gravity. And they isn't going to go outside the spaceship to make repairs. For the most part, space tourists will just going to see the sights and have a good time.

Still, there will be similarities. Regular activities be the same for astronauts and space tourists. For example, eating, washing, and sleeping will turned into exciting challenges for everyone in space. And on long trips, everyone is going to doing exercises to stay fit in zero gravity. And both astronauts and space tourists will going to have many new adventures!

7 Future Time Clauses
SETTING GOALS

OUTCOMES
• Describe the order between future events, using a future time clause
• Follow the sequence of two future events in a reading
• Follow the time order of events in a conversation
• Discuss future plans and goals
• Write a description of future plans and goals

STEP 1 · GRAMMAR IN CONTEXT

BEFORE YOU READ

Look at the photo and at the title of the article. Discuss the questions.

1. The girl wants to become a businesswoman. What do you think she will do to reach her goal?

2. What are some other typical goals that people have?

3. What's one of *your* goals?

READ

07|01 Read this article.

From Dream to Reality

We all have dreams, but how can we make them a reality? We change them into goals and make an action plan. Read about how one student, Latoya Jones, turned *her* dreams into goals and made an action plan.

PUT YOUR DREAMS ON PAPER. After you write a dream down, it will start to become a goal. Your path will then be a lot clearer.

Latoya Jones wrote this:
• Before I turn 30, I'm going to be a successful businessperson.

LIST YOUR REASONS. When things get difficult, you can read this list to yourself and it will help you go on.

This is what Latoya put at the top of her list:
• My parents will be proud of me when I'm a successful businessperson.

WRITE AN ACTION PLAN. Once you know what your goal is and why you want to achieve it, you must write an action plan.

This is Latoya's action plan:
- I'm going to go to business school as soon as I save enough money to pay for it.
- When I graduate, I'll get a job with a big company.
- After I get some experience, I'll find a better job.

TAKE YOUR FIRST STEPS TODAY. Don't wait. As soon as you have an action plan, take steps to achieve it.

Here are the first steps Latoya is going to take:
- Before I apply to schools, I'm going to download some catalogs.
- After I apply, I'll prepare carefully for interviews.

You can do exactly what Latoya did to achieve your goals and turn them into reality. It's not always easy, but remember: The longest journey starts with the first step!

AFTER YOU READ

A VOCABULARY Choose the word or phrase that best completes each sentence.

1. When you **achieve** something, you get it _____.
   a. as a gift
   b. after hard work
   c. from your family

2. Sam got a college **catalog** because he wanted to _____.
   a. pay his bill
   b. do his homework
   c. learn about classes

3. A **goal** is something you _____.
   a. don't want very much
   b. plan and work for
   c. buy at a store

4. A **path** is a way to _____ your goals.
   a. reach
   b. buy
   c. choose

5. At a college **interview**, someone _____.
   a. asks you questions
   b. shows you the school
   c. gives you a job

B COMPREHENSION For each pair of statements about Latoya's action plan, choose the action (*a* or *b*) that comes first.

1. a. She will download school catalogs.
   b. She will apply to schools.

2. a. She will save money.
   b. She will go to business school.

3. a. She will get a job with a big company.
   b. She will graduate.

4. a. She will find a better job.
   b. She will get some experience.

5. a. She will turn 30.
   b. She will become a successful businesswoman.

C DISCUSSION Work with a partner. Compare your answers in B. Explain why you think your answers are correct.

FUTURE TIME CLAUSES

Statements

Main Clause			Time Clause	
I **will** I **am going to**				I **graduate**.
She **will** She **is going to**	**get** a job	**when**	she **graduates**.
They **will** They **are going to**				they **graduate**.

Yes/No Questions

Main Clause			Time Clause	
Will you	**get** a job	**when**	you **graduate**?
Are you **going to**			

Short Answers

Affirmative			Negative		
Yes,	I	**will**. **am**.	No,	I	**won't**. **'m not**.

Wh- Questions

Main Clause				Time Clause	
Where	**will** you **are** you **going to**	**get** a job	**when**	you **graduate**?

GRAMMAR NOTES

1 Function of a Future Time Clause

Use a future time clause to show the **time order between two future events**.

A future time clause begins with a **time expression** such as *when, after, as soon as, before, until,* or *while*.	MAIN CLAUSE TIME CLAUSE He**'s going to move** *after* he **graduates**. *(First he'll graduate. Then he'll move.)*
The time expression shows which of two future events **will happen first**.	MAIN CLAUSE TIME CLAUSE We**'ll visit** him *before* he **leaves**. *(First we'll visit him. Then he'll leave.)*
BE CAREFUL! A **future time clause** is about a **future event**, but its verb is in the **simple present**. Do not use *be going to* or *will* in a future time clause. Use the simple present.	He's going to move after he **graduates**. NOT after he ~~is going to graduate~~ We'll miss him when he **leaves**. NOT when he~~'ll leave~~

2 Position of the Future Time Clause

The **time clause** can come **at the beginning or the end** of the sentence. The meaning is the same.

• at the **beginning**	***Before* she applies,** she'll visit schools.
• at the **end**	She'll visit schools ***before* she applies.**

IN WRITING Use a **comma after the time clause** when it comes at the **beginning** of the sentence. Do not use a comma after the main clause when the main clause comes first.

***After* he graduates,** he'll look for a job.
He'll look for a job ***after* he graduates.**
NOT He'll look for a job**ₓ** after he graduates.

USAGE NOTE In **conversation**, we often answer a *when* question with **just the time clause**.

A: When will she visit schools?
B: ***Before* she applies.**

3 Time Words for the First Event

When, *after*, and *as soon as* introduce the **first event**.

***When* I graduate,** I'll look for a job.
I'll look for a job ***after* I graduate.**
(First I'll graduate. Then I'll look for a job.)

USAGE NOTE Use *as soon as* to emphasize that the second event will happen immediately after the first event.

***As soon as* I graduate,** I'll look for a job.
(First I'll graduate. Immediately after that, I'll look for a job.)

4 Time Words for the Second Event

Before and *until* introduce the **second event**.

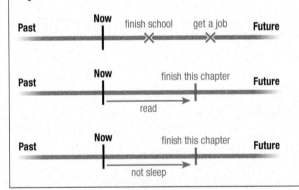

***Before* I get a job,** I'll finish school.
(First I'll finish school. Then I'll get a job.)

I'll read ***until* I finish this chapter.**
(I'll keep reading, but only up to the time that I finish this chapter. Then I'll stop.)

I won't sleep ***until* I finish this chapter.**
(I'll stay awake, but only up to the time that I finish this chapter. Then I'll go to sleep.)

5 *While* for Same-Time Events

While introduces an event that will happen **at the same time** as another event.

Notice that you can use the **simple present** or **present progressive** with an action verb after *while*.

***While* I look for a job,** I'll go on studying.
or
***While* I'm looking for a job,** I'll go on studying.
(I'll look for a job and study at the same time.)

EXERCISE 1 DISCOVER THE GRAMMAR

GRAMMAR NOTES 1–5 Read the numbered sentence. Then choose the pair of sentences that has a similar meaning.

1. Amber will open her own business when she finishes school.
   a. Amber will open her own business. Then she'll finish school.
   (b.) Amber will finish school. Then she'll open her own business.

2. Denzell won't quit until he finds another job.
   a. Denzell will find another job. Then he'll quit.
   b. Denzell will quit. Then he'll find another job.

3. Jake is going to retire as soon as he turns 60.
   a. Jake is going to retire. Then he'll turn 60.
   b. Jake is going to turn 60. Then he'll retire.

4. After the Morrisons sell their house, they'll move to Florida.
   a. The Morrisons will sell their house. Then they'll move to Florida.
   b. The Morrisons will move to Florida. Then they'll sell their house.

5. Marisa will call you when she gets home.
   a. Marisa will call you. Then she'll get home.
   b. Marisa will get home. Then she'll call you.

6. Dimitri is going to live with his parents until he gets married.
   a. Dimitri is going to get married. Then he'll live with his parents.
   b. Dimitri will live with his parents. Then he'll get married.

7. While Li-jing is in school, she's going to work part-time.
   a. Li-jing will finish school. Then she's going to get a part-time job.
   b. Li-jing will go to school. At the same time, she's going to have a part-time job.

8. Marta will have her degree before she turns twenty-one.
   a. Marta will get her degree. Then she'll turn twenty-one.
   b. Marta will turn twenty-one. Then she'll get her degree.

9. Adel and Farah won't buy a house until their son is two years old.
   a. They'll buy a house. Then their son will turn two.
   b. Their son will turn two. Then they'll buy a house.

10. Ina will live in Paris while she's studying French cooking.
    a. First she'll study French cooking. Then she's moving to Paris.
    b. She'll study French cooking. At the same time, she'll live in Paris.

EXERCISE 2 SIMPLE PRESENT OR FUTURE

GRAMMAR NOTES 1–3 Complete this student's worksheet. Use the correct form of the verbs in parentheses.

GOAL PLANNING WORKSHEET

A. What is your most important goal?

- To find a job after graduation.

B. List the reasons you want to achieve this goal.

- When I _____*get*_____ a job, I _____*'ll have*_____ more money.
  1. (get)   2. (have)
- When I _____ enough money, I _____ a used car.
  3. (save)   4. (buy)
- I _____ happier when I _____ employed.
  5. (feel)   6. (be)
- I _____ new skills while I _____ .
  7. (learn)   8. (work)

C. What is your action plan? What path will you take to reach your goal?

- Every morning when I _____, I _____ online for
  9. (get up)   10. (check)
  employment ads.
- When I _____ to my friends, I _____ them if they know
  11. (talk)   12. (ask)
  of any jobs.

- I _____ information about résumé writing
  13. (download)
  before I _____ a new résumé.
  14. (write)
- While I _____ to find a job, I
  15. (try)
  _____ my computer skills.
  16. (improve)
- Before I _____ on an interview, I
  17. (go)
  _____ how to use Excel and PowerPoint.
  18. (know)

D. What are the steps you will take right away?

- Before I _____ anything else, I
  19. (do)
  _____ a list of people to contact
  20. (write)
  for help.
- As soon as I _____ all the
  21. (contact)
  people on my list, I _____
  22. (work)
  on fixing up my résumé.

EXERCISE 3 ORDER OF EVENTS

GRAMMAR NOTES 1–5 Combine each pair of sentences. Use the future or the simple present form of the verb. Decide which sentence goes first. Remember to use commas when necessary.

1. Sandy and Jeff will get married. Then Sandy will graduate.

   _Sandy and Jeff will get married_____ before _Sandy graduates_____.

2. Jeff is going to get a raise. Then they are going to move to a larger apartment.

   _____ as soon as _____.

3. They're going to move to a larger apartment. Then they're going to have a baby.

   After _____.

4. They'll have their first child. Then Sandy will get a part-time job.

   _____ after _____.

5. Sandy will work part-time. Then their child will be two years old.

   _____ until _____.

6. Jeff will go to school. At the same time, Sandy will work full-time.

   _____ while _____.

7. Sandy and Jeff will achieve their goals. Then they'll feel very proud.

   When _____.

EXERCISE 4 EDITING

GRAMMAR NOTES 1–5 Read this student's blog. There are eight mistakes in the use of future time clauses. The first mistake is already corrected. Find and correct seven more.

Graduation is next month! I need to make some plans now because when exams ~~will start~~ *start*,

I don't have any free time. What am I going to do when I'll finish school? What path will

I take? My roommate is going to take a vacation before she'll look for a job. I can't do

that because I need to earn some money soon. I think that after I'll graduate, I'm going to

take a desktop publishing class. As soon as I learned the software, I look for a job with

a business publisher. It's hard to find full-time jobs, though. Part-time jobs are easier to

find. Maybe I'll take a part-time job until I'll find a good full-time one. Or maybe I'll take a

workshop in making decisions before I do anything!

Present Perfect

PART 3

OUTCOMES

- Describe events that began in the past and continue into the present
- Describe the duration of events, using the present perfect + *since/for*
- Identify key details in a short biography
- Identify the length of time of events in an interview
- Ask and answer questions about life events and experiences
- Write a paragraph about experiences and accomplishments

OUTCOMES

- Use *already*, *yet*, and *still* with the present perfect
- Discuss events that happened or did not happen at some time in the past
- Identify key details in an information article and a conversation
- Recognize and discuss tasks on a to-do list or plan
- Write a paragraph about a goal and the steps needed to reach it

OUTCOMES

- Describe events that happened at an indefinite time in the past
- Describe repeated actions and states in the past
- Identify main points of an article and a conversation about travel
- Discuss famous quotes, giving explanations and reasons for opinions
- Write a paragraph in response to a quote from literature

OUTCOMES

- Recognize when to use the present perfect and the simple past
- Identify key details in a short, factual text
- Understand the time frame of important details in an interview
- Discuss past events and experiences
- Research a famous person and present findings to the class
- Write a paragraph about a personal experience

OUTCOMES

- Describe actions that started in the past and are still in progress
- Describe actions that started at an indefinite time in the past and are finished
- Identify main points of a short text on a scientific topic
- Understand the time frame of main events in conversations
- Discuss climate change
- Write an email or letter about recent activities

Present Perfect:
Since and *For*
CAREERS

OUTCOMES
• Describe events that began in the past and continue into
  the present
• Describe the duration of events, using the present perfect
  + *since/for*
• Identify key details in a short biography
• Identify the length of time of events in an interview
• Ask and answer questions about life events and
  experiences
• Write a paragraph about experiences and accomplishments

STEP 1   **GRAMMAR IN CONTEXT**

BEFORE YOU READ

Look at Bob Burnquist's sports
card. Discuss the questions.

1. What are his interests?
2. What are *your* interests?
3. What is Bob's motto?[1]
4. Do you have a motto? What is it?

READ

08|01   Read this article about a champion skateboarder.

King of Skate

When he was only 11 years old, Bob
Burnquist's life changed dramatically. A skate
park opened just three blocks from his house
in São Paulo, Brazil. Bob got his very first
skateboard and started skating. He's been a
skater since then.

---

1 *motto:* a short statement of life goals or beliefs
2 *individuality:* the way people are different from each other

SPORTS CARD
Bob Burnquist

Date of Birth	October 10, 1976
Place of Birth	Rio de Janeiro, Brazil
Residence	California, U.S.
Citizenship	Brazil and U.S.
Started Skateboarding	1987
Turned Professional	1991
Other Interests	Reading, travel, photography, snowboarding, mountain biking, surfing, skydiving
Motto	"Be good, be positive, respect individuality[2] and nature."

At first, he did it just for fun, but soon he turned pro.[3] Before long, he made enough money to support himself while doing what he loved most. His first big international competition was in Canada in 1995. Bob won. Since then, he has won many more first-place prizes. And he is still winning. Since 2002, when he was voted "King of Skate" in a California contest, Bob has won twelve gold medals—three of them in 2013.

Bob has lived in California since 1995, but he frequently returns to Brazil. He's had dual citizenship (Brazil and the United States) for many years. Does he consider himself American? Bob says, "I'm American, South American. . . . A citizen of the world."

The skateboard isn't the only board Bob uses. He also enjoys snowboarding and surfing. Since he moved to California, he has been close to snow-topped mountains and the beach. His backyard and, of course, the streets provide opportunity for skating. As he once said, "If you snowboard, surf, and skate, you pretty much cover the whole earth."

---

3 *turned pro:* became a professional (did the sport for money)

AFTER YOU READ

A VOCABULARY Choose the word or phrase that is closest in meaning to the word(s) in **bold**.

1. Bob's life changed **dramatically**.
   a. slowly and a little   b. dangerously   c. quickly and a lot

2. He earned enough money to **support himself**.
   a. pay for lessons   b. pay for things he needs   c. buy a new skateboard

3. Does Bob **consider himself** American?
   a. want to be   b. like being   c. think he is

4. The streets provide **opportunity** for skating.
   a. some dangers   b. good chances   c. a lot of contests

5. Bob's **residence** is in California.
   a. home   b. office   c. family

6. Bob always says, "Be **positive**."
   a. 100 percent sure   b. hopeful   c. strong

B COMPREHENSION Read the statements. Check (✓) *True* or *False*.

	True	False
1. Bob Burnquist doesn't skate anymore.	☐	☐
2. He has won only one first-place prize since 1995.	☐	☐
3. Bob moved to California in 1995.	☐	☐
4. Bob is a citizen of many countries.	☐	☐
5. He lives close to the beach.	☐	☐

C DISCUSSION Work with a partner. Compare your answers in B. Why did you check *True* or *False*?

PRESENT PERFECT WITH *SINCE* AND *FOR*

Statements

Subject	*Have (not)*	Past Participle		*Since/For*
I You* We They	**have (not)**	**been**	here	**since** 2002. **for** a long time.
He She It	**has (not)**	**lived**		

* *You* is both singular and plural.

Contractions

Affirmative	Negative
I have = **I've** you have = **you've** we have = **we've** they have = **they've** he has = **he's** she has = **she's** it has = **it's**	have not = **haven't** has not = **hasn't**

Yes/No Questions

Have	Subject	Past Participle		*Since/For*
Have	I you we they	**been**	here	**since** 2002? **for** a long time?
Has	he she it	**lived**		

Short Answers

Affirmative			Negative		
Yes,	you I/we you they	**have.**	**No,**	you I/we you they	**haven't.**
	he she it	**has.**		he she it	**hasn't.**

Wh- Questions

Wh- Word	*Have*	Subject	Past Participle	
How long	**have**	I you we they	**been**	here?
	has	he she it	**lived**	

Short Answers

Since 2002.
For many years.

GRAMMAR NOTES

1 Present Perfect + *Since* or *For*

Use the present perfect with *since* or *for* to show that something **began in the past and continues into the present** (and may continue into the future).

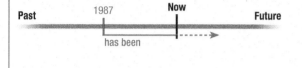

Bob **has been** a skater *since* 1987.
(He became a skater in 1987, and he is still a skater.)
He **has been** a skater *for* many years.
(He became a skater many years ago, and he is still a skater.)

2 *Since* and *For*

Since shows **when** something started. *For* shows **how long** something has lasted.

Use *since* + **point in time** (*since yesterday, since 5:00, since Monday, since 1995, since then*) to show when something started.	He **has won** many contests *since 1995*. He **has become** famous *since then*.
Since can also introduce a time clause.	He **has loved** sports *since he was a child*.
Use *for* + **length of time** (*for 10 minutes, for two weeks, for years, for a long time*) to show how long something has lasted.	Bob **has had** a restaurant *for years*. He **hasn't broken** a board *for a long time*.
Expressions with *since* or *for* can go at the **end** or the **beginning** of the sentence.	He has become famous *since then*. *Since then*, he has become famous.
USAGE NOTE It is **more common** to put the expression with *since* or *for* at the **end** of the sentence.	He has lived in L.A. *for many years*. *(more common)* *For many years*, he has lived in L.A. *(less common)*
IN WRITING Use a **comma** when the expression with *since* or *for* comes at the **beginning** of the sentence.	*Since he turned pro,* he hasn't taken a vacation. *For many years,* he's had dual citizenship.
Do not use a comma when the expression with *since* or *for* comes at the end of the sentence.	**NOT** He hasn't taken a vacation╳ since he turned pro. **NOT** He's had dual citizenship╳ for many years.

	He **has lived** there for years.
Form the present perfect with *have* + **past participle**.	They **have been** partners since 1998.

	BASE FORM	SIMPLE PAST	PAST PARTICIPLE
To form the **past participle** of **regular verbs** add *-d* or *-ed* to the base form of the verb. It is the same as the regular simple past form of the verb.	love	love**d**	love**d**
	want	want**ed**	want**ed**

IN WRITING There are often **spelling changes** when you add *-ed* to the verb.	marry	marr**ied**	marr**ied**
	stop	stop**ped**	stop**ped**

	BASE FORM	SIMPLE PAST	PAST PARTICIPLE
Many common verbs are **irregular**. They do not form the past participle by adding *-d* or *-ed* to the base form of the verb. Here is a list of some of the **irregular verbs used in this unit**. It shows both the simple past and the past participle of each verb. Notice that most irregular verbs have a past participle form that is different from the simple past form.	be	was/were	**been**
	become	became	**become**
	go	went	**gone**
	have	had	**had**
	meet	met	**met**
	take	took	**taken**
	wear	wore	**worn**
	win	won	**won**
	write	wrote	**written**

USAGE NOTE Some verbs have **two past participle forms**—one **regular** and one **irregular**. In conversation, the irregular past participle form is more common. There is one exception: For *dream*, the regular form is more common.	kneel	knelt/kneeled	**knelt/kneeled**
	light	lit/lighted	**lit/lighted**
	prove	proved	**proven/proved**
	dream	dreamed/dreamt	**dreamed/dreamt**

USAGE NOTE A few verbs have **two irregular past participles**. The form *have gotten* is very common in American English.	beat	beat	**beaten/beat**
	get	got	**gotten/got**

	He has **won** many contests.
BE CAREFUL! Do not form the **past participle of irregular verbs** by adding *-d* or *-ed* to the base form of the verb.	NOT He has ~~winned~~ many contests.

REFERENCE NOTE

For a more complete list of **irregular verbs**, see Appendix 1 on page 321.

STEP 3 FOCUSED PRACTICE

EXERCISE 1
DISCOVER THE GRAMMAR

GRAMMAR NOTES 1–3 Read the information about a skater, Caterina. Then choose the sentence (*a* or *b*) that best describes the situation.

1. Caterina has been a skater since 2008.
   a. She is still a skater.
   b. She is not a skater anymore.

2. She has lived in the same apartment for five years.
   a. She lived in a different apartment six years ago.
   b. She moved two years ago.

3. Caterina has been married for five years.
   a. She is not married now.
   b. She got married five years ago.

4. Catarina and her husband haven't been on a vacation since 2011.
   a. They are on a vacation now.
   b. They were on a vacation in 2011.

5. Caterina hasn't won a contest for two years.
   a. She won a contest two years ago.
   b. She didn't win a contest two years ago.

6. She has stayed positive about her career since she won her last contest.
   a. She expects to win more contests.
   b. She isn't hopeful anymore.

EXERCISE 2 *SINCE* OR *FOR*

GRAMMAR NOTE 2 Complete the sentences about Brazilian sportswriter Mariana Andrade. Use *since* or *for*.

1. Mariana Andrade has lived in São Paulo _____*since*_____ 2000.

2. She has supported herself as a sportswriter _____ four years.

3. _____ June, she has written several articles about skateboarding.

4. This sport has been very popular in Brazil _____ many years.

5. Mariana has met Burnquist twice _____ she started her job.

6. She loves to skate, but she hasn't had much opportunity _____ a long time.

7. She has been married to Alvaro, another skater, _____ 2008.

Present Perfect: *Since* and *For*   **79**

EXERCISE 3 FORMS OF THE PRESENT PERFECT

GRAMMAR NOTE 3 Complete this article about Lauren Jones. Use the correct form of the verbs in parentheses.

Lauren Jones _____*has loved*_____ skating since she was a little girl. She began skating
1. (love)

when she was 10, and she _____ since then. She _____ a
2. (not stop)   3. (be)

professional skater now for several years. She and her husband _____ in San
4. (live)

Diego, California since the two got married. They _____ the same one-bedroom
5. (have)

apartment for three years. They _____ a vacation for many years, but they
6. (not take)

_____ to several international skating contests since Lauren turned pro. Lauren
7. (go)

_____ in three contests since last year, and she _____ two
8. (skate)   9. (win)

second-place prizes since then. Lauren _____ to be a pro since she was a child.
10. (want)

"There aren't many professional female skateboarders," she says. "Ever since my dream came true, I

_____ myself a lucky woman."
11. (consider)

EXERCISE 4 FORMS OF THE PRESENT PERFECT WITH *SINCE* OR *FOR*

GRAMMAR NOTES 2–3 Complete the sentences. Use the present perfect form of the verbs in parentheses and *since* or *for*.

1. Skateboarding _____*has been*_____ popular _____*for*_____ more than 50 years.
   a. (be)   b.

2. Skateboards _____ around _____ a long time. In the 1930s,
   a. (be)   b.
   the first ones were simple wooden boxes on metal wheels. They _____
   c. (change)
   dramatically _____ then!
   d.

3. The first skateboarding contest took place in California in 1963. _____ then,
   a.
   thousands of contests _____ place internationally.
   b. (take)

4. In 1976, the first outdoor skate park opened in the United States. _____ then,
   a.
   hundreds of parks _____ in countries around the world such as Australia,
   b. (open)
   China, England, France, Israel, Japan, and Kenya.

5. Skateboarding can be dangerous. _____ the 1960s, hundreds of thousands of
   a.
   people _____ to hospital emergency rooms because of injuries.
   b. (go)

6. When he was seven years old, Jon Comer lost his right foot as a result of a car accident. But that
   didn't stop him. _____ then, he _____ one of the best-known
   a.   b. (become)
   professional skateboarders in the world, thanks to his great skill and very positive attitude.

7. Tony Hawk _____ professionally _____ many years, but he is
   a. (not compete)   b.
   still the most famous and successful skateboarder of all time.

EXERCISE 5 QUESTIONS, STATEMENTS, AND SHORT ANSWERS

A GRAMMAR NOTES 1–3 Amy Lu is applying for a job as a college sports instructor. Look at her résumé and the interviewer's notes. The year is 2016.

Amy Lu

525 Ahina St.
Honolulu, HI 96816

Interviewed 09/19/16

Education:

2008   Certificate (American College of Sports Medicine)
2005   M.A. Physical Education (University of Texas)

moved to Honolulu in 2006

Employment:

2007-present   part-time physical education teacher (high school)
2005-present   sports trainer (private)

teaches tennis, swimming

Skills:

speaks English, Portuguese, and Chinese
practices martial arts   *got black belt in tae kwon do 2 mos. ago*

Other Interests:

travel, sports photography, skateboarding, surfing

Awards:

2008   Teacher of the Year Award
2005   First Prize in Sunburn Classic Skate Contest

Memberships:

2008-present   member of National Education Association (NEA)

B John Sakaino is interviewing Amy Lu for a job as a college sports instructor. Use the words in parentheses to complete the questions. Use the information in Amy's résumé to write her answers. Use contractions when possible.

1. (how long / live in Honolulu)

JOHN: _How long have you lived in Honolulu?_

AMY: _I've lived in Honolulu for 10 years._ or _I've lived in Honolulu since 2006._

2. (how long / have your M.A. degree)

JOHN: _____

AMY: _____

3. (have any more training / since / you get your M.A.)

JOHN: _____

AMY: _____

4. (how long / be a physical education teacher)

JOHN: _____

AMY: _____

5. (how long / work as a sports trainer)

JOHN: _____

AMY: _____

6. (how long / have a black belt in tae kwon do)

JOHN: _____

AMY: _____

7. (win any awards since then)

JOHN: I see you won a medal in skateboarding. _____

AMY: _____ I won the Teacher of the Year Award in 2008.

8. (how long / be a member of NEA)

JOHN: _____

AMY: _____

EXERCISE 6 EDITING

GRAMMAR NOTES 1–3 Read these posts to a skateboard message board. There are ten
mistakes in the use of the present perfect with *since* and *for*. The first mistake is already
corrected. Find and correct nine more.

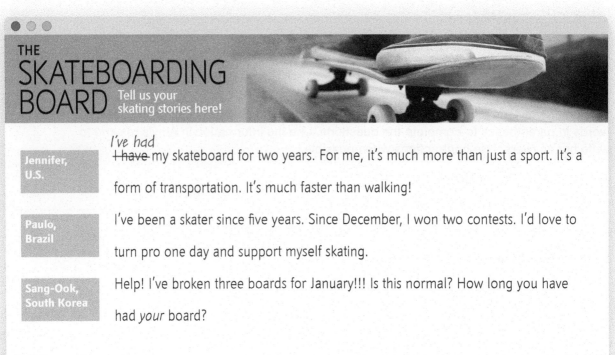

THE
SKATEBOARDING
BOARD Tell us your skating stories here!

Jennifer, U.S.

I've had
~~I have~~ my skateboard for two years. For me, it's much more than just a sport. It's a

form of transportation. It's much faster than walking!

Paulo, Brazil

I've been a skater since five years. Since December, I won two contests. I'd love to

turn pro one day and support myself skating.

Sang-Ook, South Korea

Help! I've broken three boards for January!!! Is this normal? How long you have

had *your* board?

Marta, Mexico	Broken boards?! That's nothing! Consider yourself lucky! I've break my wrist twice since I started skating!
Megan, Australia	Last year, my board hit a rock while I was skating in the street. I fell and hit my head and had to go to the emergency room. I always worn a helmet since then!
Ming, U.S.	I live in California since 2006. My first love is surfing, but when there aren't any waves, I jump on my skateboard and take to the streets! My motto is "Make the best of what you have!"
Todd, Canada	Wow! Yesterday, my friend gave me a copy of the video "OP King of Skate." I've watch it three times since then. The Burnquist part is awesome!
Sylvie, France	At last! A skate park opened near my home last week. Since then, I gone every day. It's a lot more fun than skating in the streets!

Present Perfect:
Already, Yet, and Still
PARTY PLANNING

OUTCOMES
• Use *already*, *yet*, and *still* with the present perfect
• Discuss events that happened or did not happen at some time in the past
• Identify key details in an information article and a conversation
• Recognize and discuss tasks on a to-do list or plan
• Write a paragraph about a goal and the steps needed to reach it

---

STEP 1   GRAMMAR IN CONTEXT

BEFORE YOU READ

Look at the photo. Discuss the questions.

1. How do you feel about parties?

2. Which do you prefer: giving a party or going to one? Why?

READ

▶09|01   Read this article about how to plan a party.

It's Party Time!

It's almost the end of the year, and you've already been to several parties, but you haven't given a party of your own yet. You're a little nervous, but you decide it's time to take the plunge.[1]

First things first: Have you chosen the date yet? What about the time?

OK. You've already chosen the date and the time and emailed the invitations. But you still haven't decided on the menu, and now your party is just one week away! Don't panic!

---

1 *take the plunge:* do an activity that seems difficult or frightening

We spoke to Patty Cake, a professional party planner. She says, "It *is* very important to be organized, but remember: You don't need a whole new set of skills. Think about your everyday life. You've already done many of the things you need to do for a party. You know how to shop for food, put it on plates, and introduce friends to one another. Now, all you need to do is just bring your many skills together."

Still need help? Party planners, like Patty Cake, can offer specific advice. She says, "We've already helped hundreds of people plan successful parties—big and small. If you haven't used a party-planning service yet, you should give it a try." And you don't have to spend a lot of money. Free advice is available on the Internet. There, you will also find handy² lists where you can check off things you've already done (and see the things you haven't done yet!). So, take a deep breath, relax, and enjoy the party!

2 *handy:* useful; easy to use

AFTER YOU READ

A VOCABULARY **Complete the sentences with the words from the box.**

available   organized   professional   specific   successful

1. OK. The drinks are on the table over there. Extra chairs are in the bedroom. The cake is in the refrigerator. I'll take it out at 8:00 p.m. That's it! I think I'm quite _____.

2. I can meet you for lunch any day this week to discuss plans for your party. You can also call me anytime—day or night. As you can see, I'm pretty _____.

3. The party is for my friend Marta. She's a writer. Her latest book is on the bestseller list! She's really _____.

4. Please bring two large bags of Crispy Chips. The ones in the blue bag—they're low in fat, but not low in salt. You'll find them at Shopwise in aisle 6. I know I'm being very _____, but I want to be sure you get the right ones!

5. Jake offered to paint the apartment before the party, but I prefer to hire _____ painters. They have training, job experience—and insurance if something goes wrong!

B COMPREHENSION **Reread the first three paragraphs in the article. Check (✓) the correct answers.**

The party giver . . .

☐ **1.** went to several parties

☐ **2.** gave a party of her own

☐ **3.** chose a date for the party

☐ **4.** chose the time

☐ **5.** sent invitations

☐ **6.** decided on a menu

C DISCUSSION **Work with a partner. Compare your answers in B. Why did you or didn't you check each item?**

PRESENT PERFECT: *ALREADY, YET,* AND *STILL*

Affirmative Statements: *Already*

Subject	*Have*	*Already*	Past Participle		*Already*
They	have	*already*	emailed	the invitations.	
She	has		chosen	the menu.	
They	have		emailed	the invitations	*already*.
She	has		chosen	the menu	

Negative Statements: *Yet*

Subject	*Have not*	Past Participle		*Yet*
They	haven't	emailed	them	*yet*.
She	hasn't	chosen	it	

Negative Statements: *Still*

Subject	*Still*	*Have not*	Past Participle	
They	*still*	haven't	emailed	them.
She		hasn't	chosen	it.

Yes/No Questions: *Yet*

Have	Subject	Past Participle		*Yet*
Have	they	emailed	them	*yet*?
Has	she	chosen	it	

Short Answers

Affirmative		Negative	
Yes,	they **have**.	No,	they **haven't**.
	she **has**.		she **hasn't**.
			not *yet*.

GRAMMAR NOTES

1 Present Perfect + *Already, Yet,* or *Still*

Use the present perfect with *already, yet,* or *still* to show that something **happened or did not happen at an indefinite** (not exact) **time in the past**.

• *already*	I**'ve** *already* **emailed** the invitations.
• *yet*	We **haven't ordered** the cake *yet*.
• *still*	He *still* **hasn't replied**.

BE CAREFUL! Do not use *already, yet,* or *still* with past time expressions.	**NOT** I've *already* mailed the invitations ~~last week~~.
USAGE NOTE In American English, we sometimes use the **simple past** with *already* and *yet*.	Jenna **has** *already* **left**. or Jenna *already* **left**. Ebo **hasn't left** *yet*. or Ebo **didn't leave** *yet*.

2 Statements

In **affirmative statements**, use *already*. In **negative statements**, use *yet* or *still*.

Use *already* in **affirmative statements** to show that something **has happened before now**.	Jenna **has *already* met** Carlos.
USAGE NOTE We often use the present perfect with *already* for something that happened sooner than expected.	You**'ve *already* set** the table. Great!
Use *yet* in **negative statements** to show that something **has not happened before now** (in the near past).	A: Jenna **has*n't* called *yet***. B: Oh, I'm sure we'll hear from her later.
USAGE NOTE We often use the present perfect with *not yet* for something we expected to happen earlier, but did not happen. It is possible that it will happen soon.	Where's Tom? I expected him at 8:00, but he **hasn't arrived *yet***. I hope he gets here soon.
You can also use *still* in **negative statements**. *Still* has a similar meaning to *not yet*.	Jenna *still* **hasn't called**.
USAGE NOTE We often use the present perfect with *still* to show that we are surprised or unhappy with the situation.	I don't know if Jenna is coming or not. I've texted her several times, but she *still* **hasn't answered**. She promised to help me.

3 Questions

In questions, we usually use *yet*.

Use the present perfect with *yet* in **questions** to ask if something has happened before now.	A: **Have** you **bought** the soda *yet*?
Notice the different possible ways of giving **negative answers**.	B: **No, I haven't.** or **No, *not yet*.** or ***Not yet*.**
USAGE NOTE We sometimes use *already* in questions to express **surprise** that something has happened sooner than expected.	**Has** Carlos **arrived *already*?** What's he doing here? The party doesn't start until 8:00!

4 Word Order

Already usually goes **before the past participle**. It can also go at the **end of the clause**.	I**'ve *already* made** the cake. I**'ve made** the cake *already*.
Yet usually goes at the **end of the clause**.	They **haven't arrived *yet***. She **hasn't invited** Mehmet *yet*.
Still goes **before *have not***.	They *still* **haven't arrived**. She *still* **hasn't invited** Mehmet.

REFERENCE NOTES

For a list of **irregular past participles**, see Appendix 1 on page 321.

For more information on the **indefinite past**, see Unit 10 on page 92.

For a list of **irregular past participles**, see Appendix 1 on page 321.

For more information on the **indefinite past**, see Unit 10 on page 92.

STEP 3   FOCUSED PRACTICE

EXERCISE 1 DISCOVER THE GRAMMAR

GRAMMAR NOTES 1–3 Read the first statement. Then decide if the second statement is
True (T) or *False (F)*.

1. I've already given many parties.

    _F_ This will be my first party.

2. I haven't made the cake yet.

    _____ I plan to make a cake.

3. Has Bev arrived yet?

    _____ I'm surprised that Bev is here.

4. Tom and Lisa still haven't arrived.

    _____ I expect them to arrive.

5. Has Jenna left already?

    _____ I'm surprised that Jenna left.

6. Have you had a cup of tea yet?

    _____ I don't know if you had a cup of tea.

7. Carlos has already met my sister.

    _____ I need to introduce Carlos to her.

8. I still haven't called Mehmet.

    _____ I don't plan to call him.

9. Has Tom bought the chips yet?

    _____ I think Tom is going to bring the chips.

10. I still haven't talked to the party planner.

    _____ I should call her.

11. Have you taken any photos yet?

    _____ I saw you take some photos.

12. We've already finished all the cake.

    _____ There is more cake.

EXERCISE 2 QUESTIONS, STATEMENTS, SHORT ANSWERS

Ⓐ GRAMMAR NOTES 1–3 Complete these conversations that take
place at Marta's party. Use the present perfect form of the verbs
in parentheses with *already* or *yet* and short answers. Use
contractions when possible. See Appendix 1 on page 453
for help with irregular verbs.

1. A: This is a great party. Marta made the cake. She's

    a professional baker. _____Have_____ you

    _____tried_____ it _____yet_____?
         (try)

    B: _____No_____, I _____haven't_____.

    But I'm going to have a piece now.

2. A: Jenna, I'd like you to meet my friend Carlos.

   B: We _____ _____ _____. Marta introduced us.
   (meet)

3. A: Would you like another cup of coffee?

   B: No, thanks. I _____ _____ _____ three cups!
   (have)

4. A: _____ Jenna _____ _____? It's still early!
   (leave)

   B: _____, she _____. She's in the kitchen.

5. A: _____ you _____ Tarantino's new movie _____?
   (see)

   B: _____, I _____. It's great. What about you?

   A: I _____ _____ it _____, but I want to.
   (see)

6. A: This was a great party. I'm giving my own party next week. I _____

   _____ _____ the whole thing, but I'm still nervous about it.
   (plan)

   B: Don't worry. If you organize it well, the rest will take care of itself!

🔊09|02 Ⓑ LISTEN AND CHECK **Listen to the conversations and check your answers in A.**

EXERCISE 3 WORD ORDER

GRAMMAR NOTE 4 **Unscramble the words to complete what some of the guests at Marta's party said.**

1. (tried / have / yet / the cake / you)

   Have you tried the cake yet _____?

2. (Jenna / yet / haven't / seen / I)

   _____.

3. (already / met / I've / Carlos)

   _____.

4. (yet / seen / Bruno / you / have)

   _____?

5. (still / tried / I / the cake / haven't)

   _____.

6. (some of the guests / left / already / have)

   _____.

7. (Bruno / arrived / hasn't / still)

   _____!

THINGS TO DO

- ☑ pick a date
- ☐ choose a time!!
- ☑ find a location
- ☑ write a guest list
- ☑ buy invitations
- ☐ send invitations!!
- ☐ plan the menu!!
- ☑ pick out music
- ☐ shop for food
- ☐ clean the house

EXERCISE 4 AFFIRMATIVE AND NEGATIVE STATEMENTS

GRAMMAR NOTES 1–4 Read Dante's party-planning checklist. Write statements about the things that he *has already done* and the things that he *hasn't done yet* (or the things that he *still hasn't done!*). See Appendix 1 on page 321 for help with irregular verbs.

1. *He's already picked a date.*

2. *He hasn't chosen a time yet.* or *He still hasn't chosen a time.*

3. _____

4. _____

5. _____

6. _____

7. _____

8. _____

9. _____

10. _____

EXERCISE 5 EDITING

GRAMMAR NOTES 1–4 Read this online bulletin board. There are nine mistakes in the use of the present perfect with *already*, *yet*, and *still*. The first mistake is already corrected. Find and correct eight more.

Ask the Party Planner!

Doug asked: Help! My party is next week, and I ~~already~~ *still* haven't figured out the food! I'm not at all organized. I've yet wasted three days worrying, and I still don't have any ideas. What should I do?

The Party Planner's Advice: Don't panic! Your guests haven't started arriving already, so there's still time. Ask everyone to bring something! (You've already invite people, right?) Or order pizza. I haven't met anyone already who doesn't like pizza.

Rosa asked: I'd like to find a "theme" for my next birthday party. I've already have a pasta party (10 kinds of pasta!), and I've already gave a movie party (everyone dressed up as a movie character). Both were very successful, but I haven't still decided what to do this time. Any ideas?

The Party Planner's Advice: Sure. Has you tried this one yet? Ask each guest to bring a baby photo of himself or herself. Collect the photos. People try to match the photos with the guests! Your guests will love it!

Present Perfect: Indefinite Past

ADVENTURE TRAVEL

STEP 1 GRAMMAR IN CONTEXT

BEFORE YOU READ

Look at the photos and at the title of the article. Discuss the questions.

1. What do you think the article is about?

2. Would you like to do the things in the photos? Why or why not?

READ

▷ 10|01 Read this article about unusual vacations.

Been There? Done That?

Maybe it's time for something new . . .

Today's world is getting smaller. People are traveling the globe[1] in record numbers.[2] Our readers have been to Rome. They've visited Greece. They've seen the ancient pyramids of Egypt. They've gone skiing in the Swiss Alps. Now, they're looking for new places to see and new things to do. They want adventure. *Travel Today* has just come out with its annual survey. As part of the survey, the magazine asks its readers the following question: "What would you like to do that you've never done before?"

Here are some of their answers:

---

1 *the globe:* the world
2 *in record numbers:* much more than in the past

> I've made **several trips to Egypt,** but I've never ridden **a camel.** I've always wanted **to do that.**

Hot-air ballooning! My boyfriend *has tried* this several times, but *I've never done it.*

I've ice-skated and *I've climbed* mountains, but *I've never been* ice climbing. That's something I'd definitely like to try!

Riding a camel, hot-air ballooning, ice climbing . . . These are just a few activities that travelers can choose from today. All you need is time, money (a lot of it!), and a sense of adventure.[3] But you don't have to go to a faraway place in an unusual type of transportation to have a great vacation! Have you ever spent the day walking in the woods, heard the sound of the wind, or watched the sun set over the ocean? These can be wonderful adventures, too! And a lot more affordable!

---

3 *sense of adventure:* the ability to enjoy new things

AFTER YOU READ

A VOCABULARY Match the words with their definitions.

_____ **1. adventure**	**a.**	very old
_____ **2. survey**	**b.**	an exciting, unusual experience
_____ **3. affordable**	**c.**	happening every year
_____ **4. transportation**	**d.**	a questionnaire
_____ **5. ancient**	**e.**	a way of traveling someplace
_____ **6. annual**	**f.**	not expensive

B COMPREHENSION Which activities have the readers of *Travel Today* tried? Check (✓) them.

☐ **1.** skiing in the Alps   ☐ **4.** ice-skating

☐ **2.** riding a camel   ☐ **5.** mountain climbing

☐ **3.** hot-air ballooning   ☐ **6.** ice climbing

C DISCUSSION Work with a partner. Compare your answers in B. Why did you or didn't you check each activity?

STEP 2   **GRAMMAR PRESENTATION**

PRESENT PERFECT: INDEFINITE PAST

Statements

Subject	*Have (not)*	Past Participle	
They	**have** (not)	**visited**	Egypt.
She	**has** (not)	**been**	there.

Statements with Adverbs

Subject	*Have (not)*	Adverb	Past Participle		Adverb
They	**have**	*never*	**visited**	Egypt.	
She	**has**	*just* *recently*	**been**	there.	

They	**have** (not)		**visited**	Egypt	*twice.* *lately.* *recently.*
She	**has** (not)		**been**	there	

Yes/No Questions

Have	Subject	*(Ever)*	Past Participle	
Have	they	*(ever)*	**visited**	Egypt?
Has	she		**been**	there?

Short Answers

Affirmative		Negative	
Yes,	they **have**.	No,	they **haven't**.
	she **has**.		she **hasn't**.
			never.

Wh- Questions

Wh- Word	*Have*	Subject	Past Participle	
How often	**have**	they	**visited**	Egypt?
	has	she	**been**	there?

GRAMMAR NOTES

1 Present Perfect

Use the present perfect to show that something **happened at an indefinite** (not exact) **time in the past**.

Use the present perfect when you **don't know when** something happened or when the specific **time is not important**.

Past ? Now Future

We've been to Rome.

They**'ve traveled** to Egypt.
  (You don't know the exact time.)
We**'ve been** to Rome.
  (The exact time isn't important.)

Use the present perfect (not the simple past) to show a **connection to the present**: the result of the action or state is important in the present.

The hotel **has closed**.
  (So we can't stay there now.)

USAGE NOTE For many speakers *have been to* and *have gone to* have different meanings.

He**'s been to** France.
  (At some point in the past, he visited France, but he's not necessarily there now.)
He**'s gone to** France.
  (He's in France now.)

2 Present Perfect + Adverbs of Time or Time Expressions

You can also use the present perfect with **adverbs of time** or **time expressions** to show that something happened at an **indefinite time in the past**.

For **repeated actions** at some indefinite time in the past, use adverbs of time or time expressions such as:

- *twice*
- *often*
- *many times*

They**'ve seen** the Pyramids *twice*.
We**'ve *often* stayed** at that hotel.
We**'ve stayed** there *many times*.

For **repeated actions** or **states** that continue up to the present and may continue into the future, use:

- *so far*

So far, I**'ve taken** more than 1000 photos. I'm sure I'll take many more before this trip is over!
So far, the weather **has been** great.

USAGE NOTE We often use *so far* with numbers, adverbs like *twice*, and *only*.

So far, she's bought *four* souvenirs.
So far, they've traveled to Egypt *twice*.
So far, he's *only* been to Cairo.

For states or actions that **continue in the present**, use:

- *always*
- *never*

We**'ve *always* wanted** to go to Egypt.
I**'ve *never* ridden** a camel.

CONTINUED ▶

To ask **questions** and give **negative answers**, use:	
• *ever* (= at any time before now) • *never*	**A:** **Have** you *ever* **been** to Rome? **B:** No, I'**ve** *never* **been** there. **or** No, *never*.

To stress that something happened in the very **recent past**, use:	
• *just* (= a very short time before now) • *lately/recently* (= in the near past)	I'**ve** *just* **gotten** back from China. They **haven't been** there *lately*. He'**s flown** a lot *recently*.

USAGE NOTE In American English, we often use *just* and *recently* with the **simple past**. You can't, however, use *lately* with the simple past.	I'**ve** *just* **returned** or I *just* **returned**. **NOT** I returned ~~lately~~.
BE CAREFUL! Do not use the present perfect with adverbs or expressions that refer to a **specific time in the past**. Use the simple past.	I **got** back *yesterday*. **NOT** ~~I've gotten~~ back *yesterday*.

3 Word Order

With the present perfect, most **adverbs of time** or **time expressions** can go at the **end of the clause** or **before the past participle**.

Some adverbs of time and time expressions go at the **end of the clause**:	
• *twice* • *many times* • *lately*	She'**s been** there *twice*. I'**ve been** there *many times*. I **haven't traveled** *lately* because it's too expensive.

Other adverbs go **before the past participle**:	
• *always* • *often* • *ever* • *never* • *just*	I'**ve** *always* **wanted** to stay there. We'**ve** *often* **talked** about it. **Have** you *ever* **seen** the pyramids? We'**ve** *never* **been** to Egypt. His plane **has** *just* **landed**.

Recently can go **at the end of the clause** or **before the past participle**.	They'**ve traveled** a lot *recently*. They'**ve** *recently* **traveled** a lot.
So far usually goes at the **beginning** or **end of the clause**.	*So far*, I'**ve read** 100 pages of my guide book. I'**ve read** 100 pages of my guide book *so far*.

REFERENCE NOTES

For a list of **irregular past participles**, see Appendix 1 on page 321.

For all **present perfect forms**, see Unit 8 on page 74.

For **present perfect with** *already, yet,* and *still*, see Unit 9 on page 84.

EXERCISE 1   DISCOVER THE GRAMMAR

GRAMMAR NOTES 1–3   Read the first statement. Then decide if the second statement is *True (T)* or *False (F)*. If there isn't enough information in the first statement to know the answer, put a question mark *(?)* on the line.

1. Adventure vacations have become very popular.

   _T_ They are popular now.

2. I've been to Italy twice.

   _____ I was there two years ago.

3. I have never been to the Himalayas.

   _____ I went to the Himalayas a long time ago.

4. I've just returned from China.

   _____ I was in China a short time ago.

5. Greg asks you, "Have you ever been to Costa Rica?"

   _____ Greg wants to know when you were in Costa Rica.

6. Marta asks you, "Have you read any good travel books lately?"

   _____ Marta wants to know about a travel book you read last year.

7. We have visited Egypt several times.

   _____ This is not our first visit to Egypt.

8. He's recently been to Greece.

   _____ He's been to Greece recently.

9. I've spent $100 so far.

   _____ I've spent $100 up to now.

10. I've been on an African safari.[1]

    _____ I'm on a safari now.

---

1 *safari:* a trip through the country areas of Africa in order to watch wild animals

EXERCISE 2 STATEMENTS AND QUESTIONS

A GRAMMAR NOTES 1–2 *Travel Today* (TT) interviewed travel writer Rosa García (RG).
Complete this interview. Use the present perfect form of the verbs in parentheses. Use
contractions when possible.

TT: As a travel writer, you _____ *'ve visited* _____ many places. Any favorites?
                           1. (visit)

RG: Thailand. It's a beautiful, amazing country. I _____ there five times.
                                          2. (be)

TT: What _____ your most unusual travel experience?
               3. (be)

RG: My *most* unusual? I _____ so many! I _____ near sharks (in a cage,
                     4. (have)   **5.** (swim)

    of course!), I _____ dinner next to a very active volcano, I _____ in
               6. (eat)   **7.** (sleep)

    an ice hotel in Finland . . .

TT: The world _____ a lot smaller. There are fewer and fewer "undiscovered" places.
                 8. (become)

    _____ you ever _____ a really great place and decided not to tell
                                   9. (find)

    your readers about it?

RG: No, never. I _____ about doing that a few times, but so far, I _____
              10. (think)

    never actually _____ it. I _____ always _____
                   11. (do)   **12.** (write)

    about it.

TT: Where _____ you _____ recently?
                              13. (be)

RG: I _____ just _____ from a hot-air ballooning trip in Australia. It was
                   14. (return)

    really fantastic. In fact, ballooning is my new favorite form of transportation!

TT: Where are you going next?

RG: On an African safari! I _____ never _____ on one, and I'm really
                                  15. (be)

    excited. I _____ always _____ to do that.
                            16. (want)

TT: Good luck! And I look forward to your African safari article.

▶10|02 **B** LISTEN AND CHECK **Listen to the interview and check your answers in A.**

EXERCISE 3 AFFIRMATIVE AND NEGATIVE STATEMENTS

GRAMMAR NOTES 1–3 Look at this survey. Then write sentences about things Andy *has done* and things he *hasn't done* (or *has never done*). Use contractions when possible.

Travel Time Survey

Name: *Andy Cheng*

Have you ever done the following activities? Check (✔) the ones you have done.

1. rent a car ☐
2. rent a motorcycle ✔
3. ride a camel ☐
4. go up in a hot-air balloon ✔
5. have some really unusual food ✔
6. see ancient pyramids ☐
7. sail a boat on the Nile River ✔
8. swim with dolphins in the ocean ✔
9. be on a safari ☐
10. fly around the world ☐

1. *He hasn't rented a car.* **or** *He's never rented a car.*
2. *He's rented a motorcycle.*
3. _____
4. _____
5. _____
6. _____
7. _____
8. _____
9. _____
10. _____

EXERCISE 4 WORD ORDER

A GRAMMAR NOTE 3 Complete this conversation. Put the words in parentheses in the correct order. Use the present perfect form of the verbs. Include short answers. Use contractions when possible.

EVAN: Hot-air ballooning! What's it like? *I've never done this* _____ before!
1. (I / do this / never)

ANDY: You'll love it. _____,
2. (I / a few times / go up)

   but _____.
3. (not do it / lately / I)

EVAN: _____?
4. (you / a lot / travel)

ANDY: Yes, _____. I'm a travel writer, so it's part of my job.
5.

EVAN: That's great! _____ on a safari?
          6. (you / be / ever)

ANDY: No, _____, but _____ .
          7.   8. (want / to go / always / I)

EVAN: Me too. _____ .
                    9. (I / several times / to Africa / be)

     In fact, _____ back from a trip there.
                    10. (I / get / just)

     But _____ on a safari.
              11. (so far / I / not be)

ANDY: Look. _____ getting the balloon ready. It's time to go up!
                    12. (they / finish / just)

▶10|03 **B** LISTEN AND CHECK **Listen to the conversation and check your answers in A.**

EXERCISE 5 STATEMENTS

GRAMMAR NOTES 1–3 **Look at some of Rosa's things. Write sentences using the present perfect form of the verbs from the box. Use adverbs of time or time expressions when possible.**

| ~~be~~ | ride | see | stay | travel | write |

1. <u>*She's been to Egypt twice.*</u>   **2.** _____

3. _____   **4.** _____

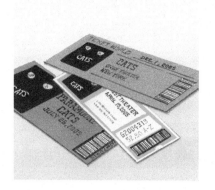

5. _____   6. _____

EXERCISE 6 EDITING

GRAMMAR NOTES 1–3 Read these comments found on a hot-air ballooning website. There are twelve mistakes in the use of the present perfect and adverbs. The first mistake is already corrected. Find and correct eleven more.

●●●

upandaway.com

    have
We ~~has~~ received many comments from our clients. We'd like to share some with you.

Britta Kessler GERMANY   I have always be afraid of heights. But after I saw the beautiful photos on your website, I knew I had to

go hot-air ballooning! This have been one of the best experiences of my life so far. Thank you!

James Hudson CANADA   We've returned just from a fantastic vacation. I've told all my friends about your company.

Antonio Vega MEXICO   I've always wanted to go up in a hot-air balloon. I was not disappointed!

Bill Hampton USA   I just seen some new photos posted on the website! Awesome!

Amalia Lopes BRAZIL   I've never went hot-air ballooning, but after visiting your wonderful website, I've decided to sign up!

Pat Calahan IRELAND   We gave our parents a balloon trip as an anniversary gift. They've just wrote to say it was fantastic.

They've ever been very adventurous, but now they want to go whitewater rafting!

Lydia Hassan NEW ZEALAND   You have ever seen the face of a kid on a hot-air balloon ride? The cost of the ride: a lot. That look on

her face: priceless!

May Roa PHILIPPINES   I broken my leg last month, so I haven't lately been able to do sports—boring! Your mountain balloon

trip has just gave me a lift—in more than one way!

11

Present Perfect and Simple Past

FAILURE AND SUCCESS

OUTCOMES
• Recognize when to use the present perfect and the simple past
• Identify key details in a short, factual text
• Understand the time frame of important details in an interview
• Discuss past events and experiences
• Research a famous person and present findings to the class
• Write a paragraph about a personal experience

STEP 1 | GRAMMAR IN CONTEXT

BEFORE YOU READ

Look at the photo of Thomas Edison. Discuss the questions.

1. What is Thomas Edison famous for?
2. Why do you think people call him a "first-time failure"?

READD

▶11|01 Read this article about failure and success.

Famous First-Time Failures

Have you ever tried and failed, and then quit something really very important to you? Thomas Alva Edison failed thousands of times before he created the first successful electric light bulb. But the famous inventor had a great attitude. He never lost hope and never gave up. "I have not failed, not once. I've discovered ten thousand ways that don't work," he said after one of many tries.

Like Edison, author Melissa de la Cruz didn't have it easy at first. She wrote her first book at age 22 and sent it to many publishers.[1] They all rejected it. Nobody wanted her next few books either. Then, when she decided to take a writing course, every school rejected her. The young writer probably wanted to give up many times, but she didn't quit. Since her early failures, de la Cruz has written more than twenty-five

Thomas Alva Edison

---

1 *publishers:* people or companies that arrange the writing, printing, and sale of books

books—many of them best sellers. She has won several awards and has sold millions of copies of her books around the world.

Have you ever quit too soon? Has your own failure really been a success that is waiting for a few more tries? Maybe you haven't failed enough times yet? Try again, and when you feel discouraged, remember Edison and de la Cruz and follow the advice in the famous saying: "If at first you don't succeed, try, try, try again."

Melissa de la Cruz

AFTER YOU READ

Ⓐ VOCABULARY **Choose the word or phrase that best completes each sentence.**

1. Edison **created** many things. This means that he _____ many new things.
   a. bought   **b.** made   **c.** wanted

2. The opposite of **failure** is _____.
   a. health   **b.** happiness   **c.** success

3. If you are **discouraged**, you don't feel _____.
   a. hopeful   **b.** nervous   **c.** tired

4. If people **reject** your ideas, they _____ them.
   a. say *yes* to   **b.** think about   **c.** say *no* to

5. Your **attitude** is how you _____ about something.
   a. act   **b.** feel or think   **c.** learn

6. You win an **award** for being _____ at something you do.
   a. pretty good   **b.** good   **c.** the best

Ⓑ COMPREHENSION **Read the statements. Check (✓) *True* or *False*.**

	True	False
1. Thomas Edison was immediately successful.	☐	☐
2. Edison never quit.	☐	☐
3. Publishers immediately accepted Melissa de la Cruz's first book.	☐	☐
4. Publishers rejected de la Cruz's next books.	☐	☐
5. De la Cruz is still writing books.	☐	☐
6. De la Cruz is very successful.	☐	☐

Ⓒ DISCUSSION **Work with a partner. Compare your answers in B. Why did you check *True* or *False*?**

PRESENT PERFECT AND SIMPLE PAST

Present Perfect
She **has been** here since 2014.
They**'ve lived** here for 20 years.
She**'s written** ten pages today.
He **hasn't flown** this month.
Has she **called** him today?

Simple Past
She **was** in the Philippines in 2013.
They **lived** there for 10 years.
She **wrote** twenty pages yesterday.
He **didn't fly** last month.
Did she **call** him yesterday?

GRAMMAR NOTES

1 Present Perfect or Simple Past + *For*

The present perfect with *for* has a **very different meaning** from the simple past with *for*.

Use the **present perfect** to show that something began in the past and **continues into the present** (and may continue into the future).

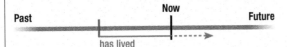

She **has lived** in the United States for more than thirty years.
(She moved to the United States more than thirty years ago, and she is still living there.)

Use the **simple past** to show that something happened in the past and has **no connection to the present**.

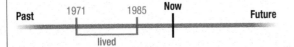

She **lived** in the Philippines for fourteen years.
(She lived there until 1985, but she no longer lives there.)

2 Indefinite Time or Specific Time in the Past

Use the **present perfect** to show that something happened at an **indefinite time** in the past. The exact time is not known or not important.

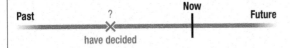

They **have decided** to write another book.
(We don't know exactly when they made the decision, or the time of the decision is not important.)

Use the **simple past** to show that something happened at a **specific time** in the past. The exact time is known and often included.

She **wrote** her first book *in 2001*.
(We know the exact time and it is important information.)

BE CAREFUL! Do not use the present perfect with a specific time in the past. The only exception is with *since*.

I **lived** in Manila *in 2007*.
NOT I've lived in Manila *in 2007*.
I**'ve lived** in Manila *since 2007*.

3 Unfinished Time or Finished Time

Use the **present perfect** to show that something happened in a time period that is **unfinished**, such as *today, this morning, this month, this year.*	Her publisher **has called** three times *today*. *(Today isn't finished, and it's possible that the publisher will call again.)*
Use the **simple past** to show that something happened in a time period that is **finished**, such as *yesterday, yesterday morning, last month, last year.*	Her publisher **called** three times *yesterday*. *(Yesterday is finished.)*
BE CAREFUL! Some time expressions such as *this morning*, *this month*, or *this year* can refer to an **unfinished** or a **finished** time period. Use the present perfect if the time period is unfinished. Use the simple past if the time period is finished.	It's 10:00 a.m. She**'s had** three cups of coffee *this morning*. *(The morning isn't finished.)* It's 1:00 p.m. She **had** three cups of coffee *this morning*. *(The morning is finished.)*

REFERENCE NOTES

For the **simple past**, see Unit 2 on page 16.
For the **present perfect** with *since* and *for*, see Unit 8 on page 76.
For the **present perfect** for **indefinite past**, see Unit 10 on page 94.
For a list of **irregular verbs**, see Appendix 1 on page 321.

STEP 3   FOCUSED PRACTICE

EXERCISE 1 DISCOVER THE GRAMMAR

GRAMMAR NOTES 1–3 Read the information about Melissa de la Cruz. Then choose the sentence (*a* or *b*) that best describes the situation.

1. Melissa de la Cruz was born in the Philippines in 1971. She lived there until she moved to the United States.
   a. She lived in the Philippines for fourteen years.
   b. She's lived in the Philippines for fourteen years.

2. She moved to the United States in 1985. She still lives there.
   a. She lived in the United States for more than thirty years.
   b. She's lived in the United States for more than thirty years.

3. She was a computer programmer for nine years.
   a. She has had a job as a computer programmer for nine years.
   b. She had a job as a computer programmer for nine years.

4. She has always loved to read.
   a. Her love of books started early.
   b. She didn't love books until she became an adult.

5. At first, many publishers rejected her books.

  a. She was not successful.

  b. She has not been successful.

6. In 2013, she returned to the Philippines for a book-signing tour.

  a. She has been there for a few weeks.

  b. She was there for a few weeks.

7. In 2002, she married architect Michael Johnston. The couple is still married.

  a. The couple has been married for many years.

  b. The couple was married for many years.

8. They write books together.

  a. They have written together for a while.

  b. They wrote together for a while.

9. Their books sell all over the world.

  a. Their books have been a great success.

  b. Their books were a great success.

10. It's April and they are on their third book-signing tour.

  a. They went on several trips this year.

  b. They've been on several trips this year.

EXERCISE 2 PRESENT PERFECT OR SIMPLE PAST

GRAMMAR NOTES 1–3 Complete this article about best-selling author Stephen King (1947–). Circle the correct verb forms.

Stephen King (has written) / wrote more than 60 novels and almost
                        1.
200 short stories. As a child in Portland, Maine, he has enjoyed / enjoyed
                                                              2.
reading horror comics.[1] He has begun / began writing in school, where
                                          3.
he has sold / sold his stories to his friends. But his early
          4.
success as a writer did not continue without problems.

In 1973, he has written / wrote his first novel, *Carrie*,
                        5.
about a teenage girl with frightening magical powers. It
has received / received thirty rejections. Discouraged, King
          6.
has thrown / threw the book away. Luckily for him and
          7.
his many future fans, his wife has removed / removed it
                                          8.
from the trash and encouraged him to submit it again.

This time the publishers have accepted / accepted it.
                                    9.

---

1 *horror comics:* magazines (often for children) that use pictures
  to tell very frightening stories

Stephen King

Since 1974, King <u>has sold</u> / sold more than 350 million books around the world.

10.

In addition to his books, he <u>has written</u> / wrote scripts for movies and television.

11.

He <u>has received</u> / received many awards including the World Fantasy Award for Life

12.

Achievement, which he <u>has won</u> / won in 2004. In spite of his huge success, King lives a

13.

simple life. He <u>has continued</u> / continued to live in Maine and he <u>has remained</u> / remained

14.   **15.**

married to the same woman who <u>has rescued</u> / rescued *Carrie* from the trash can many

16.

years ago. In a 2014 interview with *Rolling Stone Magazine*, the interviewer <u>has asked</u> / asked

17.

King about his fear of failure. "I'm afraid of failing at whatever story I'm writing," King

<u>has admitted</u> / admitted. His fear, however, never stops him. King continues to be one of the

18.

best-selling authors in the world.

EXERCISE 3 PRESENT PERFECT OR SIMPLE PAST STATEMENTS

GRAMMAR NOTES 1–3 Complete this entry in a writer's online journal. Use the present perfect or simple past form of the verbs in parentheses.

Thursday, 4:00 p.m.

It ____*has been*____ a very difficult day, and it's not over yet! I _____

    1. (be)   **2.** (begin)

working at 8:00 a.m. this morning. I _____ to finish the next chapter of my

                                         3. (want)

book, but I _____ only two pages all day! It's so frustrating. It's already

                4. (write)

Thursday, and I _____ a good idea all week. (Last week, I _____

                        5. (not have)   **6.** (write)

two whole chapters!) Yesterday, I _____ so discouraged that I almost

                                             7. (feel)

_____. But then I _____ Thomas Edison and the trouble he

  8. (quit)   **9.** (remember)

_____ when he was trying to create the light bulb. He _____

10. (experience)   **11.** (have)

such a great attitude about failure and success. It really _____ me to go on. I

                                             12. (help)

guess I can look at today in a positive way and say, "This morning, I _____

                                             13. (discover)

another way not to finish this chapter!"

EXERCISE 4 PRESENT PERFECT OR SIMPLE PAST QUESTIONS

A GRAMMAR NOTES 1–3 *Success Magazine* (SM) is interviewing a famous author, Emil Karlsson (EK). Complete the interview questions. Use the words in parentheses. Choose between the present perfect and simple past.

SM: *How long have you been an author?*
      1. (how long / you / be an author)

EK: Oh, for about fifteen years.

SM: And _____
      2. (when / you / write your first book)

EK: I wrote my first book when I was twenty-one.

SM: _____
      3. (be / it / immediately successful)

EK: Yes. I was very lucky. And very surprised!

SM: _____
      4. (how many copies / it / sell during its first year)

EK: More than a million.

SM: More than a million copies? That's a lot of copies! Now, tell me about your most recent book.

_____
      5. (when / it / come out)

EK: It came out about a year ago.

SM: And _____ since then?
      6. (it / win / any awards)

EK: Yes. It won *Mystery Mag's* Best Book of the Year Award.

SM: Congratulations! _____?
      7. (how many copies / it / sell)

EK: I'm not sure. You'll have to ask my publisher!

▶11|02 **B** LISTEN AND CHECK Listen to the interview and check your answers in A.

EXERCISE 5 EDITING

GRAMMAR NOTES 1–3 **Read these online comments about a book called** *Failure and Success*. **There are twelve mistakes in the use of the present perfect and simple past. The first mistake is already corrected. Find and correct eleven more.**

Comments from Readers

November 4

I've just finished reading *Failure and Success* by Nila Sciretta. Actually, ~~I read~~ *I've read* several of her

books this year. The book is great! It's no surprise that it sold so many copies. **—Marta Lopez**

I was a big fan of this author for many years, so I was very happy to find her latest book

online. I've downloaded it last week and I finished it in two days. It's a great book—perhaps

the best book I read so far this year. I highly recommend it. **—Burak Mardin**

Have these other people read the same book as me? I haven't liked it at all. I thought it was

boring. I've finished it last night, but I'm sorry I bought it. Save your money! **—Felipe Casa**

For the last few months, I tried suggestions from *Failure and Success*. This book has changed

my attitude about failure. Everyone has failed at some time, but the author has not failed in

communicating her message: Failure can be a great teacher! **—Soon-Bok Park**

I only read two chapters so far, but I think it's a very interesting and helpful book. I've already

learned a lot from it. I especially like all the examples about famous people, like Edison, who

have failed at first before they became successful. **—Jason Morgen**

My husband and I are both college professors. Before we finally have found teaching jobs at

the same school, we had to live in different cities. It was a very difficult time for us. A friend

recommended one of Sciretta's earlier books and it really helped. We're also authors, but we

didn't find a publisher yet. But thanks to Sciretta's advice, we won't give up! **—Ann Braid**

Present Perfect Progressive and Present Perfect

CLIMATE CHANGE

OUTCOMES
- Describe actions that started in the past and are still in progress
- Describe actions that started at an indefinite time in the past and are finished
- Identify main points of a short text on a scientific topic
- Understand the time frame of main events in conversations
- Discuss climate change
- Write an email or letter about recent activities

| STEP 1 | GRAMMAR IN CONTEXT |

BEFORE YOU READ

Look at the photo and at the title of the article. Discuss the questions.

1. What is happening to the Earth?
2. Why does the Earth have a thermometer in it?
3. What is a hot topic?

READ

▶ 12|01   Read this article about climate change.

Global Warming:[1] A Hot Topic

The Earth's climate has changed many times. Warm oceans covered the Earth for millions of years. Then those oceans turned to ice for millions more. If the climate has been changing for five billion years, why is global warming such a hot topic today?

Almost everyone agrees that the Earth has been getting hotter. But not everyone agrees about the cause. Most climate experts think that human activities have added to global warming. The coal and oil we burn for energy have been sending more and more gases into the air around the Earth. The gases keep the

---

1 *global warming:* the continuing increase in the Earth's temperatures (including air and oceans) since the 1950s

heat in the atmosphere[2] and also cause air pollution.[3] These experts believe humans can slow global warming.

Others say global warming is mostly the result of natural causes, such as changes in the sun. They don't believe that human activities can make things better or worse.

Human or natural, the effects of global warming have been powerful. Here are just two examples:

- In the Arctic,[4] ice has been melting quickly. As a result, polar bears and other animals have become endangered species.[5] Arctic towns and villages are also in danger as sea levels rise.

- In parts of Africa, rainfall has decreased. Water and food have become very hard to find. Both people and animals have been suffering badly.

Recently, people have been taking steps to slow these dangerous trends. They have been developing ways to use clean solar energy. In addition, they have been designing homes and cars that use less energy.

Does it really matter what causes global warming? Environmentalists[6] believe that it does, and they say that if we have been part of the cause, then we can also be part of the solution.

---

2 *atmosphere:* the air that surrounds the Earth
3 *air pollution:* something dirty and unhealthy in the air
4 *the Arctic:* the most northern part of the Earth
5 *endangered species:* a type of animal or plant that may not continue to exist
6 *environmentalists:* people who want to protect the environment (land, water, and air)

AFTER YOU READ

A VOCABULARY Match the words with their definitions.

_____ 1. **expert**   a. the power that makes machines work

_____ 2. **climate**   b. to create a drawing that shows how to build something

_____ 3. **develop**   c. someone with special knowledge of a subject

_____ 4. **energy**   d. the typical weather in an area

_____ 5. **design**   e. the way a situation is generally changing

_____ 6. **trend**   f. to work on a new idea or product to make it successful

B COMPREHENSION Read the statements. Check (✓) *True* or *False*.

	True	False
1. Climate change is something new.	☐	☐
2. Almost everyone believes that the Earth used to be cooler.	☐	☐
3. Coal and oil are still sending gases into the air around the Earth.	☐	☐
4. Ice in the Arctic has stopped melting.	☐	☐
5. In parts of Africa, people and animals are still suffering.	☐	☐
6. People are no longer developing ways to use solar energy.	☐	☐

C DISCUSSION Work with a partner. Compare your answers in B. Why did you check *True* or *False*?

PRESENT PERFECT PROGRESSIVE AND PRESENT PERFECT

Present Perfect Progressive

Statements

Subject	Have (not)	Been	Base Form of Verb + -ing	(Since/For)
I You* We They	have (not)	been	working	(since 2009). (for years).
He She It	has (not)			

* *You* is both singular and plural.

Yes/No Questions

Have	Subject	Been	Base Form of Verb + -ing	(Since/For)
Have	you	been	working	(since 2009)? (for years)?
Has	she			

Short Answers

Affirmative				Negative		
Yes,	I/we	have.		No,	I/we	haven't.
	she	has.			she	hasn't.

Wh- Questions

Wh- Word	Have	Subject	Been	Base Form of Verb + -ing
How long	have	you	been	working?
	has	she		

Present Perfect Progressive and Present Perfect

Present Perfect Progressive
They **have been living** here for many years.
I've been reading this book since Monday.
Dr. Owen **has been writing** articles since 2000.
She**'s been working** in Kenya for a year.

Present Perfect
They **have lived** here for many years.
I've read two books about solar energy.
Dr. Owen **has written** many articles.
She**'s worked** in many countries.

GRAMMAR NOTES

1 Present Perfect Progressive or Present Perfect

The present perfect progressive and the present perfect usually have **different meanings**.

Use the **present perfect progressive** to show that something is **unfinished**. It started in the past and is still continuing. The focus is on the **continuation** of the action.

I**'ve been reading** a book about solar energy.
 (I'm still reading it.)
She**'s been writing** an article.
 (She's still writing it.)

Use the **present perfect** to show that something is **finished**. It happened at an indefinite time in the past. The focus is on the **result** of the action.

I**'ve read** a book about solar energy.
 (I finished the book.)
She**'s written** an article.
 (She finished the article.)

USAGE NOTE We also use the **present perfect progressive** for finished actions that **ended in the very recent past**. You can often still see the results of the action.

Look! The streets are wet. It**'s been raining**.
 (It stopped raining very recently.)
NOT It's rained.

BE CAREFUL! We usually do not use **non-action verbs**, such as *be*, *have*, and *know* in the progressive.

She**'s had** the same job since 2000.
NOT She's been having the same job since 2000.

2 With Time Expressions, Quantifiers, and Numbers

Use the **present perfect progressive** with *for +* **time expression** to show *how long* something has been happening.

I**'ve been reading** books about wind energy *for two months*.

Use the **present perfect** with a **quantifier or number** to show:

- *how much* someone has done
- *how many things* someone has done
- *how many times* someone has done something

I**'ve read** *a lot* about it.
She**'s written** *three* articles.
I**'ve read** that book *twice*.

BE CAREFUL! Do not use the present perfect with a **specific time in the past**. The only exception is with *since*.

She**'s read** three articles.
NOT She's read three articles *last week*.
She**'s read** three articles *since last week*.

With verbs that show **duration** such as *live*, *study*, *teach*, and *work*, you can use the **present perfect progressive** or the **present perfect** with *for* or *since*. The meaning is the same: something is **unfinished**.

• **present perfect progressive**	He**'s been studying** global warming *for* ten years.
	or
• **present perfect**	He**'s studied** global warming *for* ten years.
	(In both examples, he is still studying it.)

USAGE NOTE We often use the **present perfect progressive** to show that something is **temporary**.	They**'ve been living** here *since* 1995, but they are moving next month.
USAGE NOTE We often use the **present perfect** to show that something is **permanent**.	They**'ve lived** here *since* they were children, and they're not planning on moving.

REFERENCE NOTES

For a list of **non-action verbs**, see Appendix 2 on page 322.

For the **present perfect with *since* and *for***, see Unit 8 on page 76.

For the **present perfect for the indefinite past**, see Unit 10 on page 94.

For the **present perfect and simple past**, see Unit 11 on page 104.

EXERCISE 1 DISCOVER THE GRAMMAR

GRAMMAR NOTES 1–3 Read each statement. Decide if something is finished or unfinished. Check (✓) *Finished* or *Unfinished*.

	Finished	Unfinished
1. I've been reading a book about global warming.	☐	☑
2. I've read a book about global warming.	☐	☐
3. She's written two magazine articles about air pollution.	☐	☐
4. She's been waiting for some supplies.	☐	☐
5. They've lived in Ontario since 2002.	☐	☐
6. They've been living in Ontario since 2002.	☐	☐
7. We've been developing plans with the leaders of many countries.	☐	☐
8. We've developed these plans with many leaders.	☐	☐
9. Look out the window—it's been raining.	☐	☐
10. Look. Someone has watered the plants.	☐	☐

EXERCISE 2 PRESENT PERFECT PROGRESSIVE OR PRESENT PERFECT

GRAMMAR NOTES 1–3 Complete the statements about an expert on climate change, Professor Jane Owen, and her work. Circle the correct words. Sometimes both answers are correct.

1. *Green Earth* magazine has been publishing /(has published)Professor Owen's third annual report on environmental trends. It's an excellent report.

2. Professor Owen is working on two articles for the next issue of *Green Earth* magazine. She has been writing / has written these articles since Monday.

3. She has been writing / has written about global warming many times.

4. Professor Owen has been speaking / has spoken at our school several times about climate change.

5. She has been speaking / has spoken since 8:00 p.m., and she still has a lot more to tell us.

6. Professor Owen has a lot of work to do. Lately, she has been studying / has studied the use of solar energy for homes. She's learning about pollution from buildings.

7. She was late for a meeting with the members of her group. When she arrived they said, "At last, you're here. We've been waiting / We've waited for you."

8. Professor Owen has been living / has lived in Kenya for the last two years, but she will return to the United States in January.

9. She has been working / has worked with environmentalists in Kenya and Tanzania.

10. Kenyans have been planting / have planted 30 million trees since the 1970s.

EXERCISE 3 PRESENT PERFECT PROGRESSIVE

GRAMMAR NOTES 1-2 Look at the two pictures of Professor Owen. Complete the sentences describing what has been happening. Use the present perfect progressive form of the verbs in parentheses. Choose between affirmative and negative.

1. She _____'s been working_____ in her office.
   (work)

2. She _____ a book.
   (write)

3. She _____ TV.
   (watch)

4. She _____ her computer.
   (use)

5. She _____ coffee.
   (drink)

6. She _____ tea.
   (drink)

7. She _____ her sandwich.
   (eat)

8. She _____ her new black sweater.
   (wear)

9. She _____ hard.
   (work)

10. It _____ all day.
    (rain)

EXERCISE 4 STATEMENTS

GRAMMAR NOTES 1–3 Complete Professor Owen's blog about the European Solar
Decathlon, a competition for the best solar houses (homes that get all their energy from
the sun). Use the present perfect progressive or the present perfect form of the verbs in
parentheses. Sometimes both forms are possible.

One of the solar houses in
this year's competition

Green Mail

JUNE 28, 2014   VERSAILLES, FRANCE — A beautiful solar village ____*has appeared*____ on
1. (appear)

the grounds of the Versailles Palace. Twenty teams from universities in Europe, Asia, and North and

South America _____ these houses here for an international competition of
2. (bring)

solar houses. Universities _____ in this competition since 2007. For all the
3. (participate)

contests, talented students _____ the energy-efficient houses, and they
4. (design)

_____ them as well. Over the years, the homes _____
5. (build)   **6.** (get)

more energy efficient *and* more beautiful. This year, twenty houses _____ the
7. (enter)

competition. I _____ the houses since I got here. I still have several more to
8. (visit)

see, and I am looking forward to it. I _____ also _____ to many of the
9. (talk)

student designers. So far, what I hear most often is, "I could *totally* live in this house!" I agree.

Check back in about two weeks for the winners.

JULY 14 — Well, the contest is finally over and Team RhOME (RhOME = Rome home) from Italy

_____ this year's first prize. The teams from France and the Netherlands also
10. (win)

_____ prizes for their creative work. Tomorrow, it's back to Kenya for me. This
11. (receive)

_____ a really great event.
12. (be)

EXERCISE 5
QUESTIONS AND ANSWERS

GRAMMAR NOTE 2 Professor Owen
is interviewing one of the student
designers at Solar Decathlon Europe.
Use the words in parentheses to write
Professor Owen's questions. Use
her notes to complete the student's
answers. Choose between the present
perfect progressive and the present
perfect. Use contractions when possible.

> started project two years ago
> cost – $250,000
> house tours – all afternoon
> visitors this week – so far about 30,000
> interest in solar energy – started three
>   years ago
> total energy production today – more than
>   the house needs!
> the team's first competition – 2010
> one prize for lighting design

1. (how long / your team / work / on this project)

   OWEN: _How long has your team been working on this project?_

   STUDENT: _We've been working on this project for two years._

2. (how much money / the team / spend / on the house)

   OWEN: _____

   STUDENT: _____

3. (how long / you / lead tours / today)

   OWEN: _____

   STUDENT: _____

4. (how many people / visit / this week)

   OWEN: _____

   STUDENT: _____

5. (how long / you / be / interested in solar energy)

   OWEN: _____

   STUDENT: _____

6. (how much energy / the house / produce today)

   OWEN: _____

   STUDENT: _____

7. (how long / your team / compete)

   OWEN: _____

   STUDENT: _____

8. (how many prizes / your team / win)

   OWEN: _____

   STUDENT: _____

EXERCISE 6 EDITING

GRAMMAR NOTES 1–3 Read this student's email. There are eight mistakes in the use of the present perfect progressive and the present perfect. The first mistake is already corrected. Find and correct seven more.

Hi guys,

Sorry I haven't ~~wrote~~ *written* sooner. I haven't been having any free time since we arrived in Versailles for the solar house competition. (Our house got here before us!) I'm really excited and also really tired. Since we arrived, we've been lived on pizza and coffee. I haven't sleeping more than a few hours since . . . well, I can't remember when. Our team has been working day and night for the last two weeks, and today the house looks wonderful. I'm so proud—we've designed a home that's beautiful AND reduces pollution. We're finally ready for the judges, so I've spent most of the day looking at other teams' houses. I've been visiting ten houses today. They are so interesting and creative! I hope they help start a new trend in housing that is good for the environment. For the last hour, I've just been hanging out in a café with some people from the other teams. I've already been drinking three cups of coffee—it's delicious, but really strong! We been practicing our French. I still don't understand too much, but our teammate Jacques Renard is from Quebec, Canada, and he's been helped me out a lot. Wish us luck and check your text messages for photos of the house.

Katie

Modals and Similar Expressions

PART 4

OUTCOMES

- Express ability and possibility in the past, present, and future
- Identify main points in a social sciences text
- Identify important details in a job interview
- Compare and contrast different possibilities for improving language skills
- Discuss an academic topic
- Write a paragraph about past, present, and future abilities

OUTCOMES

- Ask for, give, or deny permission
- Identify main points in a short reading
- Recognize when a speaker gives permission or refuses permission
- Come to a resolution with others by asking for and giving permission to do something
- Write a short note, explaining a situation and asking for permission to do something

OUTCOMES

- Make and respond to requests
- Identify important details related to requests in emails and text messages
- Identify details related to a schedule in a conversation
- Discuss a daily schedule that involves making requests of others
- Write and respond to a request in a text or email message

OUTCOMES

- Give and ask for advice
- Identify main points in a short text about rules and advice
- Recognize statements of advice in a radio show
- Discuss possible solutions to everyday situations, giving reasons and explanations
- Write an email or letter of complaint, giving advice on making improvements

Ability and Possibility: *Can, Could, Be able to*

MULTILINGUALISM

OUTCOMES
- Express ability and possibility in the past, present, and future
- Identify main points in a social sciences text
- Identify important details in a job interview
- Compare and contrast different possibilities for improving language skills
- Discuss an academic topic
- Write a paragraph about past, present, and future abilities

STEP 1   GRAMMAR IN CONTEXT

BEFORE YOU READ

Look at the photo. Discuss the questions.

1. What do you think a *polyglot* is?
2. Do you recognize any of these languages?
3. Which languages can *you* speak?

READ

▶13|01   Read this article about multilingualism.

Hello!

Bonjour!

Bom dia!

¡Hola!

Hamjambo!

Multilingualism

Do you speak English? Parlez-vous français? Fala português? ¿Habla Usted español? Unaongea Kiswahili? As a child, retired basketball player, Dikembe Mutombo Mpolondo Mukamba Jean-Jacques Wamutombo (known as Dikembe Mutombo for short), could speak several languages. Growing up in a multilingual home in Zaire (today called the Democratic Republic of the Congo), he learned some languages at home and others at school. Today, he can speak nine: English, French, Portuguese, Spanish, Swahili, and four other African languages. Dikembe Mutombo is just one example of the more than 50% of the world population who can communicate in two or more languages. And as the world "gets smaller," thanks to the Internet, increased travel, and large numbers of people moving to other countries, this number will continue to grow.

Bilingualism describes people who speak two languages; *multilingualism* usually describes the ability to speak more than two languages. Being multilingual, or a polyglot, such as Mutombo, does not always mean that a person is able to communicate like a native speaker in each language. In fact, most foreign language speakers, especially people who learn a language as adults, cannot speak like native speakers. The majority of people, even if they become fluent,[1] are not able to totally

---

1 *fluent:* able to speak or write a language very well

**Polyglot
Dikembe Mutombo**

lose their foreign accents, and they will usually make some mistakes when they use the language. But they will be able to communicate well enough to understand and allow people to understand them.

Multilingualism has many advantages in today's world. Speaking other languages can help you get a job in many fields such as tourism, health services, banking, teaching, and sales. And recent research shows that learning a new language can make you smarter and help slow down the signs of aging. But, most of all, learning and knowing other languages can be fun and exciting. You can use your languages when you travel, and you can learn more about other people and cultures. Dikembe Mutombo loves to travel. In an interview with the magazine *Condé Nast Traveler*, he said, "People think of travel for work or play, but it can also be a lesson that will change your life." However, even if you don't travel, you still can enjoy songs, books, and movies in other languages—without ever leaving home.

AFTER YOU READ

Ⓐ VOCABULARY Choose the word or phrase that best completes each sentence.

1. A **retired** language teacher _____ .
   a. teaches many classes   b. used to teach   c. works very hard

2. An **adult** is a person who _____ .
   a. is not a child   b. is good at languages   c. speaks well

3. People do **research** when they want to _____ about a subject.
   a. learn new facts   b. forget   c. complain

4. One **advantage** of speaking several languages is _____ .
   a. a good dictionary   b. hard work   c. more job opportunities

5. "What **field** are you in?" is a question about your _____ .
   a. native language   b. occupation   c. country

6. If the **majority** of people speak more than one language, this means that _____ are multilingual.
   a. less than 50%   b. 50%   c. more than 50%

Ⓑ COMPREHENSION Circle the correct information to complete each statement.

1. As a child, Dikembe Mutombo had the ability to speak two / more than two languages.

2. Today, one of the many languages he speaks is French / Chinese.

3. A multilingual person usually speaks / doesn't speak like a native speaker.

4. Most multilingual people lose / don't lose their foreign accent.

5. Knowing other languages helps you in the field of sports / tourism.

6. Learning another language is often enjoyable / difficult.

Ⓒ DISCUSSION Work with a partner. Compare your answers in B. Why did you choose each answer?

ABILITY AND POSSIBILITY: *CAN* AND *COULD*

Statements

Subject	Can / Could (not)	Base Form of Verb	
I You He She We You They	can (not)	speak French	now.
	could (not)		last year.

Contractions

cannot or can not	=	can't
could not	=	couldn't

Yes / No Questions

Can / Could	Subject	Base Form of Verb
Can	I you he she	speak French?
Could	we you they	

Short Answers

Affirmative				Negative		
Yes,	you I he	can.		No,	you I he	can't.
	she you we they	could.			she you we they	couldn't.

Wh- Questions

Wh- Word	Can / Could	Subject	Base Form of Verb
How well	can	she	speak French?
	could	you	

ABILITY AND POSSIBILITY: *BE ABLE TO*

Statements

Subject	Be	(Not) Able to	Base Form of Verb
I	am	(not) able to	practice.
You	are		
He She	is		
We You They	are		

Yes/No Questions

Be	Subject	Able to	Base Form of Verb
Is	she	**able to**	**practice?**
Are	you		

Short Answers

Affirmative				Negative			
Yes,	she	**is.**		**No,**	she	**isn't.**	
	I	**am.**			I'm	**not.**	

Wh- Questions

Wh- Word	Be	Subject	Able to	Base Form of Verb
When	**is**	she	**able to**	**practice?**
How often	**are**	you		

GRAMMAR NOTES

Can and its past form *could* are modals. *Be able to* is an expression similar to a modal. Modals are auxiliaries: we use modals with other verbs.

Like all modals, *can* and *could*:

- are followed by the base form of a verb: **modal + base form of verb**

  Marti **can speak** Arabic.
  Marti **could speak** Arabic when he was a child.

- have only **one form**
  (Do not use *-s* for the third-person singular, and do not add *-s* to the base form of the verb.)

  I **can** speak French, and she **can** speak Arabic.
  NOT She ~~cans~~ speak Arabic.
  NOT She can ~~speaks~~ Arabic.

- form the **negative with** *not*
  (Do not use *do, does,* or *did.*)

  She **can't** understand me.
  NOT She ~~doesn't can~~ understand me.

- go **before the subject** in **questions**
  (Do not use *do, does,* or *did.*)

  Can Antonio speak Italian?
  NOT ~~Does~~ can Antonio speak Italian?

Be able to is similar to a modal, but it has different forms (*am, is, are; was, were; will be*).

Was she **able to speak** French as a child?
Will I **be able to learn** French by next year?

IN WRITING *Can* and *could* are more common in conversation than in writing. *Be able to* is more common in formal writing.

A lot of people **can speak** several languages.
  (conversation)
Many people **are able to speak** several languages.
  (formal writing)

2 Can, Could, Be able to: Meanings

A modal adds meaning (such as the meaning of ability or possibility) to the verb that follows it. For example, *can*, *could*, or *be able to* shows that somebody has the **ability** and/or the **possibility** to do something.

• **ability** (natural or learned)	She **can speak**, but she **can't hear**. We **could read**, but we **couldn't write**. Soon, you**'ll be able to write** to me in English.
• **possibility**	You **can take** English as a second language this year. I **couldn't take** it last year. My school didn't offer it. You**'ll be able to take** that course next semester.
Can, *could*, and *be able to* often have both meanings of **ability and possibility**. This is especially true when we use them with a human or animal subject.	I **can help** you study for your French test. *(I have the ability and the possibility to help you.)*
We sometimes use *can* with a non-human or non-animal subject, but in this case the meaning is just **possibility**.	Speaking a foreign language **can be** fun. *(It has the possibility of being fun.)*

3 Present Ability or Possibility

Use *can* or *am/is/are able to* for present ability or possibility.

• *can* • *am/is/are able to*	She **can speak** English, but she **can't speak** French. She **is able to speak** English, but she **isn't able to speak** French.
USAGE NOTE *Can* is very common. It is much more common than *be able to* in everyday **conversation** about present ability.	**Can** you **speak** French? *(more common)* **Are** you **able to speak** French? *(less common)*
USAGE NOTE We often use *be able to* when the ability to do something comes after a lot of **hard work**.	French was difficult for me, but now I**'m able to have** a conversation because I spent a year studying in France.

4 Future Ability or Possibility

Use *can* or *will be able to* for future ability or possibility.

• *can*	I hope I **can understand** people when I'm in France next month.
• *will be able to*	I hope I**'ll be able to understand** people when I'm in France next month.
BE CAREFUL! Use *will be able to* (not *can*) for things you **learn**.	When I finish this course, I**'ll be able to** speak French well. **NOT** When I finish this course, I ~~can~~ speak French well.

Use *could* or *was/were able to* for past ability or possibility.

• *could*	**Could** he **speak** Spanish when he was a child?
• *was/were able to*	**Was** he **able to speak** Spanish when he was a child?

BE CAREFUL! Do not use *could* in affirmative statements for a **single event in the past**. Use *was/were able to*.	After a lot of hard work, they **were able to pass** the French test.
	NOT ... they ~~could~~ pass the French test.
However, it is possible to use the negative *couldn't* for single past events.	They studied hard, but they **couldn't pass** the test.

REFERENCE NOTES

For *can* and *could* for **permission**, see Unit 14 on page 135; for **requests**, see Unit 15 on page 144.
For *can't* and *could* for **present conclusions**, see Unit 32 on page 312.
For *could* for **future possibility**, see Unit 31 on page 305.
For a list of **modals and their functions**, see Appendix 19 on page 328.

STEP 3 FOCUSED PRACTICE

EXERCISE 1 DISCOVER THE GRAMMAR

A GRAMMAR NOTES 1–5 Read this article about two famous polyglots. Underline all the verbs that express ability or possibility.

Julio Iglesias

Singing in Another Language

What do Spanish-born Julio Iglesias and Canadian-born Celine Dion have in common? They are both world-famous superstars who can sing in many languages. As a young man, Iglesias played football professionally until a serious car accident changed everything. He couldn't walk for two years, and he wasn't able to play football anymore. But he soon discovered that he could sing. Now more than seventy years old, he can still entertain audiences of all ages. He has recorded songs in fourteen languages, including French, Portuguese, German, and Japanese. Did he miss football? Maybe, but he's happy with his career. He realized long ago, he said in a recent interview, "I can sing until the end. I won't be able to play football until the end."

Celine Dion

Celine Dion dreamed at an early age of becoming a professional singer, and by the time she was 14, she was able to turn that dream into reality. She entered many singing competitions and was able to take home prizes, including the World Music Award for the best-selling female singer of all time. At first, she only sung in her native French, but she took lessons and soon she was able to sing and record in English. Today, she mostly records in French and English, but, like Julio Iglesias, she can also sing in many languages, including Spanish, German, Italian, Japanese, and Mandarin Chinese. Because of family health problems, she stopped performing for a while. After taking a break from her career, she resumed her schedule. Her fans hope that she will be able to continue entertaining them for many more years.

B Look at the words you underlined in A. Write three sentences about Julio Iglesias and three sentences about Celine Dion. Write one sentence about the present, one sentence about the past, and one sentence about the future.

Julio Iglesias

present: _He can sing in many languages._ _____

past: _____

future: _____

Celine Dion

present: _____

past: _____

future: _____

EXERCISE 2 STATEMENTS AND QUESTIONS

A GRAMMAR NOTES 2–5 Some language students are talking in the school cafeteria.
Circle the correct words to complete their conversations.

Conversation 1

A: I heard your sister wants to take Chinese lessons before her trip. (Could she find) / Is she able to find
a class?
1.

B: Yes. In fact, she started classes last month. She can understand a little now, but even with lessons

and a lot of practice, she still <u>can say / can't say</u> very much.
2.

Conversation 2

A: How is Chang doing with his English?

B: Good. He's made a lot of progress. Last semester, he <u>can't order / couldn't order</u>
3.
a meal in a restaurant or talk on the phone. His friends helped him do everything.

Now he <u>can speak / could speak</u> English in a lot of situations. It won't be long before
4.
<u>he was able to get / he'll be able to get</u> a part-time job here.
5.

Conversation 3

A: What about Emma? <u>Was she able to pass / Could she pass</u> her final exam?
6.
B: Yes, but she had trouble with her presentation because she got so nervous. She really

<u>can communicate / can't communicate</u> well in small groups, but she still doesn't feel
7.
comfortable in big ones. She plans to take a course in public speaking.

A: That's good. I'm sure that with her dedication <u>she was able to improve / she'll be able to improve</u>
8.
very quickly.

Conversation 4

A: <u>Can you speak / Could you speak</u> Russian as a child, Alex?
9.
B: Yes. We spoke it at home, so <u>I'm able to speak / I could speak</u> it fluently when I was very young.
10.
A: Do your children speak Russian, too?

B: No. Unfortunately, they don't. We always only spoke French at home, so, sadly, they never

<u>was able to become / were able to become</u> really fluent. But they're going to take Russian
11.
lessons next year, so I hope that someday <u>they can speak / they'll be able to speak</u> and
12.
understand it. Languages are so important!

🔊 13|02 **B** LISTEN AND CHECK Listen to the conversations and check your answers in A.

Ability and Possibility: *Can, Could, Be able to* **129**

EXERCISE 3
CAN AND COULD: AFFIRMATIVE AND NEGATIVE STATEMENTS

GRAMMAR NOTES 1–3 Look at the English Language Ability Checklist. Complete the teacher's comments about Andreas. Use *can*, *can't*, *could*, and *couldn't* and the correct verb from the checklist.

English Language Ability Checklist

Student: Andreas Koblin

	LAST YEAR	NOW
read a newspaper	☑	☑
read a book	☒	☑
write an essay	☑	☑
write an academic paper	☑	☑
understand a movie	☒	☒
understand the words to songs	☒	☑
understand the news on TV	☒	☑
discuss the news with classmates	☒	☑
give a presentation	☒	☒

1. Last year, Andreas _____*could read*_____ a newspaper in English, but he ___*couldn't understand*___ the news on TV.

2. Now, he _____ the news on TV.

3. Last year, he _____ the news with his classmates, but now he _____ the news with other students.

4. Andreas _____ a book in English now. Last year, he _____ a book in English.

5. Andreas _____ an essay now. And he _____ an academic paper, too.

6. Last year, he _____ a movie in English. He still _____ a movie in English today.

7. Now, he _____ the words to songs in English very well, but last year he _____ them.

8. Andreas has improved a lot, but he still _____ a presentation in English. I am sure he will be able to do this with a little more practice.

EXERCISE 4 CAN, COULD, OR BE ABLE TO

GRAMMAR NOTES 1–5 Complete this FAQ (Frequently Asked Questions) about language learning. Use *can*, *could*, or *be able to* and the correct form of the verb in parentheses. There is often more than one correct answer.

_____*Can*_____ everyone _____*become*_____ multilingual?
                                    1. (become)

Yes. Almost everyone has the ability to learn more than one language, but some people

_____ languages more easily than others.
   2. (learn)

What are some characteristics of good language learners?

Good learners _____ mistakes. This means they accept mistakes as a
                  3. (tolerate)

natural part of the language-learning process. They don't feel frustrated or get embarrassed.

They understand that people learn through mistakes. Good learners also enjoy learning

languages. They know that it is hard work, but they also know that after they learn a new

language, they _____ many advantages.
               4. (enjoy)

What is the best way to learn a language?

There is no one "best way." Polyglot, author, language teacher, and world traveler Susanna

Zaraysky says that people _____ any language anywhere. As an example,
                          5. (learn)

she describes how people in post-war Bosnia _____ their English by
                                            6. (practice)

listening to weak radio or TV signals. She also strongly believes that listening to music

_____ with the learning process. In fact, research shows that singing in a
   7. (help)

foreign language _____ people in their fluency and pronunciation.
                 8. (assist)

Does knowing one foreign language help you learn another?

Definitely. People who speak a second language _____ a third or fourth
                                               9. (pick up)

language more easily.

I'm studying French this semester. _____ I _____ Italian
                                                          10. (learn)

more easily next semester?

Yes. Especially because French and Italian have a lot in common—similar vocabulary for

example. But even if the third language is unrelated to the second, as with Spanish and

Chinese, it helps to have the experience of "learning to learn" another language.

What about age? Can people learn at any age?

Yes, again. Most people find it much easier to learn when they are younger, but people

_____ a new language at any age. I had a student who, after a lot of hard
   11. (acquire)

work, _____ Portuguese when she was 82. She _____
      12. (learn)   **13.** (not lose)

her accent, but today she _____ with Portuguese language speakers when
                          14. (communicate)

she travels.

EXERCISE 5 EDITING

GRAMMAR NOTES 1–5 Read these postings from an online language-learning message board. There are ten mistakes in the use of *can*, *could*, and *be able to*. The first mistake is already corrected. Find and correct nine more.

I just read an article about polyglot Dikembe Mutombo. It's an amazing story. When he first went to the

United States, he was able to speak French and several other languages, but he couldn't ~~spoke~~ ^{speak} a word of

English. He studied six hours a day and soon he is able to join in discussions in his classes at Georgetown

University. He was also able become a professional basketball player—something he never really planned to

do. Today, he can speak nine languages, and he is able to help a lot of people with the money he made as a

star basketball player! —Martha O'Neill, Canada

I grew up in Finland, where children learn at least two foreign languages. By the time I was 18, I was able

speaking Finnish, Swedish, English, and German. I'm studying Russian now. Last week, I could get an A on my

final exam. And in a few years, I can speak my fourth foreign language. I think everyone should learn foreign

languages! —Matias Laine, Finland

In India, we grow up speaking many languages. I was born in Bangalore. As a child, I spoke Gujarati at home

with my parents. In school, I also learned Kannada (the state language) and India's two official languages

(Hindi and English). As a result, today I able to communicate in four languages. —Tanvi Patel, India

My mother could understands both English and Spanish, but she only spoke Spanish with me. I never really

knew if she couldn't speak English or if she just didn't want to. It had an advantage for me, though. I learned

English at school at an early age, but I was also able to keep my family's native language. Now, I'm fluent in

both languages. —Lia Gomez, USA

Here in Europe, we generally learn more than one language because there are so many different countries

close together. As a result, we can often communicate with other Europeans when we travel. When I went

to Germany last year, I were able to speak to the people there and I learned a lot about their country. That

wasn't true on my trip to Hungary, though. Hungarian is very different from French. I can't understand a

word when I was there! —Philippe Michaud, France

PERMISSION: *CAN, COULD, MAY, DO YOU MIND IF*

Yes/No Questions: *Can/Could/May*

Can/Could/May*	Subject	Base Form of Verb	
Can **Could** **May**	I he she we they	**stay**	here?

Short Answers

Affirmative	Negative
Certainly. Of course. Sure. No problem.	Sorry, but . . .

*Can, could, and *may* are modals. Modals have only one form. They do not have *-s* in the third-person singular.

Wh- Questions: *Can/Could/May*

Wh- Word	Can/Could/May	Subject	Base Form of Verb
When	**can** **could** **may**	I he she we they	**call?**

Statements: *Can/May*

Subject	Can/May (not)	Base Form of Verb	
You He She	**can (not)** **may (not)**	**stay**	here.

Contractions*

cannot or can not	=	**can't**

**There is no contraction for *may not*.

Questions: *Do you mind if*

Do you mind if	Subject	Verb	
Do you mind if	I we they	**stay**	here?
	he she it	**stays**	

Short Answers

Affirmative	Negative
Not at all. **No**, I **don't**. Go right ahead.	Sorry, but . . .

GRAMMAR NOTES

1 Can, Could, May

Use the modals *can*, *could*, and *may* to ask for **permission**.

- *can*
- *could*
- *may*

Can I **borrow** your book?	LESS FORMAL
Could he **come** tomorrow?	
May we **leave**, Professor Lee?	MORE FORMAL
(student speaking to teacher)	

USAGE NOTE *May* is not very common. It is much **more formal** and polite than *can* and *could*. We sometimes use it when we are speaking to a person in authority (for example, a teacher, police officer, doctor, librarian, counselor, etc.).

USAGE NOTE We often use *please* when we ask for permission. Notice the word order.

Could I **ask** a question, *please*?
or
Could I *please* **ask** a question?

Could refers to the **present** or the **future**. It does not refer to the past (even though *could* is the past form of *can*).

Could I **call** you *tomorrow*?

IN WRITING **Asking for permission** is much more common in **conversation** than in writing, but you can ask for permission in **informal notes**, **emails**, and **text messages**.

Can I **make** an appointment to discuss my presentation with you? *(conversation)*
Hi Professor Chin. **Could** I **make** an appointment to discuss my presentation with you? *(note / email)*

2 Answers

There are **several ways to answer** when someone asks for permission.

When we **give permission**, we usually use **informal expressions** instead of modals in answers.

A: **Could** I close the window?
B: *Sure.* or *Of course.* or *Go ahead.*

When we use a **modal** in an **affirmative answer**, we almost always use *can*. We do not use *could*, and we rarely use *may* in short answers.

A: **Could** I borrow this pencil?
B: *Yes*, of course you **can**.
NOT Yes, of course you ~~could~~.

A: **May** I please see your notes?
B: *Sure* you **can**. or *Yes*, you **may**. *(rare)*

USAGE NOTE When we **refuse permission**, we usually **apologize** and give an **explanation**.

A: **Can** I please use your computer?
B: *I'm sorry, but* I need it today.

USAGE NOTE *No, you can't* and *No, you may not* are **not common** answers, and they don't sound polite. People sometimes use these short negative answers when they are angry. And adults sometimes use them when talking to children.

A: **Can** I wear your new sweater?
B: *No, you can't!* I haven't even worn it yet!

A: Mommy, **can** I have ice cream for breakfast?
B: *No, you can't.*

Use the expression *do you mind if* to ask for permission when an **action may annoy** or inconvenience someone.

Use the **simple present** of the verb after *do you mind if*.	A: **Do you mind if** he *cleans up* later? B: No, I don't. He can do it tomorrow.
BE CAREFUL! Do not use *please* with *do you mind if*.	**Do you mind if** I **ask** a question? **NOT** Do you mind if I ask a question ~~please~~?

BE CAREFUL! When we **give permission**, we use *Not at all* or *No, I don't*, but we're really saying: *It's OK*.
 	
When we **refuse permission**, we can use *Yes, I do*, but we're really saying: *It's not OK*.
	A: **Do you mind if** Ian comes over tonight?
	B: ***Not at all.*** or ***No, I don't.***
	    (It's OK for Ian to come over tonight.)
	
	B: ***Yes, I do.***
	    (It's not OK for Ian to come over tonight.)

USAGE NOTE It's **not common** to refuse permission with *Yes, I do*. As with questions with *can*, *could*, and *may*, when we refuse permission to a question with *do you mind if*, we usually **apologize** and give an **explanation**.	A: **Do you mind if** Ian comes over tonight? B: ***Sorry, but*** I have to study tonight.
IN WRITING As with *can*, *could*, and *may*, *do you mind if* is much more common in **conversation** than in writing, but you can use it in **informal notes**, **emails**, and **text messages**.	Hi. **Do you mind if** I **invite** Paulo to have dinner with us tomorrow night? *(email)*

REFERENCE NOTES

For general information on **modals**, see Unit 13, Grammar Notes 1–2, on page 125.

For *can* and *could* for **ability and possibility**, see Unit 13 on page 124; for **requests**, see Unit 15 on page 144.

For *could* and *may* for **future possibility**, see Unit 31 on page 305; for **present conclusions**, see Unit 32 on page 312.

For a list of **modals and their functions**, see Appendix 19 on page 328.

EXERCISE 1 DISCOVER THE GRAMMAR

GRAMMAR NOTES 1–3 Read the quiz. Underline all the modals and expressions for permission. Then if you'd like to, you can take the quiz. The answers are below.

Are You a Good Roommate?

Take this short quiz and find out.

1. **You want to use your roommate's computer.**
   You say:
   ○ **a.** I may use your computer tonight.
   ○ **b.** Can I use your computer tonight?
   ○ **c.** I'm using your computer tonight.

2. **You don't have any food in the house.**
   You say:
   ○ **a.** Can you make dinner for me?
   ○ **b.** I don't mind eating some of your food.
   ○ **c.** Do you mind if I have some of your food?

3. **You may not have time to wash the dishes tonight.**
   You say:
   ○ **a.** Could you wash the dishes?
   ○ **b.** I can't wash the dishes.
   ○ **c.** Can I wash the dishes tomorrow?

4. **Your roommate asks you: "Could my best friend stay overnight?"**
   You answer:
   ○ **a.** Can she stay in a hotel instead?
   ○ **b.** Sure she can!
   ○ **c.** I'm sure she could, but I don't want her to!

5. **You can find nothing to wear to the party next Friday.**
   You say:
   ○ **a.** Could I borrow your new sweater?
   ○ **b.** I may borrow your new sweater.
   ○ **c.** You could lend me your new sweater.

6. **You want to hang your favorite poster in your dorm room.**
   You say:
   ○ **a.** Could I hang my poster here?
   ○ **b.** Maybe you could hang my poster here.
   ○ **c.** I assume I can hang my poster here.

ANSWERS: 1. b, 2. c, 3. c, 4. b, 5. a, 6. a

EXERCISE 2 QUESTIONS AND ANSWERS

GRAMMAR NOTES 1–3 Look at the signs. Complete each question and answer. Use the words in parentheses and the correct pronouns. Write appropriate short answers. There can be more than one correct short answer.

1. PIERRE: ___Do you mind if___ I _____eat_____ my lunch here

   <u>a. (do you mind if / eat)</u>

   while I get on the Internet? I'll be neat.

   ASSISTANT: _____Sorry_____ . Please look at the sign.

   <u>b.</u>

Computer Lab

2. SÉBASTIEN: Those guys next door are making a lot of noise!

   _____ they _____ that?

   <u>a. (can / do)</u>

   NATHANIEL: _____ . They aren't going to gain any friends

   <u>b.</u>

   that way, but according to the guidelines, it's OK to play

   music now. It's 8:00 a.m.

   SÉBASTIEN: Well, _____ I _____ your

   <u>c. (can / borrow)</u>

   earplugs? I have to prepare for my English presentation.

Quiet Hours
11:00 p.m. - 7:00 a.m.
Sunday - Saturday

3. CARMEN: _____ we _____ our bikes on

   <u>a. (may / ride)</u>

   this path?

   GUARD: _____ .

   <u>b.</u>

4. DONOVAN: _____ I _____ my dog next

   <u>a. (could / bring)</u>

   semester? My roommate doesn't mind.

   COUNSELOR: _____ . But some of the other dorms

   <u>b.</u>

   allow pets.

Kent Hall

5. GABRIELLE: _____ I _____ my cell phone

   <u>a. (may / use)</u>

   in here?

   LIBRARIAN: _____ . People get really annoyed by cell

   <u>b.</u>

   phone conversations.

EXERCISE 3 QUESTIONS AND ANSWERS

GRAMMAR NOTES 1–3 Heather and her roommate Tara are planning a party in Kent Hall.
Use the words in parentheses to ask for permission. Answer the questions.

1. Tara's friend Troy is in town. She wants him to come to the party.

   TARA: *Do you mind if Troy comes to the party?*
   (do you mind if)

   HEATHER: *Not at all.* _____ I'd love to meet him.

2. Heather wants to borrow her roommate's black sweater.

   HEATHER: I have nothing to wear. _____
   (can)

   TARA: _____ I'm planning to wear it myself!

3. Tara's sister is coming from out of town. Tara wants her to stay in their room.

   TARA: _____
   (do you mind if)

   HEATHER: _____ She can sleep on the couch.

4. Heather and Tara would like to have the party in the dormitory lounge. Heather asks her

   dormitory counselor for permission.

   HEATHER: _____
   (may)

   COUNSELOR: _____ It's available next Friday. We just have to

   establish some guidelines.

5. Heather and Tara would like to hang decorations from the ceiling of the lounge.

   HEATHER: _____
   (could)

   COUNSELOR: _____ Fire regulations won't allow it.

6. Heather and Tara want the party to go until midnight.

   HEATHER: _____
   (could)

   COUNSELOR: _____ Quiet hours start at 11:00 on Friday.

7. Tara wants to play some of her friend Erica's CDs at the party.

   TARA: _____
   (could)

   ERICA: _____ Which ones should I bring?

8. It's Friday night. A student wants to study in the lounge.

   STUDENT: _____
   (can)

   HEATHER: _____ We're having a party. Want to join us?

EXERCISE 4 EDITING

GRAMMAR NOTES 1–3 Read Sharif's English test. There are seven mistakes in the use of *can*, *could*, *may*, and *do you mind if*. The first mistake is already corrected. Find and correct six more.

Class: _English 102_

Name: _Sharif Halabi_

Directions: These conversations take place on a train. Find and correct the mistakes.

1. A: May we board the train now?

   B: Sorry, you ~~couldn't~~ can't board until 12:30.

2. A: Can he comes on the train with me?

   B: Sorry. Only passengers can board.

3. A: Do you mind if I'm sitting here?

   B: No, I don't. My friend is sitting here.

4. A: Could I looked at your newspaper?

   B: Yes, of course you could.

5. A: Do you mind if my son play his computer game?

   B: No, not at all. It won't disturb me.

   A: Thanks.

   B: No problem.

Requests: *Can, Could, Will, Would, Would you mind*
MESSAGES

OUTCOMES
- Make and respond to requests
- Identify important details related to requests in emails and text messages
- Identify details related to a schedule in a conversation
- Discuss a daily schedule that involves making requests of others
- Write and respond to a request in a text or email message

STEP 1   GRAMMAR IN CONTEXT

BEFORE YOU READ

Look at the title of the text messages and the emails. Discuss the questions.

1. What do you think the title means?

2. Why do people use abbreviations in text messages?

3. Do you prefer text messages or emails? Why?

READ

▶15|01   Read these text messages between Marta and her mother. Then read the emails to Marta from her boss and from Marta to her assistant.

Messages 4 u!

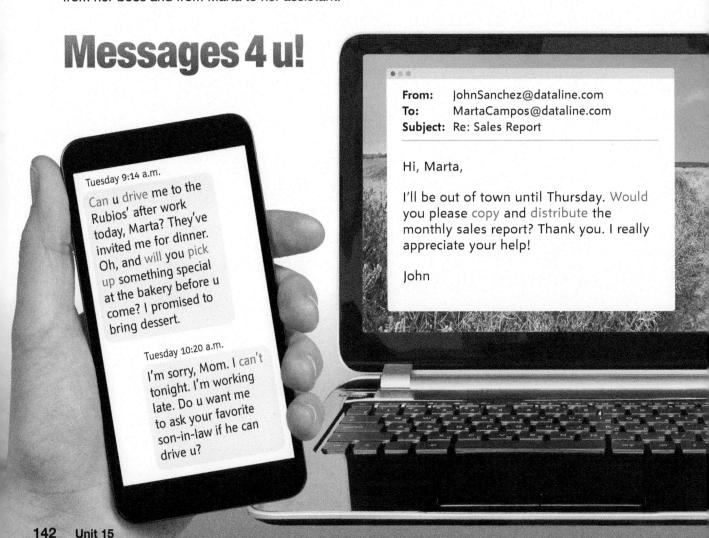

Tuesday 9:14 a.m.

Can u drive me to the Rubios' after work today, Marta? They've invited me for dinner. Oh, and will you pick up something special at the bakery before u come? I promised to bring dessert.

Tuesday 10:20 a.m.

I'm sorry, Mom. I can't tonight. I'm working late. Do u want me to ask your favorite son-in-law if he can drive u?

From: JohnSanchez@dataline.com
To: MartaCampos@dataline.com
Subject: Re: Sales Report

Hi, Marta,

I'll be out of town until Thursday. Would you please copy and distribute the monthly sales report? Thank you. I really appreciate your help!

John

AFTER YOU READ

Ⓐ VOCABULARY Choose the word or phrase that best completes each sentence.

1. A **request** is a polite way of _____ something.
   a. asking for   b. doing   c. answering

2. When you **deliver** a report, you _____ it to someone.
   a. promise   b. describe   c. bring

3. When you **respond** to a message you give a(n) _____.
   a. answer   b. report   c. opinion

4. When a question is **urgent**, you need to react to it _____.
   a. carefully   b. immediately   c. slowly

5. When you **distribute** reports, you _____ one to each person in a group.
   a. give   b. read   c. talk about

6. When you **appreciate** what someone does for you, you feel _____.
   a. worried   b. sorry   c. thankful

Ⓑ COMPREHENSION Read the statements. Check (✓) *True* or *False*.

	True	False
1. Marta's mother made three requests to her daughter.	☐	☐
2. Marta's mother needs a ride.	☐	☐
3. Marta is going to drive her.	☐	☐
4. John is going to copy and distribute the sales report.	☐	☐
5. Marta wants Ann to give her the copies of the sales report.	☐	☐
6. Marta wants to know how her boss responds to a request.	☐	☐

Ⓒ DISCUSSION Work with a partner. Compare your answers in B. Why did you check *True* or *False*?

FROM: MartaCampos@dataline.com
TO: AnnChen@dataline.com
SUBJECT: Re: Sales Report

Hi, Ann,

I'm sending you a copy of our sales report. Could you please make 25 copies? And would you mind delivering them to me as soon as you're finished? It's urgent.

One more thing—Will you tell me how the boss responds to our request for another office assistant?

Thanks.

Marta

REQUESTS: *CAN, COULD, WILL, WOULD, WOULD YOU MIND*

Questions: *Can/Could/Will/Would*

Can/Could/ Will/Would*	You	Base Form of Verb	
Can Could Will Would	you	distribute	this report for me?
		drive	me to the doctor?
		pick up	some groceries?

Short Answers

Affirmative	Negative	
Sure. Certainly. No problem. Of course. I'd be glad to.	I'm sorry, (but)	I can't.
	I'm afraid	

* *Can*, *could*, *will*, and *would* are modals. Modals do not have *-s* in the third-person singular.

Questions: *Would you mind*

Would you mind	Gerund	
Would you mind	distributing	this report for me?
	driving	me to the doctor?
	picking up	some groceries?

Short Answers

Affirmative	Negative	
Not at all. I'd be glad to. No problem. Of course not.	I'm sorry, (but)	I can't.
	I'm afraid	

GRAMMAR NOTES

1 *Can, Could, Will, Would*

Use the modals *can*, *could*, *will*, and *would* to make a **request**.

• *can*	**Can** you **email** me?
• *could*	**Could** you **copy** Danica?
• *will*	**Will** you **call** me tomorrow?
• *would*	**Would** you **remind** me to call Mason?

USAGE NOTE *Could* and *would* are more polite than *can* and *will*. We use *could* and *would* to soften requests.	John, **can** you mail this for me? Ms. Lee, **could** you mail this for me? *(more polite)*
USAGE NOTE You can also use *please* to make the request even more polite. Notice the word order.	**Would** you **close** the door, ***please***? or **Would** you ***please*** **close** the door?
IN WRITING **Requests** are much more common in **conversation** than in writing, but you can use requests in **informal notes**, **emails**, and **text messages**.	**Can** you **get** two oranges? *(conversation)* Laura, **could** you **pick up** some bread on the way home? *(text message)*

2 Answers

There are **several ways to respond** to requests.

In **affirmative answers** to requests, we usually use expressions such as *sure*, *of course*, *certainly*, *I'd be glad to*, and *no problem*.

> A: **Would** you **shut** the window, please?
> B: *Sure.* or *Of course.* or *Certainly.*

USAGE NOTE *Certainly* and *I'd be glad to* are more formal than other answers. *No problem* is the least formal.

> A: Dan, **could** you **help** me carry these books?
> B: *I'd be glad to*, Professor Chin. *(more formal)*
>
> A: **Can** you **lend** me your pen?
> B: **No problem.** *(least formal)*

USAGE NOTE In **negative answers**, we usually **apologize** and give an **explanation**.

> A: **Could** you **deliver** this to Ron, please?
> B: *I'm sorry*, *but* I **can't**. I'm expecting a client.

BE CAREFUL! Do not use *would* or *could* in response to polite requests.

> NOT Sure I ~~would~~.
> NOT I'm sorry, but I ~~couldn't~~.

3 Would you mind

We also use the expression *would you mind* to make **polite requests**.

Use a **gerund** (verb + *-ing*) after *would you mind*.

> Would you mind *making* a copy of the report?

Would you mind is even more polite than *could* or *would*.

> A: **Would you mind waiting**? Mr. Caras is in a meeting.

BE CAREFUL! When we answer this type of request with *Not at all* or *Of course not*, it means that we will do what the person requests.

> B: *Not at all.* or *Of course not.*
>   (OK. I'll do it.)

USAGE NOTE In **negative answers**, we usually **apologize** and give an **explanation**.

> C: *I'm sorry*, I **can't**. I have another appointment in a half an hour.

PRONUNCIATION NOTE

15 02
Pronunciation of Could you, Would you, Will you, Can you

In **informal conversation**, we often pronounce *could you*, *would you*, *will you*, and *can you* as "couldja," "wouldja," "willya," and "canya."

> A: **Could you** mail this for me?
>   *(couldja)*
> B: Sure. **Would you** remind me later?
>   *(wouldja)*
>
> A: **Will you** type this for me?
>   *(willya)*
> B: No problem. **Can you** leave it on my desk?
>   *(canya)*

REFERENCE NOTES

For general information on **modals**, see Unit 13, Grammar Notes 1–2, on page 125.

For *can* and *could* for **ability and possibility**, see Unit 13 on page 124; for **permission**, see Unit 14 on page 135.

For *can't* and *could* for **present conclusions**, see Unit 32 on page 312.

For *could* for **future possibility**, see Unit 31 on page 305.

For *will* for the **future**, see Unit 6 on page 55 and Unit 7 on page 67.

For a list of **modals and their functions**, see Appendix 19 on page 328.

STEP 3   FOCUSED PRACTICE

EXERCISE 1 DISCOVER THE GRAMMAR

GRAMMAR NOTES 1–3 Raul's roommate, Emil, is having problems today. Underline Emil's requests. Then choose the appropriate response to each request.

1. Raul, <u>would you please drive me to Cal's Computer Shop?</u> I have to bring my computer in.

   a. Yes, I would.   (**b.**) I'd be glad to.

2. Would you mind lending me five dollars? I'm getting paid tomorrow.

   a. Not at all.   **b.** Yes.

3. Raul, can you lend me your laptop for a minute? I have to email my teacher.

   a. Sorry, but I can't.   **b.** No, I can't.

4. Will you pick up some milk on the way home this afternoon?

   a. No, I won't.   **b.** I'm sorry, I can't. I'll be at work until 8:00.

5. Would you explain this text message from Kora? She uses weird abbreviations.

   a. I'd be glad to.   **b.** No, I wouldn't.

6. Could you text me Jana's address? I lost it.

   a. No, I couldn't.   **b.** Sorry, but I don't have it.

7. I'm in a real hurry. Will you help me do the dishes?

   a. Certainly.   **b.** Of course not.

8. Could you lock the door on your way out? My hands are full.

   a. Yes, I could.   **b.** Sure.

9. Kora, can you tell Ethan to come to the phone? It's important.

   a. No problem.   **b.** Not at all.

EXERCISE 2 REQUESTS

A GRAMMAR NOTES 1, 3 Look at the pictures. What is each person thinking? Write the letter of the correct thought from the box.

a. Repair the copier.	d. File these reports.	g. Buy some cereal.
b. Call back later.	e. Shut the door.	h. Wait for a few minutes.
c. Get that book.	f. Close the window.	i. Wash your cups and dishes.

1. ___d___

2. _____

3. _____

4. _____

5. _____

6. _____

7. _____

8. _____

9. _____

B What are the people in the pictures in A going to say? Complete their requests. Use the words in parentheses and the information from the pictures.

1. _____*Could you file these reports, please?*_____ I've finished reading them.
   (could)

2. _____ I can't think with all that noise in the hall.
   (would)

3. _____ on the way home? We don't have any left.
   (will)

4. _____ It's freezing in here.
   (can)

5. _____ Mr. Rivera is still in a meeting.
   (would you mind)

6. _____ It's getting messy in here.
   (would you mind)

7. _____ I have to leave for a meeting now.
   (could)

8. _____ I can't reach it.
   (can)

9. _____ I need to make copies right away.
   (could)

EXERCISE 3 REQUESTS AND ANSWERS

GRAMMAR NOTES 1–3 Write polite requests. Use *can, could, will, would,* or *would you mind* and the correct form of the words in parentheses. Write appropriate answers. There can be more than one correct answer.

1. MAN: _____*Would you mind lending me your phone*_____? The battery in mine is dead.
   a. (lend me your phone)

   WOMAN: _____*No problem*_____. But I'm in a hurry.
   b.

   _____?
   c. (please / keep your conversation short)

   MAN: _____. I just need to text my friend.
   d.

2. STUDENT: Excuse me, Professor Ruiz. _____?
   a. (explain reflexive pronouns)

   I don't understand them.

   PROFESSOR: _____ right now. I'm expecting a call.
   b.

   _____?
   c. (come back in 20 minutes)

3. WOMAN: _____? It's blocking my driveway.
   a. (move your car)

   MAN: _____. I'll do it right away. I'm really
   b.

   sorry. I didn't notice.

4. MANAGER: _____? Our sales people need it for their
   a. (please / distribute this report)

   meeting this afternoon.

   ASSISTANT: _____. I can't leave my desk right now.
   b.

   But I can ask Tania to do it.

EXERCISE 4 *COULD YOU, WOULD YOU (MIND), WILL YOU, CAN YOU*

PRONUNCIATION NOTE Listen to the short informal conversations. What do you hear?
Complete the requests with *could you, would you (mind), will you,* and *can you.*

1. _____*Could you*_____ lend me some money?

2. _____ call me when you get home?

3. _____ turning the TV down?

4. _____ explain the meaning of this word to me?

5. _____ give me a ride home?

6. _____ help me carry these books?

EXERCISE 5 EDITING

GRAMMAR NOTES 1–3 Read Marta's response to an email from her boss. (Her answers are
in red.) There are eight mistakes in making and responding to requests. The first mistake is
already corrected. Find and correct seven more.

Date: 04-11-16 12:14:39 EST
From: MartaCampos@dataline.com
To: JohnSanchez@dataline.com
CC: AnnChen@dataline.com
Subject: sales meeting—Reply

>>><JohnSanchez@dataline.com> 04/11/16 10:37 am>>>

The meetings are going well, but they are going to go on an extra day. Could you

please call
~~call please~~ Doug Rogers to try to reschedule our sales meeting?

Not at all. I'll do it right away.

We'll need three extra copies of the monthly sales report. Would you ask Ann to take

care of that?

Yes, I would. (Ann—could you do this?)

I won't have time to return Emma Lopes's call this week. Would you mind to call her and

telling her I'll call her back next week?

No problem. Could you email me her phone number?

I hate to ask, but will you mind working on Saturday? We'll need the extra time to go

over the new information I've gotten.

Sorry, but I couldn't. My in-laws are coming for a visit. But Rob Lin says he can come into the office to help out.

One last thing. I was going to pick up those new business cards, but I won't be back in time. Would you mind asking the printer to deliver them to the office? I'd really appreciate that.

Yes, I would. I'll call and ask him to do it right away.

And this will cheer you up—it looks like our office will receive the award for Communication Excellence this year.

Great! Can I told everyone, or is it a secret?

UNIT 16

Advice: *Should, Ought to, Had better*

INTERNET RULES

OUTCOMES
- Give and ask for advice
- Identify main points in a short text about rules and advice
- Recognize statements of advice in a radio show
- Discuss possible solutions to everyday situations, giving reasons and explanations
- Write an email or letter of complaint, giving advice on making improvements

STEP 1   GRAMMAR IN CONTEXT

BEFORE YOU READ

How do you communicate with people on the Internet? Discuss the questions.

1. Is it important to be polite on the Internet? Why or why not?

2. Do you behave differently online than face-to-face with people?

3. What are some rules you follow?

READ

16|01 Read this article about being polite on the Internet. If you don't understand a cyber[1] word, look up its meaning on the next page.

Netiquette 101

Email, bulletin boards, and chat rooms open up a new world of communication—and sometimes misunderstanding. To avoid problems, you should know these simple rules of netiquette:

- When should you post to a bulletin board or chat room? Newbies shouldn't jump in right away—they really ought to lurk a little first. Look through old messages for answers to common questions. Many websites also have FAQs for basic information. After that, post when you have something new to say. You should keep your post short and simple.

- Should you use capital letters to make a strong statement? NO! A MESSAGE ALL IN CAPITAL LETTERS SEEMS LIKE SHOUTING. You should follow the normal rules for capital (big) and lowercase (small) letters.

- Did someone make you angry? Wait a minute! You'd better not reply right away. Count to 10 first. Don't flame another board or chat room member. You should never forget that people on the Internet are real people with real feelings.

- Emoticons can help avoid misunderstandings. You should learn how to use them to show your feelings.

- Internet safety is part of netiquette. When you post to a bulletin board or a chat room, you should always protect your identity by using a screen name. Never give your real name or other personal information.

Practice these five rules of netiquette, and most of your emoticons will be smileys!

---

1 *cyber:* about computers or the Internet

Cyber Words

bulletin board an Internet site where members can post ideas about a special interest

chat room a site for online conversations in "real" time

emoticon a picture of a feeling, for example:

FAQs Frequently Asked Questions

flame to send insulting messages to someone

lurk to read messages on a bulletin board but not post any messages

netiquette Internet etiquette (rules for polite behavior)

newbie (or newb) someone new to an Internet site

post to send messages to a bulletin board or chat room

AFTER YOU READ

A VOCABULARY **Complete the sentences with the words from the box.**

avoid	behavior	communication	identity	normal	protect

1. Never give your real _____ in a chat room. Always use a screen name.

2. It's _____ for newbies to lurk on a site before they post. Many people do that.

3. _____ websites where members flame other members.

4. Emoticons improve your online _____. They show your feelings.

5. People's _____ in chat rooms is often different from how they act in real life.

6. _____ yourself on the Internet. Never tell anyone your passwords.

B COMPREHENSION **Read the statements. Check (✓) OK or Not OK.**

	OK	Not OK
1. Read some messages before you post.	☐	☐
2. Reply immediately when you're angry.	☐	☐
3. Use all capital letters in your posts.	☐	☐
4. Use emoticons to show feelings.	☐	☐
5. Use your real name in chat rooms.	☐	☐
6. Write long, complicated messages.	☐	☐
7. Think about people's feelings when you post a message.	☐	☐

C DISCUSSION **Work with a partner. Compare your answers in B. Why did you check OK or Not OK?**

ADVICE: *SHOULD, OUGHT TO, HAD BETTER*

Statements

Subject	Should / Ought to / Had better*	Base Form of Verb
I You He She We You They	should (not) ought to had better (not)	reply.

Contractions

should not	=	shouldn't
had better	=	'd better

* *Should* and *ought to* are modals. *Had better* is similar to a modal.
  These forms do not have -*s* in the third-person singular.

Yes/No Questions

Should	Subject	Base Form of Verb
Should	I he she we they	reply?

Short Answers

Affirmative			Negative		
Yes,	you he she you they	should.	No,	you he she you they	shouldn't.

Wh- Questions

Wh- Word	Should	Subject	Base Form of Verb	
How When Where	should	I he she we they	send	it?

GRAMMAR NOTES

1 Should and Ought to

Use the modals *should* and *ought to* to say that something is **advisable** (a good idea).

• *should*	Derek **should answer** that email.
• *ought to*	You **ought to send** Mia a copy, too.

USAGE NOTE *Should* is much more **common** than *ought to* in conversation.

You **should check out** this website!

IN WRITING *Should* is common in both informal and formal writing.

You **should post** some of your vacation photos. *(email)*

Internet users **should be** aware of proper Internet etiquette. *(newspaper)*

USAGE NOTE We often soften advice with *maybe*, **perhaps**, or *I think*.

Ryan, *maybe* you **should spend** less time on the Internet.

2 Had better

Use the expression *had better* for **strong advice**—when you believe that something bad will happen if the person does not follow the advice.

• *had better*	Kids, you'**d better get** offline now or you won't have time for your homework.

USAGE NOTE We mostly use the expression *had better* in **conversation**, and we usually use the contraction '*d better*. The full form *had better* is very formal.

You'**d better** choose a screen name. *(common)*

You **had better** choose a screen name. *(rare)*

Had better always refers to the **present** or the **future**. It never refers to the past (even though it uses the word *had*).

You'**d better call** them *now*. They're waiting.

You'**d better post** that *tomorrow* or it'll be late.

3 Negative Statements

Use *should not* and *had better not* in negative statements.

The negative of *should* is *should not* or *shouldn't*.

You **shouldn't post** right away.

The negative of *had better* is *had better not* or '*d better not*. Notice the word order.

You'**d better not use** your real name.

NOT You'd not better use your real name.

USAGE NOTE We do not usually use the negative of *ought to* in American English. We use *shouldn't* instead.

We **shouldn't** post long messages.

We **ought not to** post long messages. *(rare)*

Use *should* for questions. We do not usually use *ought to* or *had better* for questions.

• *should*	When **should** I **sign on**?
Use *should* to ask for advice.	A: **Should** I **join** this chat room?
USAGE NOTE You can use *should* in **short answers**, but we often use other **expressions**.	B: Yes, you **should**. It's fun.
	C: *Sure. Why not?*
	D: *Not really.* It's a waste of time.

PRONUNCIATION NOTE

16|02   Pronunciation of *Ought to* and *Had better*

In **informal conversation**, we often pronounce *ought to* "oughta." Notice that the "t" in "oughta" sounds like a quick "d."	A: I **ought to get** a new computer. *(I oughta get)*
For *had better*, we usually pronounce *had* as the contraction *'d*, and sometimes we leave out *had* and just say "better."	B: You **had better get** a flash drive, too. *(You'd better get* or *You better get)*

REFERENCE NOTES

For general information on **modals**, see Unit 13, Grammar Notes 1–2, on page 125.

For a list of **modals and their functions**, see Appendix 19 on page 328.

EXERCISE 1 DISCOVER THE GRAMMAR

Ⓐ GRAMMAR NOTES 1–4 Read these posts to an online bulletin board for high school students. Underline the words that give or ask for advice.

Subject: HELP!

From: Hothead

MY BRAIN IS EXPLODING!!! SAVE ME!! <u>What should I do?</u> I'm taking all honors courses this year, and I'm on the debate team, in the school congress, and on the soccer team. OH! And, I'd better not forget piano lessons! I'm so busy I shouldn't even be online now. 😣

From: Tweety

First of all, you should stop shouting. You'll feel better. Then you really ought to ask yourself, "Why am I doing all this?" Is it for you, or are you trying to please somebody else?

From: Loki

Tweety's right, Hothead. Do you really want to do all that stuff? No? You'd better not do it then. You'll burn out before you graduate. 😊

From: gud4me

You're such a loser. You should get a life. I mean a NORMAL life. Do you have any friends? Do you ever just sit around and do nothing?

From: Tweety

Hey, gud4me, no flaming allowed! That's bad cyber behavior. We really shouldn't fight—it never helps communication. 😊

Ⓑ Check all the advice from the posts in A.

☐ **1.** Take all honors courses.

☑ **2.** Stop shouting.

☐ **3.** Feel better.

☐ **4.** Don't do things you don't want to do.

☐ **5.** Get a life.

☐ **6.** Don't fight.

EXERCISE 2 STATEMENTS WITH *SHOULD, OUGHT TO,* AND *HAD BETTER*

GRAMMAR NOTES 1–3 Read these posts to a chat room about learning English. Complete the posts. Use the correct form (affirmative or negative) of the words in parentheses. Use contractions when possible.

CURLY: I think I _____*should watch*_____ more movies to improve my English. Any ideas?
1. (should / watch)

USEDIT: I loved *The Uninvited*. But you _____ it if you don't like scary films.
2. (had better / rent)

AGURL: That's right. And you _____ the remote in your hand. That way you
3. (had better / keep)

can fast-forward through the scary parts.

592XY: I think you _____ *Groundhog Day*. The same thing happens again and
4. (ought to / see)

again. It's an old movie, but it's great listening practice—and it's funny!

PATI: You _____ the English subtitles. They really help.
5. (should / turn on)

USEDIT: But you _____ the subtitles right away. At first, you really
6. (should / use)

_____ a few times. That's what rewind buttons are for!
7. (should / listen)

592XY: Good advice. And you really _____ a plot summary before you
8. (ought to / read)

watch. You can find one online. It's so much easier when you know the story.

AGURL: Curly, you're a math major, right? Then you really _____ my favorite
9. (ought to / watch)

movie, *The Da Vinci Code*. It's about solving a mystery with math clues.

CURLY: Thanks, guys. Those are great ideas. But you _____ me any more
10. (had better / give)

advice, or I'll never work on my other courses!

EXERCISE 3 STATEMENTS WITH *SHOULD, OUGHT TO,* AND *HAD BETTER*

GRAMMAR NOTES 1–3 Rewrite the Internet safety tips in parentheses. Use *should*, *ought to*, or *had better*. Choose between affirmative and negative.

> The Internet is a wonderful place to visit and hang out.
> Here are some tips to make your trip there a safe one!

1. I often use my real name online. Is that a problem?

   Yes! *You should always use a screen name.*_____
   (Always use a screen name.)
   Protect your identity!

2. Someone in my chat group just asked for my address.

   _____
   (Don't give out any personal information.)
   People can use it to steal your identity and your money.

3. My brother wants my password to check out a group before joining.

_____
(Don't give it to anyone.)

Not even your brother! He might share it, and then people can steal your information.

4. I sent a file to someone, and she told me it had a virus.

_____
(Get virus protection and use it.)

A virus can hurt your computer and destroy important files (and other people's too).

5. I update my virus protection every month. Is that really necessary?

Yes! _____
(Always keep your virus protection up-to-date.)

Program it to update automatically. Remember: _Old_ virus protection is _no_ virus protection!

6. I got an email about a home-based business. I could make $15,000 a month.

_____
(Don't believe any "get rich quick" offers.)

They sound good, but people almost always lose money.

7. I got an interesting email. I don't know who sent it, but it's got a file attached.

_____
(Don't open any email attachments from strangers.)

They could contain dangerous viruses.

8. The Internet sounds too dangerous for me!

Not really. _____,
(Be careful!)

but enjoy yourself—it's an exciting world out there!

EXERCISE 4 QUESTIONS AND SHORT ANSWERS WITH *SHOULD*

GRAMMAR NOTE 4 Complete these posts to an online bulletin board. Use the words from the box to complete the questions. Give short answers.

buy one online	forward the email	~~try to repair it~~
check the spelling	say to make them stop	use emoticons
flame him	start posting	use my birthday

1. Q: My computer is seven years old and has problems. _____Should I try to repair it_____?

   A: _____No, you shouldn't_____. That's very old for a computer! Buy a new one!

2. Q: I just joined an online discussion group. When _____? Right away?

   A: You should really just read for a while. It's always a good idea to "lurk" before you post.

3. Q: I just received a warning about a computer virus. The email says to tell everyone I know

   about it. _____?

   A: _____. These warnings are almost always false.

4. Q: I hate to go shopping, but I really need a jacket. _____?

   A: _____. It's safe. Just buy from a company you know.

158   Unit 16

5. Q: I type fast and make spelling mistakes. Is that bad? _____?

   A: _____ . Use a spell checker! Mistakes are bad netiquette!

6. Q: My friends email me a lot of jokes. I don't want to hurt their feelings, but I *really* don't want to keep getting these jokes. What _____?

   A: You should be honest and say you are too busy to read them. These jokes can waste an awful lot of time!

7. Q: I always forget my password. _____ so I don't forget?

   A: _____ . It's too easy to guess. Protect your identity.

8. Q: A newb on our board is asking dumb questions. _____?

   A: _____ ! Your behavior should be as polite online as offline.

9. Q: _____ in emails? Those smileys are awfully cute.

   A: Sure, go ahead. They're fun. But don't use them in business emails.

EXERCISE 5 EDITING

GRAMMAR NOTES 1–4 **Read these posts to a bulletin board for international students in the United States. There are twelve mistakes in the use of** *should*, *ought to*, **and** *had better*. **The first mistake is already corrected. Find and correct eleven more.**

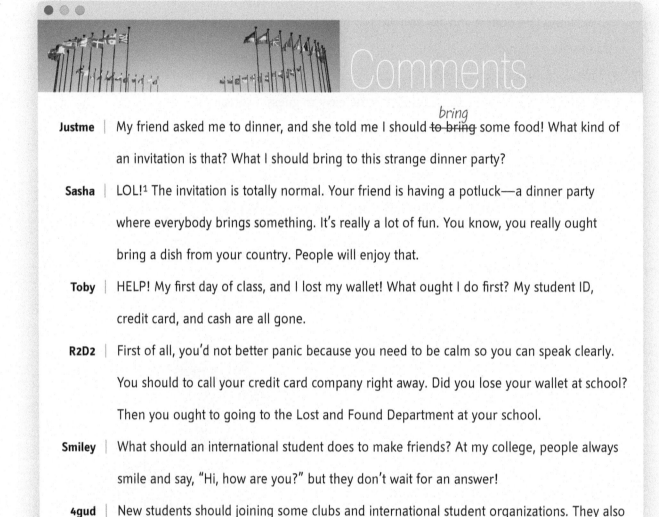

Justme	My friend asked me to dinner, and she told me I should ~~to bring~~ bring some food! What kind of an invitation is that? What I should bring to this strange dinner party?
Sasha	LOL![1] The invitation is totally normal. Your friend is having a potluck—a dinner party where everybody brings something. It's really a lot of fun. You know, you really ought bring a dish from your country. People will enjoy that.
Toby	HELP! My first day of class, and I lost my wallet! What ought I do first? My student ID, credit card, and cash are all gone.
R2D2	First of all, you'd not better panic because you need to be calm so you can speak clearly. You should to call your credit card company right away. Did you lose your wallet at school? Then you ought to going to the Lost and Found Department at your school.
Smiley	What should an international student does to make friends? At my college, people always smile and say, "Hi, how are you?" but they don't wait for an answer!
4gud	New students should joining some clubs and international student organizations. They also ought to find a student in each class to study with and ask about homework assignments.
Newguy	Hi. I'm new to this board. I'm from Vietnam, and I'm going to school in Canada next year. How should I will get ready?
Smiley	Welcome Newguy! I'm at school in Montreal, and you won't believe how cold it gets here. You're better bring a lot of warm clothes!
Sasha	You ought check the school's website. They might have a Vietnam Students Association. If they do, you should email the association with your questions. Good luck!

---

1 *LOL:* abbreviation for *Laughing out Loud*

Nouns, Quantifiers, and Articles

PART 5

OUTCOMES

- Use proper, common, count, and non-count nouns
- Describe quantities and use quantifiers with nouns
- Identify the main points in a text on a scientific topic
- Identify details in a conversation about a day-to-day topic
- Discuss quotes and proverbs
- Write a note or letter that lists and describes quantities of items

OUTCOMES

- Use indefinite and definite articles to describe nouns
- Identify main ideas in a story
- Identify important details in a conversation
- Summarize and give opinions on the moral of a fable
- Write a paragraph about a personal experience that illustrates the meaning of a moral

Nouns and Quantifiers
TIME CAPSULES

OUTCOMES
- Use proper, common, count, and non-count nouns
- Describe quantities and use quantifiers with nouns
- Identify the main points in a text on a scientific topic
- Identify details in a conversation about a day-to-day topic
- Discuss quotes and proverbs
- Write a note or letter that lists and describes quantities of items

---

STEP 1	GRAMMAR IN CONTEXT

BEFORE YOU READ

Look at the photos and at the title of the article. Discuss the questions.

1. What items are in the time capsule?
2. Why is the article called "Time in a Bottle"?

READ

17|01 Read this article about time capsules.

The Westinghouse Time Capsule at the 1939 New York World's Fair

Time in a Bottle

A baseball, a light bulb, a child's doll, a camera, and an electric shaver. Some money (a dollar bill and a few coins). Seeds (such as rice and corn). The Bible, a written message from Albert Einstein, and hundreds of books and newspapers on microfilm.[1]

What do these items have in common? They all went into a capsule 50 feet (15 meters) underground in Flushing Meadows Park, in New York City. The year was 1939; the occasion was the New York World's Fair; and the instructions were not to open the capsule for 5,000 years!

The Westinghouse Time Capsule is just one of many capsules all over the world. They hold hundreds of everyday objects, but they have just one purpose: to tell people of the future about life in the past. To help make this happen, Westinghouse published a book, printed on special paper with ink that will not fade[2] over time. The book tells how to find and open the capsule. It even explains how to interpret the capsule's English, which will be very different from languages 5,000 years from now!

The Westinghouse Time Capsule is an example of an intentional time capsule, but history has given us unintentional time capsules, too. The most famous is the ancient Roman city of Pompeii, in Italy. In the year 79, Vesuvius, a nearby volcano,

---

1 *microfilm:* a special type of film used for making very small photos of important papers
2 *fade:* lose color

erupted.[3] It buried the city under 60 feet (18 meters) of ash and created an instant time capsule. Archaeologists[4] are still studying it today.

Intentional or unintentional, time capsules give us the chance to "communicate" with people from other times. What will people think of us when they open the Westinghouse Time Capsule in 5,000 years? Will they be as impressed with our civilization as we are with ancient Pompeii? Only time will tell—although we certainly won't be there to find out!

---

3 *erupted:* exploded and sent out smoke, fire, and rocks into the sky
4 *archaeologists:* people who study ancient cultures by examining their buildings and objects

Replica of the Westinghouse Time Capsule

AFTER YOU READ

A VOCABULARY Choose the word or phrase that best completes each sentence.

1. A _____ is an example of an **occasion**.
   a. time capsule   b. location   c. party

2. The **purpose** of the party was a _____.
   a. cake   b. present   c. birthday celebration

3. Emily was **impressed**. She thought the time capsule was _____.
   a. depressing   b. great   c. terrible

4. If an action was **intentional**, you _____ to do it.
   a. planned   b. forgot   c. didn't want

5. I really couldn't **interpret** Einstein's message. What was the _____?
   a. reason   b. language   c. meaning

6. _____ is an example of an ancient **civilization**.
   a. Flushing Meadows Park   b. Pompeii   c. Westinghouse

B COMPREHENSION Read the statements. Check (✓) *True* or *False*.

	True	False
1. Time capsules contain unusual items.	☐	☐
2. There are time capsules all over the world.	☐	☐
3. The Westinghouse Time Capsule is in Italy.	☐	☐
4. The ancient city of Pompeii is an unintentional time capsule.	☐	☐
5. Time capsules teach us about different civilizations.	☐	☐
6. People will soon be able to see the contents of the Westinghouse Time Capsule.	☐	☐

C DISCUSSION Work with a partner. Compare your answers in B. Why did you check *True* or *False*?

NOUNS AND QUANTIFIERS

Count Nouns			
	Noun	Verb	
One	**capsule**	is	in New York.
Two	**capsules**	are	

Non-Count Nouns		
Noun	Verb	
Money	is	inside.

Quantifiers and Count Nouns		
	Quantifier	Noun
It holds	some enough a lot of a few several (a great) many	coins.
It doesn't hold	any enough	coins.
Does it hold	a lot of many	coins?

Quantifiers and Non-Count Nouns		
	Quantifier	Noun
It holds	some enough a lot of a little a great deal of	money.
It doesn't hold	any enough	money.
Does it hold	a lot of much	money?

GRAMMAR NOTES

1   Proper Nouns and Common Nouns

Proper nouns are the **names** of particular people, places, or things.	
• **people:** *Albert Einstein, Columbus, Emily*	**Albert Einstein** was a famous scientist.
• **places:** *New York, Germany, Europe, Vesuvius*	He was born in **Germany**.
• **things:** *Coca Cola, the Statue of Liberty*	We visited **the Statue of Liberty**.
Proper nouns are usually **singular**.	**Pompeii** *is* an amazing place.
IN WRITING **Capitalize** the **first letter** of each word in a proper noun.	**Westinghouse** built a time capsule. It's in **New York City**.
Common nouns refer to people, places, and things, but not by their names.	
• **people:** *scientist, teacher, explorer*	Albert Einstein was a famous **scientist**.
• **places:** *city, country, continent, volcano*	He left his **country** in 1933.
• **things:** *soda, monument, magazine, wool*	The Statue of Liberty is a popular **monument**.
Common nouns can be **singular or plural**.	The time **capsule** *is* in New York. How many time **capsules** *are* there?
IN WRITING Do **not capitalize** the **first letter** of a common noun.	Einstein was a **scientist**. **NOT** Einstein was a ~~Scientist~~.

2 Count Nouns and Non-Count Nouns

Common nouns can be **count nouns** or **non-count nouns**.

Count nouns refer to people, places, or things that you **can count separately**: *one book, two books, three books . . .*	
• **people:** *one teacher, twenty students* • **places:** *one country, five cities* • **things:** *one bookcase, a hundred books*	Mr. Lee is my favorite **teacher**. He's lived in three different **countries**. He reads more than fifty **books** a year.
Count nouns can be **singular** or **plural**. They take **singular** or **plural verbs**.	He read one **book**. She read two **books**. The **book** *is* new, but the **newspapers** *are* old.
You can use *a, an,* or *the* before singular count nouns. You can use *the* before both singular and plural nouns.	There's *a* **doll** and *an* **electric shaver** in *the* box. *The* **box** contains *the* **objects** I described.
Non-count nouns refer to things that you **cannot count separately**. For example, you can say *rice,* but you cannot say ~~one rice~~ or ~~two rices~~. Here are some categories of non-count nouns:	
• **abstract words:** *education, love, time* • **activities:** *exploring, farming, sailing* • **courses of study:** *art, history, math* • **foods:** *corn, milk, rice* • **fabrics:** *cotton, silk, wool*	**Education** is very important. **Farming** is a difficult occupation. **Math** was my favorite subject in school. They grow **rice**, but they don't grow **corn**. That sweater is made of **cotton**.
Some **common non-count nouns** do not fit into categories: *equipment, furniture, homework, information, news, work.*	Today's **homework** was very easy. The **information** in this article is interesting. The **news** is on TV now. Let's watch it.
Most non-count nouns have **no plural forms**.	She bought a lot of **rice**. **NOT** She bought a lot of ~~rices~~.
They take **singular verbs** and **pronouns**.	**Archaeology** *is* an interesting subject. *It was* his favorite subject.

3 Quantifiers

Quantifiers are **words** or **phrases** such as *some* or *a few* that **show quantity**. Use quantifiers with nouns to express *how many* or *how much*.	
Some quantifiers go only with **count nouns**.	*Many* **people** worked on the capsule. *(count)*
Other quantifiers go only with **non-count nouns**.	They did *a great deal of* **work**. *(non-count)*
A few quantifiers can go with both **count** and **non-count nouns**.	It took *a lot of* **people** to finish. *(count)* It took *a lot of* **time**. *(non-count)*

In **affirmative statements**, use these quantifiers:

- *many*, *a lot of*, *a great many*, and *a great deal of* for a large quantity

- *some* and *several* for a moderate quantity (not very large, not very small)

- *enough* for a necessary quantity

- *a few/few* and *a little/little* for a small quantity

PLURAL COUNT NOUNS	NON-COUNT NOUNS
many / *a lot of* coins	*a lot of* money
a great many jobs	*a great deal of* work
some socks	*some* wool
several books	*some* paper
enough apples	*enough* rice
a few years	*a little* time

BE CAREFUL! The meaning of *a few* and *a little* is different from *few* and *little*. *A few* and *a little* mean *some*.

Few means *not many*. *Little* means *not much*. *Few* and *little* often mean *not enough* or *less than expected*.

We had *a little* time to complete the project. *(We had some time, but not a lot.)*

We had *little* time to complete the project. *(We almost didn't have enough time.)*

USAGE NOTE Sometimes people use *much* instead of *a lot of* in affirmative sentences. This is very formal and not common.

They spent *a lot of* money. *(very common)*
They spent *much* money. *(not common)*

USAGE NOTE In **informal conversation**, we sometimes use *lots of* instead of *a lot of* with both **plural count nouns** and **non-count nouns**.

We have *lots of* coins.
We have *lots of* time.

IN WRITING You can use *a lot of* and *lots of* in **informal writing**.

However, people **do not use** these quantifiers in very **formal writing**.

The Westinghouse time capsule contains *a lot of* everyday objects. *(less formal)*

The Westinghouse time capsule contains *many* everyday objects. *(more formal)*

In **negative statements** and **questions**, use:

- *many*, *a lot of*, *any*, and *enough* with **count nouns**

There weren't *many* **students** in class.
Did you put *any* **seeds** in the capsule?
There weren't *enough* **books**.

- *much*, *a lot of*, *any*, and *enough* with **non-count nouns**

We didn't have *much* **time** to study.
Did you put *any* **rice** in the capsule?
There wasn't *enough* **paper**.

REFERENCE NOTES

For a list of **irregular plural nouns**, see Appendix 6 on page 324.

For a list of **non-count nouns**, see Appendix 7 on page 324.

For **categories of proper nouns**, see Appendix 8 on page 325.

For **spelling rules** for **regular plural nouns**, see Appendix 25 on page 331.

For **capitalization rules**, see Appendix 27 on page 333.

EXERCISE 1 DISCOVER THE GRAMMAR

Ⓐ GRAMMAR NOTES 1–5 **Read this article about Pompeii. Underline the nouns. Circle the quantifiers.**

Pompeii: A Window to Ancient History

Pompeii was a rich and lively city on the bay of Naples, south of Rome. Wealthy Romans came to spend the summer there in large and beautiful villas.[1] Then on August 24 in the year 79, Vesuvius erupted. The volcano buried the city under 60 feet (18 meters) of ash and killed thousands of people. It also destroyed (a great many) buildings. But not all of them. The ash preserved many houses, streets, theaters, statues, and a lot of beautiful art.

Pompeii's ruins stayed buried for almost 2,000 years. Then one day in 1748, a Spanish engineer discovered them. Since that time, archaeologists have dug up many everyday objects from this ancient civilization. Furniture, jewelry, money, and even a little food remain from that terrible day. Today, we can "see" the daily lives of people in the first century in a couch made of wood, beautiful bracelets and rings, and bowls and cups made of glass. Preserved fruit, vegetables, bread, eggs, and olives tell us meals then were not so different from meals now!

Today, Pompeii is "alive" again. Millions of tourists walk its streets each year. This amazing unintentional time capsule shows them what everyday life in ancient Rome was like. It is their window to ancient history.

---

1 *villas:* ancient Roman houses or farms with land surrounding them

Ⓑ **Put nouns from the article into the correct columns. Choose only sixteen count nouns.**

Proper Nouns	Common Nouns			
	Count Nouns		**Non-Count Nouns**	
1. *Pompeii*	1. *window*	9. _____	1. *history*	8. _____
2. _____	2. _____	10. _____	2. _____	9. _____
3. _____	3. _____	11. _____	3. _____	10. _____
4. _____	4. _____	12. _____	4. _____	11. _____
5. _____	5. _____	13. _____	5. _____	12. _____
6. _____	6. _____	14. _____	6. _____	13. _____
	7. _____	15. _____	7. _____	
	8. _____	16. _____		

EXERCISE 2 NOUN AND VERB AGREEMENT

GRAMMAR NOTE 2 Emily and James are planning a trip to Pompeii. They are checking a travel website for some tips on packing. Complete these tips. Use the correct form of the words in parentheses. See Appendix 7 on page 324 for help with non-count nouns.

Pompeii Packing Posts

On the road

Your ___*feet need*___ your help! Good _____ a must! Remember your
   1. (foot / need)   **2.** (shoe / be)

purpose here—you'll be walking for _____ to see the _____
                                      3. (hour)   **4.** (ruin)

of this ancient civilization. And those _____ very, very old—almost 2,000
                                           5. (street / be)

_____ old!
   6. (year)

Hey, it's hot out there!

_____ essential. You can't buy it once you're inside, so don't forget to take
   7. (water / be)

several _____ with you. The _____ very, very hot, so
          8. (bottle)   **9.** (sun / be)

_____ very important, too. And don't forget your _____! Both
   10. (sunblock / be)   **11.** (hat)

of these _____ protect you from the sun.
            12. (thing / help)

Pompeii—it's picture perfect!

Pompeii is amazing, and you'll want to take lots of _____. So bring a
                                                      13. (picture)

camera and an extra memory card. Extra _____ important, too!
                                         14. (battery / be)

What to wear

The right _____ a big difference. Pompeii often _____ cool at
            15. (clothing / make)   **16.** (get)

night, so bring a sweater.

Tempus fugit

That's Latin for _____. Most _____ a whole day at Pompeii.
                   17. (time / fly)   **18.** (people / spend)

The _____ huge. Take a map, and take your time!
      19. (ruin / be)

EXERCISE 3 QUANTIFIERS

(A) GRAMMAR NOTES 3–5 Emily and James are now in Pompeii. Circle the correct words to complete their conversations.

1. EMILY: There were so (many) / much people at the ruins today. Was it some kind of special

   a.

   occasion or something?

   JAMES: I don't think so. I heard the guide say it's the most popular tourist attraction in Italy.

   EMILY: And I can understand why. I've never seen so (much) / many fascinating things.

   b.

2. EMILY: My feet hurt! We did a lot of / much walking today!

   a.

   JAMES: Tell me about it! But it sure was amazing.

   EMILY: How many / much pictures did you take?

   b.

   JAMES: I took a few / lots of pictures—over 200!

   c.

3. JAMES: It sure was hot. I'm glad we took some / any water with us. I really drank

   a.

   a lot / much.

   b.

   EMILY: Me too. And I used several / a great deal of sunblock. The sun was *really* strong.

   c.

   JAMES: Do we have some / any water left? I'm still thirsty.

   d.

4. EMILY: Are you hungry? I saw a little / a few nice-looking restaurants nearby.

   a.

   JAMES: OK. But we need to stop at an ATM first. We only have a little / a few money left.

   b.

   EMILY: That's not a problem. Very little / few restaurants don't accept credit cards these days.

   c.

5. JAMES: You know, we should spend some / any time in Naples. Our guidebook says they

   a.

   have a lot of / much art from Pompeii at the Archaeological Museum.

   b.

   EMILY: Do we have little / enough time to do that? Tomorrow is our last day.

   c.

   JAMES: True. But I think we can spend few / a few hours there. We don't need

   d.

   enough / much time to pack, do we?

   e.

   EMILY: No, but I haven't bought some / any souvenirs yet, and I feel like we're running out

   f.

   of time.

   JAMES: Don't worry. We can do some / a few shopping before dinner. How much / many

   g.   h.

   gifts do you need to buy?

   EMILY: Not much / many, I guess. Just some / any things for the family.

   i.   j.

6. EMILY: I'm impressed with our guidebook. It does a great job of interpreting the art.

JAMES: Yes. It has <u>a lot of / many</u> useful information. Maybe it can recommend a restaurant.
a.

EMILY: What do you feel like eating?

JAMES: I'd love <u>some / any</u> pasta. What about you?
b.

EMILY: Sounds good. And <u>a little / a few</u> dessert would be nice, too. Maybe they have that
c.

Roman apple cake.

▶ 17|02 **B** LISTEN AND CHECK **Listen to the conversations and check your answers in A.**

EXERCISE 4 EDITING

GRAMMAR NOTES 1–5 Read Emily's email to her family. There are fifteen mistakes in the use of nouns and quantifiers and in the use of verb and pronoun agreement. The first mistake is already corrected. Find and correct fourteen more.

● ● ●

Hi Everyone!

                                           a few

James and I got back from Pompeii ~~few~~ days ago. We bought a little souvenirs, which I'll mail to

you all very soon. We're still unpacking and looking over the many, many photograph (hundreds!)

we took of this amazing place. Our Guidebook calls pompeii a "time capsule," and I truly felt that

we were somehow communicating with this rich and vibrant cultures. There are never enough

times for everything on vacation, but that's especially true of Pompeii. Really, there are few places

in the world this amazing. You should all try to go. I was so impressed!

I plan to do a several blog posts and put up a lot photos to show you what I mean. Speaking of

time capsules, I was just in the attic putting away any suitcases, and I discovered a trunk with

much old stuff. The old clothing were still in great shape—I might wear some of the skirts and

blouses. Oh, and I found a great deal of letters that Grandpa wrote to grandma when he was

working in Italy on an archaeological dig. A few of them made me cry, and one of them had a

recipe for Roman apple cake! I think we'll try to make it, and we'll let you know how it turns out.

Love,
Emily

Articles: Indefinite and Definite

STORIES

OUTCOMES
• Use indefinite and definite articles to describe nouns
• Identify main ideas in a story
• Identify important details in a conversation
• Summarize and give opinions on the moral of a fable
• Write a paragraph about a personal experience that illustrates the meaning of a moral

STEP 1 GRAMMAR IN CONTEXT

BEFORE YOU READ

Look at the picture and at the title of the story. Discuss the questions.

1. What kind of a story is a fable?
2. Which mouse is the town mouse? Which is the country mouse? Give reasons for your answers.

READ

18|01 Read this fable.

A Fable by Aesop

Aesop was a famous storyteller in Greece more than 2,000 years ago. The fables he told are still famous all over the world.

The Town Mouse and the Country Mouse

A town mouse went to visit his cousin in the country. The country cousin was poor, but he gladly served his town cousin the only food he had—some beans and some bread. The town mouse ate the bread and laughed. He said, "What simple food you country mice eat! Come home with me. I'll show you how to live." The moon was shining brightly that night, so the mice left immediately.

As soon as they arrived at the town mouse's house, they went into the dining room. There they found the leftovers of a wonderful dinner. The mice were soon eating jelly and cake and many nice things. Suddenly, the door flew open, and an enormous dog ran in. The mice ran away quickly. "Good-bye, Cousin," said the country mouse. "Are you leaving so soon?" asked the town mouse. "Yes," his honest cousin replied. "This has been a great adventure, but it's been a little too dangerous for me."

Moral:[1] It's better to eat bread in peace than cake in fear.

---

1 *moral:* a practical lesson that you learn from a story or from something that happens to you

AFTER YOU READ

A VOCABULARY Complete the sentences with the words from the box.

enormous	famous	honest	immediately	wonderful

1. Aesop's fables are _____ all over the world. Millions of people have read them.

2. I think *The Town Mouse and the Country Mouse* is a(n) _____ fable. I really enjoyed it.

3. To be _____, I didn't really understand the moral of the fable.

4. After I read the fable, I _____ went online to search for other ones. I couldn't wait to read more!

5. I ordered a book of Aesop's fables. It's _____—almost 400 pages!

B COMPREHENSION Read the statements. Check (✓) *True* or *False*.

	True	False
1. The country mouse made a wonderful meal for his cousin.	☐	☐
2. The town mouse was happy with the meal.	☐	☐
3. It was a beautiful, bright night.	☐	☐
4. The mice left the country and went to the town mouse's house.	☐	☐
5. They ate in the town mouse's kitchen.	☐	☐
6. A dog came in and frightened the mice away.	☐	☐

C DISCUSSION Work with a partner. Compare your answers in B. Why did you check *True* or *False*?

ARTICLES: INDEFINITE AND DEFINITE

Indefinite

Singular Count Nouns

	A/An	(Adjective) Noun
Let's read	a	**story**.
This is	an	**old story**.

Plural Count Nouns / Non-Count Nouns

	(Some)	(Adjective) Noun
Let's listen to	(some)	**stories** on this CD.
This CD has		**nice music**, too.

Definite

Singular Count Nouns

	The	(Adjective) Noun
Let's read	the	**story** by Aesop.
It's		**oldest story**.

Plural Count Nouns / Non-Count Nouns

	The	(Adjective) Noun
Let's listen to	the	**stories** by Aesop.
I like		**old music** on this CD.

GRAMMAR NOTES

1 Indefinite and Definite Nouns

Nouns can be **definite** or **indefinite**.

A noun is **indefinite** when you and your listener do not have a specific person, place, or thing you are thinking about.	A: Let's buy **a book**. B: Good idea. Which one should we buy? *(A and B are not thinking about a specific book.)*
A noun is **definite** when you and your listener both know which person, place, or thing you are talking about.	A: I bought **the book** yesterday. B: Good. You've wanted it for a while. *(A and B are talking about a specific book.)*

2 Indefinite Article *A/An*, No Article, and *Some*

To show that a noun is **indefinite**, use the indefinite article *a/an*, **no article**, or *some*.

Use the **indefinite article** *a/an* with **singular count nouns** that are indefinite.	A: I'm reading **a fable**. B: Oh really? Which one?
• *a* before **consonant** sounds • *an* before **vowel** sounds	*a* mouse, *a* simple meal *an* adventure, *an* enormous dog
BE CAREFUL! It is the **sound**, not the letter, that determines if you use *a* or *an*.	*a* European writer (a "Yuropean") NOT ~~an~~ European writer *an* honest man (an "ahnest") NOT ~~a~~ honest man
Use **no article** or *some* with **plural count nouns** and with **non-count nouns** that are indefinite. *Some* means an indefinite number or amount.	PLURAL COUNT NON-COUNT A: We could have **beans** and maybe **salad** for dinner. B: All we have are *some* peas and *some* spinach.

3 Indefinite Article or No Article for Identification and General Statements

Use *a/an* or **no article** to identify people or things and to make general statements.

To **identify people or things** (say what someone or something is), use:	A: What do you do?
• *a/an* with **singular count nouns**	SINGULAR COUNT B: I'm ***a cook***.
• **no article** with **plural count nouns** and **non-count nouns**	A: What are you doing? PLURAL COUNT NON-COUNT B: I'm baking **cookies** and making **tea**.
BE CAREFUL! A singular count noun always needs an article (*a*, *an*, or *the*) before it.	I'm **a cook**. NOT I'm ~~cook~~.
Do not use *a* or *an* before non-count nouns.	I'm making **tea**. NOT I'm making ~~a tea~~.
To **make general statements**, use:	
• *a/an* with **singular count nouns**	SINGULAR COUNT ***A cook*** has a difficult job.
• **no article** with **plural count nouns** and **non-count nouns**	PLURAL COUNT NON-COUNT Ava loves **stories** and **music**. *(stories and music in general)*

4 Definite Article *The*

To show that a noun is **definite**, use the definite article *the*.

Use the **definite article** *the* with most **common nouns** (count and non-count, singular and plural) when:	
• a person, place, or thing is **unique**—there is only one	***The*** **author of this fable** is very famous. ***The*** **moon** was shining brightly.
• the **context** or situation makes it clear which person, place, or thing you mean	A: Who is she? B: She's ***the teacher***. *(A and B are in class. A is a new student.)*
• you mention the noun for the **second time** (it is often indefinite the first time you mention it)	**A mouse** lived in the town. One day, ***the*** **mouse** went to the country to visit his cousin.
• a phrase or adjective such as *first, best, right, wrong,* or *only* identifies the noun	It was ***the first*** time he visited his cousin. He served ***the only*** food he had.
Use the **definite article** *the* with some **proper nouns**, for example, the names of:	
• certain books and documents	**the** *Encyclopedia Britannica*, **the** U.S. Constitution
• countries and geographical features	**the** United Arab Emirates, **the** Alps

REFERENCE NOTES

For a list of **non-count nouns**, see Appendix 7 on page 324.

For more information on *the* with **proper nouns**, see Appendix 8 on page 325.

EXERCISE 1 DISCOVER THE GRAMMAR

GRAMMAR NOTES 1–4 **Read the conversations. Choose the statement that best describes each conversation.**

1. CORA: Dad, could you read me a story?
   DAD: Sure, I'd love to.
   a. Dad knows which story Cora wants him to read.
   (b.) Cora isn't talking about a particular story.

2. IGOR: Mom, where's the new book?
   MOM: Sorry, I haven't seen it.
   a. Mom knows that Igor bought a new book.
   b. Mom doesn't know that Igor bought a new book.

3. DAD: I'll bet it's in the hall. You always drop your things there.
   IGOR: I'll go look.
   a. There are several halls in the house.
   b. There is only one hall in the house.

4. DAD: Was I right?
   IGOR: You weren't even close. It was on a chair in the kitchen.
   a. There is only one chair in the kitchen.
   b. There are several chairs in the kitchen.

5. DAD: Wow! Look at that! The pictures are great.
   IGOR: So are the stories.
   a. All books have great pictures and stories.
   b. The book Igor bought has great pictures and stories.

6. IGOR: Oh, I forgot . . . I also got a video game. Do you want to play?
   DAD: You know I love video games. But, to be honest, I'm too tired right now.
   a. Dad is talking about video games in general.
   b. Dad is talking about a particular video game.

EXERCISE 2 DEFINITE ARTICLE OR NO ARTICLE

A GRAMMAR NOTES 1–4 Pilar is in a bookstore to buy books for her young niece. An assistant, Jason, is trying to help her. Complete their conversation. Use *the* where necessary. Leave a blank if you don't need an article.

PILAR: I'm looking for _____ books for my
___1.___
14-year-old niece. Do you have

any recommendations?

JASON: Let's go to ___*the*___ young adult
___2.___
section. Does she like _____
___3.___
mysteries? Doris Duncan wrote some

good ones for teenagers.

PILAR: She's read all _____ mysteries by
___4.___
Duncan. She's _____ fastest reader
___5.___
in our family!

JASON: It's hard to keep up with _____ fast
___6.___
readers. Here's a good one by Gillian

Cross—*Born of* _____ *Sun*. It's about finding a lost Inca city.
___7.___

PILAR: She'll like that one. She loves _____ books about _____ history—and
___8.___ ___9.___
science, too.

JASON: Then how about *A Short History of* _____ *Universe*? It's in _____
___10.___ ___11.___
science section.

PILAR: This is great! She likes _____ books with beautiful pictures.
___12.___

JASON: Well, _____ pictures in this one are wonderful. *Nature Magazine* called this book
___13.___

_____ best introduction to this subject.
___14.___

PILAR: OK, I'll take _____ mystery by Cross and _____ science book. Anything else?
___15.___ ___16.___

JASON: Well, _____ kids have fun with _____ trivia games. Here's a good one.
___17.___ ___18.___

PILAR: Great. I'll get _____ trivia game, too. Thanks. You've been very helpful.
___19.___

▶18|02 **B** LISTEN AND CHECK Listen to the conversation and check your answers in A.

EXERCISE 3 INDEFINITE OR DEFINITE ARTICLE

A GRAMMAR NOTES 1–4 Read this story about a famous character in Turkish literature, Nasreddin. Complete the text with *a*, *an*, or *the*.

Nasreddin lived ____a____ long time ago in Turkey. He is one of _____ most famous
                    1.   **2.**

characters in literature. People often thought he was _____ fool, but he was _____
                                                         3.   **4.**

very wise man. Here is _____ funny story about him:
                          5.

Nasreddin Solves _____ Difficult Problem
                         6.

Nasreddin had _____ little donkey. There was _____ market
                 7.   **8.**

in _____ only nearby town, and Nasreddin and his grandson often
      9.

went there with _____ donkey. One day, they were traveling to
                   10.

_____ market when _____ group of people passed by. Someone
  11.   **12.**

shouted, "Look! _____ old man is walking while _____ boy
                   13.   **14.**

rides!" So _____ boy got down, and Nasreddin rode. Then they
              15.

passed _____ storyteller sitting under _____ tree. _____
          16.   **17.**   **18.**

storyteller called out, "Why is that poor child walking in _____
                                                              19.

hot sun?" So they both rode. Next, they met _____ old woman.
                                               20.

"_____ little donkey is tired!" she shouted. So Nasreddin said,
  21.

"_____ best thing is for both of us to walk." Soon they met
  22.

_____ merchant. _____ merchant's donkey was carrying
  23.   **24.**

_____ enormous bag. _____ merchant laughed and said,
  25.   **26.**

"Why are you two walking? That's _____ strong little
                                    27.

donkey!" Nasreddin immediately picked up _____
                                            28.

donkey and carried it on his shoulders. "These people

will never leave us alone," he told his grandson. "So

this is _____ only way to solve _____ problem."
          29.   **30.**

18|03 **B** LISTEN AND CHECK Listen to the story
about Nasreddin. Check your answers in A.

EXERCISE 4 INDEFINITE, DEFINITE, NO ARTICLE, OR *SOME*

GRAMMAR NOTES 1–4 Read this short biography of Aesop, the famous Greek storyteller. Circle the correct article or *some* to complete the text. Circle Ø if you don't need an article.

People all over (the) / Ø world know a / the fables of Aesop, but
       1.   2.

there is very little information about the / Ø life of this famous Greek
                                        3.

storyteller. Scholars agree that Aesop was born around 620 B.C.E.[1] In

his early years, he was a / the slave, and he lived on Samos, an / a island
                        4.   5.

in an / the Aegean Sea. Even as a / the slave, Aesop had the / Ø wisdom
    6.   7.   8.

and knowledge. His master respected him so much that he freed him.

When Aesop became a / Ø free man, he traveled to many countries in
                      9.

order to learn and to teach. In Lydia, the / Ø king invited him to stay in
                                        10.

that country and gave Aesop some / a difficult jobs in a / the government.
                                11.   12.

In his work, Aesop often struggled to convince people of

his ideas. Sometimes he used a / Ø fables to help people
                               13.

understand what he meant. One time, a / the king sent
                                       14.

Aesop to Delphi with a / some gold for a / the people of
                        15.   16.

that city. Aesop became disgusted with the / Ø people's
                                           17.

greed, so he sent the / Ø gold back to a / the king.
                      18.   19.

A / The people of Delphi were very angry at
  20.

Aesop for this, and they killed him. After his

death, a / the famous sculptor made a / the
       21.   22.

statue of Aesop you see in a / the photo.
                            23.

---

1 B.C.E.: the abbreviation for *Before Common Era*, a year-numbering
  system used in many parts of the world

EXERCISE 5 INDEFINITE, DEFINITE, OR NO ARTICLE

GRAMMAR NOTES 1–4 This is a trivia game. Complete the clues for each item. Then, using the clues and the appropriate picture, write the answer. Use *a*, *an*, or *the* where necessary. Leave a blank if you don't need an article. The answers to this trivia game are on page 183.

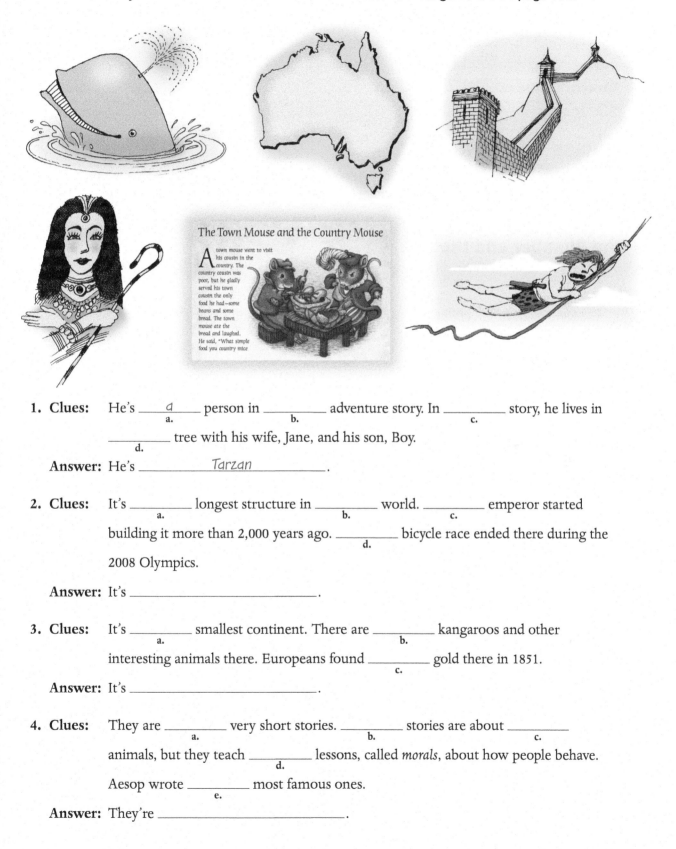

The Town Mouse and the Country Mouse

A town mouse went to visit his cousin in the country. The country cousin was poor, but he gladly served his town cousin the only food he had—some beans and some bread. The town mouse ate the bread and laughed. He said, "What simple food you country mice

1. **Clues:** He's ___*a*___ person in _____ adventure story. In _____ story, he lives in
   a.   b.   c.
   _____ tree with his wife, Jane, and his son, Boy.
   d.

   Answer: He's _____ *Tarzan* _____.

2. **Clues:** It's _____ longest structure in _____ world. _____ emperor started
   a.   b.   c.
   building it more than 2,000 years ago. _____ bicycle race ended there during the
   d.
   2008 Olympics.

   Answer: It's _____.

3. **Clues:** It's _____ smallest continent. There are _____ kangaroos and other
   a.   b.
   interesting animals there. Europeans found _____ gold there in 1851.
   c.

   Answer: It's _____.

4. **Clues:** They are _____ very short stories. _____ stories are about _____
   a.   b.   c.
   animals, but they teach _____ lessons, called *morals*, about how people behave.
   d.
   Aesop wrote _____ most famous ones.
   e.

   Answer: They're _____.

5. Clues: She was _____ intelligent and beautiful woman. She was _____ most famous
              a.   b.

         queen of Egypt. She ruled _____ country with her brother.
                                      c.

   Answer: She was _____.

6. Clues: They are _____ biggest living animals on Earth. They live in all the oceans of
                        a.

         _____ world, but they aren't _____ fish.
           b.   c.

   Answer: They're _____.

EXERCISE 6 EDITING

GRAMMAR NOTES 1–4 Read this article about video games. There are twelve mistakes in the
use of *a*, *an*, and *the*. The first mistake is already corrected. Find and correct eleven more.

The Plumber and the Ape

Once there was a plumber named Mario.

The plumber
~~Plumber~~ had beautiful girlfriend. One day, a ape fell in love with the girlfriend and kidnapped

her. The plumber chased ape to rescue his girlfriend. This simple tale became *Donkey Kong*, a

first video game with a story. It was invented by Shigeru Miyamoto, an artist with Nintendo, Inc.

Miyamoto loved the video games, but he wanted to make them more interesting.

He liked fairy tales, so he invented story similar to a famous fairy tale. Some

story was an immediate success, and Nintendo followed it with *The*

Mario Brothers and then with *Super Mario*. The third game became

popular all over a world, and it is still one of the most famous games

in video history. Nintendo has continued to add

the new adventures and new ways to play game.

Now players can follow Mario to outer space and

play the game on their Wii.[1] But success and

space travel do not change Mario. He is

still brave little plumber in a red hat.

---

1 *Wii (pronounced "we"):* a game system in which
   players hold a wireless controller and control the
   game by their movements and by pressing buttons

Mario and his creator,
Shigeru Miyamoto

- the Great Wall of China

- Australia

- Fables

- Cleopatra

- whales

Adjectives and Adverbs

PART 6

OUTCOMES

- Describe people, objects, and places, using adjectives and adverbs
- Form and use basic adverbs and participial adjectives
- Recognize important points in an advertisement
- Identify speakers' opinions in a conversation
- Discuss places to live, comparing and contrasting different options
- Write a description of one's ideal home

OUTCOMES

- Form and use comparative adjectives
- Express how two people, places, or things are similar or different
- Identify main ideas in a short newspaper article
- Recognize speakers' preferences in a conversation
- Discuss different food options
- Write a paragraph that compares and contrasts foods from different cities or countries

OUTCOMES

- Form and use superlative adjectives
- Compare one person, place, or thing to others in a group
- Identify key details in an article about a city
- Identify places and locations by their descriptions in a conversation
- Describe and express opinions about places
- Write a description of one's hometown or city

OUTCOMES

- Form and use comparative and superlative adverbs
- Express how two actions are similar or different
- Identify main ideas in an opinion article and in a debate
- Discuss issues in a debate, supporting opinions
- Describe and compare people's abilities
- Write arguments for and against a statement

Adjectives and Adverbs

HOME

OUTCOMES
- Describe people, objects, and places, using adjectives and adverbs
- Form and use basic adverbs and participial adjectives
- Recognize important points in an advertisement
- Identify speakers' opinions in a conversation
- Discuss places to live, comparing and contrasting different options
- Write a description of one's ideal home

STEP 1   GRAMMAR IN CONTEXT

BEFORE YOU READ

Look at the photo of a house. Discuss the questions.

1. Is this a good place to live? Why or why not?
2. What is important when looking for a home?

READ

19|01 Read this ad for two apartments in a private house.

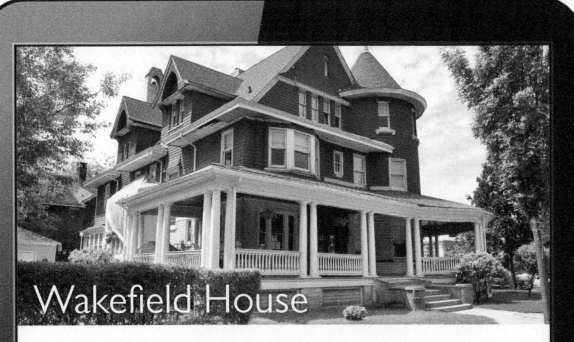

Wakefield House

Are you looking for a nice neighborhood with safe, quiet streets? Do you love the big sunny rooms and high ceilings in interesting old buildings—but want modern appliances[1] and high-speed Internet, too? Apartments in Wakefield House offer that and more. Here's your place to relax completely after a long hard day at school or work. We are located in a peaceful residential area near famous Lake Forest Park. And it's so convenient! An easy drive or bus ride takes you downtown and to the university. Exciting nightlife, shopping, and museums are only minutes away.

_____

1 *appliances:* pieces of equipment, such as washing machines or stoves, that people use in their homes

It sounds very expensive, right? But it's not! A comfortable one-bedroom apartment is surprisingly affordable. We have two beautifully furnished apartments available right now. But don't wait! Our apartments rent very quickly.

Call 555-1234 now for an appointment.

Here's what some of our satisfied tenants[2] are saying about life at Wakefield House:

"The neighborhood is like a small village with really friendly people and beautiful, charming[3] houses."

—Maggie Chang

"This place is absolutely perfect. I can easily get everywhere on my bike. It's my ideal home away from home. It's awesome."

—Luis Rivera

"Weekends here are so peaceful—no annoying traffic noise. I love sitting on the front porch and reading a good book."

—Alice Thompson

2 *tenants:* people who live in a house, apartment, or room and pay rent to the owner
3 *charming:* very nice or attractive

AFTER YOU READ

Ⓐ VOCABULARY Choose the word or phrase closest in meaning to the word in **bold.**

1. We found the **ideal** house today.
  a. perfect **b.** expensive **c.** nearby

2. The bus to town is very **convenient**.
  a. safe **b.** easy to use **c.** comfortable

3. The house is **located in** a residential area.
  a. close to **b.** far from **c.** part of

4. It's on a **peaceful** street.
  a. dangerous **b.** quiet **c.** crowded

5. We were very **satisfied** with the neighborhood.
  a. happy **b.** unhappy **c.** relaxed

6. It's **absolutely** perfect for us.
  a. almost **b.** completely **c.** very

COMPREHENSION Read the statements. Check (✓) *True* or *False*.

	True	False
1. Wakefield House is in a dangerous neighborhood.	☐	☒
2. It's in an exciting area of the city.	☒	☐
3. The apartments are not dark.	☒	☐
4. You'll be surprised that the rent is so low.	☒	☐
5. It's difficult to get to the university.	☐	☒
6. One tenant likes to spend weekends at home.	☒	☐

C DISCUSSION Work with a partner. Compare your answers in B. Why did you check *True* or *False*?

STEP 2   GRAMMAR PRESENTATION

ADJECTIVES AND ADVERBS

Adjectives	Adverbs of Manner	Adverbs of Degree
They are **quiet** tenants.	They talk **quietly**.	They're **very** quiet. They talk **very** quietly.
The house is **nice**.	They decorated it **nicely**.	It's **so** nice. They decorated it **so** nicely.
It looks **good**.	She described it **well**.	This looks **really** good. She described it **really** well.
It's a **fast** elevator.	It moves **fast**.	It's **awfully** fast! It moves **awfully** fast!

Participial Adjectives

-ing Adjective	*-ed* Adjective
The apartment is **interesting**.	One couple is **interested** in the apartment.
It's an **interesting** one-bedroom apartment.	The **interested** couple called again.
My neighbor is **annoying**.	I'm **annoyed** by his loud music.
He's an **annoying** neighbor.	Another **annoyed** tenant complained.

Word Order: Adjectives before Nouns

	Opinion	Size	Age	Shape	Color	Origin	Material	Purpose	Noun (as Adj.)	NOUN
a	**peaceful**	**little**						**residential**		area
some	**interesting**		**young**							tenants
your				**round**	**blue**	**Chinese**				vase
the		**large**	**old**				**wooden**		**kitchen**	table

GRAMMAR NOTES

1 Adjectives and Adverbs

Adjectives and adverbs **describe** or give information about **other words**.

Use **adjectives** to describe **nouns** (people, places, or things).	ADJECTIVE NOUN NOUN ADJECTIVE They are *safe* **streets**. or The **streets** are *safe*. (Safe *gives you information about the streets.*)

Use **adverbs** to describe:

• verbs	VERB ADVERB The manager **talks** *quietly*.
• adjectives	ADVERB ADJECTIVE He's *extremely* **quiet**.
• other adverbs	ADVERB ADVERB He works *very* quietly.

BE CAREFUL! Use an adjective after a **non-action verb** such as *be*, *look*, *seem*, *appear*, *smell*, or *taste*. Do not use an adverb.	VERB ADJECTIVE This house **looks** *beautiful*. **NOT** The house looks ~~beautifully~~.

2 Adverbs of Manner

Adverbs of manner **describe** or give information about **action verbs**.

Adverbs of manner often **answer the question** *"How?"*	A: How did they decorate the apartment? ACTION VERB ADVERB B: They **decorated** it *beautifully*.
Form most adverbs of manner by **adding -ly** to the adjective.	ADJECTIVE ADVERB I need a **quick** decision. Please decide *quickly*.

Some adverbs of manner also have a **form** **without -ly**. The form is the **same as** the adjective.	**ADVERB WITH -LY**		**ADVERB WITHOUT -LY**
	slowly	or	slow
	quickly	or	quick
	loudly	or	loud
	clearly	or	clear

USAGE NOTE The adverb form **without -ly** is **less formal**.	Don't speak so **loudly**. *(more formal)* Don't speak so **loud**. *(less formal)*
BE CAREFUL! Some **adjectives** also end in **-ly**, for example, *friendly*, *lonely*, *lovely*, and *silly*.	ADJECTIVE It's a **lovely** apartment.
Some common adverbs of manner are **not** **formed by adding -ly** to adjectives: The adverb form of *good* is *well*.	ADJECTIVE He's a **good** building manager. ADVERB He manages the building **well**.
Early, *fast*, *hard*, *late*, and *wrong* have the **same** adjective and adverb forms.	ADJECTIVE ADVERB She is a **hard** worker. She works **hard**.
BE CAREFUL! *Hardly* is not the adverb form of *hard*. *Hardly* means "almost not."	There's **hardly** enough room for a bed. *(There's almost not enough room for a bed.)*
Lately is not the adverb form of *late*. *Lately* means "recently."	We haven't seen any nice houses **lately**. *(We haven't seen any nice houses recently.)*

3 Adverbs of Degree

Adverbs of degree make adjectives, other adverbs, and verbs **stronger** or **weaker**.

100%	*absolutely, completely, totally*	
	awfully, terribly, too	
	really, so, very, extremely	
	pretty, quite, fairly	
0%	*not at all*	

ADVERB   VERB
A: I ***absolutely* love** it here.

               ADVERB   ADVERB
B: You can get to work ***awfully* easily**.

            ADVERB ADJECTIVE
A: We are ***pretty* lucky** to live here.

        ADVERB   ADJECTIVE
B: And it's ***not at all* expensive**!

USAGE NOTE *Awfully* and *terribly* can describe something good or bad.

The apartment was ***awfully* nice**.
The landlord was ***awfully* rude**.

USAGE NOTE In informal conversation, we often use *real* instead of *really* before an adjective.

The house is in a ***real* good** neighborhood.
   (The house is in a really good neighborhood.)

Not at all means "totally not."

I did***n't* like** the apartment ***at all***.
   (I totally didn't like it.)

Notice the word order for *not at all*.
- **after a verb** or verb + object
- **after or before an adjective** or another adverb

They did***n't* decorate** (the place) ***at all***.

It was***n't* nice *at all***. or It was***n't* at all* nice**.

BE CAREFUL! Not all adverbs of degree can go with verbs. Do not use *extremely, very, pretty, awfully, terribly, fairly,* or *too* before a verb.

I ***absolutely* love** it.
NOT I ~~extremely~~ love it.
I ***totally* agree** with you.
NOT I ~~terribly~~ agree with you.

4 Participial Adjectives

Participial adjectives are adjectives that **end with -*ing* or -*ed***.

Participial adjectives **come from verbs**.

                 VERB
This neighborhood **amazes** me.
     ADJECTIVE   ADJECTIVE
It's an **amazing** neighborhood. I'm **amazed**.

Use participial adjectives to **describe feelings**:
- the -*ing* form shows that someone or something **causes** a feeling

The house is **disappointing**.
   (The house causes a feeling of disappointment.)

- the -*ed* form shows that someone **has** a feeling

I'm **disappointed**.
   (I have a feeling of disappointment.)

5 Word Order with One Adjective

An **adjective** usually goes right **before the noun** it describes.

      ADJECTIVE NOUN
This is a ***beautiful* house**.

It can also go **after a non-action verb** such as *be, look, seem, appear, smell,* or *taste*.

         VERB   ADJECTIVE
This house **looks *beautiful***.

6 Word Order with Several Adjectives

Sometimes we use **two or three adjectives before a noun**.

If adjectives belong to **different categories**, we usually **follow this order**: **opinion + size + age + shape + color + origin + material + purpose + noun (used as adjective) + NOUN**	(OPINION) (AGE) (PURPOSE) It's in a **beautiful old residential** neighborhood. (OPINION) (COLOR) (MATERIAL) I bought a **nice black leather** couch.
Size adjectives (such as *big* and *small*) are an exception. They often go first in a series of adjectives.	(SIZE) (OPINION) (NOUN AS ADJ.) It's a **small affordable one-room** apartment. or (OPINION) (SIZE) (NOUN AS ADJ.) It's an **affordable small one-room** apartment.
IN WRITING **Do not use commas** between adjectives that belong to different categories.	(SIZE) (SHAPE) (ORIGIN) I got a **large round Mexican** mirror. **NOT** I got a large‚ round‚ Mexican mirror.
For adjectives that belong to the **same category**, the **order is not important**. IN WRITING **Use commas** between adjectives that belong to the same category.	She's a **friendly, helpful, nice** woman. or She's a **helpful, friendly, nice** woman. or She's a **nice, helpful, friendly** woman. *(All the adjectives are opinion adjectives, so the order can change.)*

7 Word Order with Adverbs of Manner or Degree

An **adverb of manner** usually goes **after the verb** it describes.	VERB ADVERB The apartment **rented** *quickly*.
When the verb has an object, the adverb goes **after the object**. BE CAREFUL! Do not put an adverb between the verb and the object.	VERB OBJECT ADVERB She **decorated** the house *nicely*. **NOT** She decorated ~~nicely the house~~.
An **adverb of degree** usually goes right **before the adjective, adverb, or verb** it describes.	ADVERB ADJECTIVE It's an *extremely* nice house. ADVERB ADVERB They found it *very* quickly. ADVERB VERB They *really* liked it.

REFERENCE NOTES

For a list of **non-action verbs**, see Appendix 2 on page 322.

For **adverbs of frequency**, see Unit 1, Grammar Note 3, on page 7.

For a list of **participial adjectives**, see Appendix 11 on page 326.

For the **order of adjectives before a noun**, see Appendix 12 on page 326.

For **spelling rules** for **adverbs ending in -ly**, see Appendix 24 on page 331.

EXERCISE 1 DISCOVER THE GRAMMAR

GRAMMAR NOTES 1–7 Read this notice from a university bulletin board. Underline the adjectives and circle the adverbs. Then draw an arrow from the adjective or adverb to the word it is describing.

APARTMENT FOR RENT
140 Grant Street, Apt. 4B

Are you looking for a place to live? This amazing apartment is in a new

building and has two large comfortable bedrooms and a small sunny

kitchen. The building is very quiet—absolutely perfect for two serious

students. It's near the campus on a peaceful street. There's convenient

transportation. The bus stop is an easy, pleasant walk, and the express bus

goes directly into town. You can run or ride your bike safely in nearby

parks. The rent is very affordable. Small pets are welcome. The apartment

is available on June 1. Interested students should call Megan at 555-5050.

We're sure you'll be satisfied. Don't wait! This beautiful new apartment

will rent fast. Nonsmokers, please.

EXERCISE 2 ADJECTIVE OR ADVERB

GRAMMAR NOTES 1–4 Circle the correct words to complete Maggie's email to her brother.

Hi Roger!

I wasn't sure I'd like living in a **large** / largely city, but I real / **really** love it! Maybe that's
            1.   **2.**

because my new / newly neighborhood is located in such a beautiful / beautifully residential
             3.   **4.**

area with lots of nice old trees.

Last Saturday, I worked hard / hardly and unpacked all my stuff. Then I spent Sunday
                       5.

happy / happily exploring my new neighborhood. I couldn't believe the gorgeous / gorgeously
   6.   **7.**

houses on these streets. I feel very lucky / luckily to live in one of them.
                             8.

Here's a photo of "my" house. What do you think?

My apartment is on the second floor. It's really great / greatly. I'm total / totally satisfied
                                                  9.   10.
with it. The other tenants are very nice / nicely. My next-door neighbor, Alice, seemed pretty
                                            11.
shy / shyly at first, but I think we're going to become good / well friends very quick / quickly.
12.   13.   14.
She's an art student, and she likes to visit museums. We're going to the Modern Art Museum

together next Saturday. Life in the city is exciting / excitingly, but I get terrible / terribly
                                                 15.   16.
homesick. So I real / really hope you visit me soon!
            17.

Love,
Maggie

EXERCISE 3 ADVERBS BEFORE ADJECTIVES AND OTHER ADVERBS

GRAMMAR NOTES 2–3 Many different people went to see the apartment described in
Exercise 1. Complete their comments about the apartment. Use the correct form of
the words in parentheses. See Appendix 24 on page 331 for help with spelling adverbs
ending in *-ly*.

1. I am very interested. I think the apartment is _____ *extremely nice* _____.
                                                      (extreme / nice)

2. I was expecting much bigger rooms. I was _____.
                                            (terrible / disappointed)

3. I thought it would be hard to get to, but the bus was _____.
                                                        (surprising / convenient)

4. I think it's a great place. I'm sure it will rent _____.
                                                    (incredible / fast)

5. The ad said it was quiet, but I heard the neighbors _____.
                                                      (very / clear)

6. I heard them, too. I thought their voices were _____.
                                                  (awful / loud)

7. The ad described the apartment _____.
                                  (pretty / accurate)

8. To be honest, this place is _____ for me!
                             (absolute / perfect)

9. I'm going to feel _____ if I don't get it.
                    (real / upset)

EXERCISE 4 PARTICIPIAL ADJECTIVES

Ⓐ GRAMMAR NOTE 4 Luis is talking to his friend Sylvie. Read their conversation. Complete it with the correct participial adjective form (-ing or -ed) of the verbs in parentheses.

SYLVIE: These apartment ads are really ___*annoying*___ . Just look at this one.
                                                    1. (annoy)

LUIS: Hmmm. It says, "cozy and _____ apartment." Why are you
                                    2. (charm)

_____ at that?
3. (annoy)

SYLVIE: I saw the place—it's *tiny*, not cozy! And I wasn't _____ at all. In fact, I was
                                                              4. (charm)

pretty _____ .
        5. (disgust)

LUIS: Take it easy. It sounds like you had an _____ day. Let's relax and watch a
                                              6. (exhaust)

movie tonight.

SYLVIE: You're right. I'm completely _____ . I could use a _____
                                      7. (exhaust)   **8.** (relax)

evening. What do you want to watch?

LUIS: There's a movie called *Lake House*. I hear it's pretty _____ .
                                                             9. (interest)

SYLVIE: *Lake House*? Great title! I'm _____ already. What's it about?
                                       10. (interest)

LUIS: Well, the story's a little _____ , but it happens in a beautiful glass house on
                                 11. (confuse)

a peaceful lake.

SYLVIE: Glass? That sounds like an _____ house. I wonder if *they're* looking
                                   12. (amaze)

for tenants.

▶19|02 Ⓑ LISTEN AND CHECK Listen to the conversation and check your answers in A.

EXERCISE 5 WORD ORDER

GRAMMAR NOTES 5, 7 Put the words in the correct order to complete the entry from Sylvie's journal.

I'm a ____*fairly cheerful person*____ most of the time, but I must say that yesterday some
        1. (cheerful / person / fairly)

_____ happened. The bus _____ ,
2. (things / upsetting / pretty)   **3.** (late / arrived / really)

so I missed an _____ at work. However, to my surprise, my boss
               4. (important / meeting / awfully)

_____ . She _____ . Later I
5. (well / quite / reacted)   **6.** (at all / angry / didn't / seem)

looked at a(n) _____ . I thought it was exactly what I wanted, but I
               7. (apartment / charming / absolutely)

needed to _____ . When I called early this morning, I found out
          8. (it / think about / carefully / very)

that the apartment was already rented! Wow! It _____ ! Next time I
                                               9. (so / happened / quickly)

see a _____ , I won't wait!
      10. (place / great / really)

EXERCISE 6 WORD ORDER WITH SEVERAL ADJECTIVES

GRAMMAR NOTE 6 Sylvie has found a great place, and she's already moved in. Put the words in the correct order to complete the new entry in her journal. Remember to use commas when necessary.

I found a ___*nice, comfortable apartment*___ in this _____!
1. (apartment / nice / comfortable)   2. (old / house / charming)

It's in a _____, just a short bus ride into town. And I can see a(n)
3. (residential / neighborhood / peaceful)

_____ outside my _____.
4. (tree / enormous / old)   5. (bedroom / wide / window)

There's even a very lovely garden with a _____. The apartment is
6. (stone / bench / Japanese)

nicely furnished, too. The kitchen has a(n) _____. I always do my
7. (beautiful / table / antique / large)

homework there. And the people here are really great. The manager, Alberto Velazquez, is a

_____. I've already met most of my neighbors. Across the hall
8. (man / friendly / helpful)

from me is a _____. My first night here, she took me to a(n)
9. (Polish / young / woman)

_____ for dinner. I know I'll be happy in this apartment.
10. (nice / neighborhood / restaurant / Italian)

EXERCISE 7 EDITING

GRAMMAR NOTES 1–7 Read reviews of school dormitories. There are fifteen mistakes in the use of adjectives and adverbs. The first mistake is already corrected. Find and correct fourteen more.

RATE YOUR DORM

★★★★★★ **Jeff W.** The Northwood dorms are pretty ~~awesomely~~ *awesome*. They're clean and modern, and they're a convenient walk to class and the dining hall. The halls get noisy terribly sometimes, though. When I'm studying hardly for exams, I have to go to the library.

★★★★★★ **Sheryl** Miller Hall is the ideal dorm for freshmen. It's quite small, so I was able to make friends fastly there. Also, the floor counselors are great. Ours explained clearly the rules. She was a young French nice woman, and she was always available when you needed to talk. I was extreme satisfied. I recommend absolutely this dorm amazing to anyone.

★★★★★★ **Tania** Warning! Keep away! Wyeth Hall is totally disgusted. The lounges are incredible dirty. The toilets don't work good, and the halls smell badly. I had a small brown depressing room on the ground floor. My parents were shocking when they saw the place.

Adjectives: Comparisons with *As...as* and *Than*

FOOD

OUTCOMES
- Form and use comparative adjectives
- Express how two people, places, or things are similar or different
- Identify main ideas in a short newspaper article
- Recognize speakers' preferences in a conversation
- Discuss different food options
- Write a paragraph that compares and contrasts foods from different cities or countries

---

STEP 1   GRAMMAR IN CONTEXT

BEFORE YOU READ

Look at the photo. Discuss the questions.

1. Would you like to order the pizza in the photo? Why or why not?
2. How often do you eat out?
3. What types of restaurant food do you enjoy?

READ

▶20|01   Read this newspaper restaurant review.

A New Place for Pizza

Pizza Place, the chain of popular restaurants, has just opened a new one on Main Street, two blocks from the university. The last time that I ate there, the service was not as good as at the other Pizza Place restaurants in town. The young staff (mostly students) probably needs time to become more professional. It's evident they don't have much experience. But

As fresh as it gets!

the pizza was incredible! It seemed bigger and better than at the other six locations in town. As with all food, the fresher the ingredients,[1] the better the pizza. The ingredients at the new Pizza Place are as fresh as you can get (absolutely no mushrooms from a can here!), and the choices are much more varied than at their other locations. We ordered two different types. The one with mashed potatoes and garlic was a lot more interesting than the traditional pizza with cheese and tomato sauce, but both were delicious.

Each Pizza Place is different. The one on Main Street is a little larger (and louder) than the others. It's also a lot more crowded because students love it. At lunchtime, the lines outside this new eatery are getting longer and longer. Go early for a quieter, more relaxed meal.

---
1 *ingredients*: things that go into a recipe (example: tomatoes, cheese, mushrooms, salt...)

AFTER YOU READ

A VOCABULARY Choose the word or phrase that best completes each sentence.

1. **Delicious** food _____ .
   a. is healthy   b. tastes good   c. costs a lot

2. If something is **evident**, you can easily _____ it.
   a. understand   b. eat   c. pay for

3. If a meal is **relaxed**, you don't feel _____ .
   a. in a hurry   b. too full   c. comfortable

4. A **varied** menu has _____ .
   a. pizza and hamburgers b. very good food   c. many different types of food

5. In a **crowded** restaurant, people or things are _____ .
   a. close together   b. not interesting   c. far apart

B COMPREHENSION Check (✓) all the words that describe each item.

1. **the restaurant** ☐ crowded   ☐ new   ☐ quiet   ☐ popular
2. **the staff**   ☐ professional   ☐ young   ☐ relaxed   ☐ loud
3. **the food**   ☐ delicious   ☐ fresh   ☐ expensive   ☐ good
4. **the choices**   ☐ boring   ☐ small   ☐ varied   ☐ interesting

C DISCUSSION Work with a partner. Compare your answers to the questions in B. Why did you check these words?

ADJECTIVES: COMPARISONS WITH *AS...AS* AND *THAN*

Comparisons with *As...as*

	(Not) As	Adjective	*As*	
The new restaurant is	(not) as	large busy good	as	the other ones.
		interesting expensive		

Comparisons with *Than*

	Comparative Adjective Form	*Than*	
The new restaurant is	larger busier better	than	the other ones.
	more interesting less expensive		

GRAMMAR NOTES

1 Comparisons with *As...As*

Use *as* + **adjective** + *as* to show how people, places, or things are **the same or equal**.	The new menu is **as good as** the old. *(The new menu and the old menu are equally good.)*
You can add *just* before the comparison to make it stronger.	The new menu is *just* **as good as** the old. *(The new menu and the old menu are really equally good.)*
Use *not as* + **adjective** + *as* to show how people, places, or things are **not the same or equal**.	The new menu isn't **as varied as** the old. *(The old menu was more varied.)*
USAGE NOTE We often leave out the second part of the comparison when the meaning is clear.	A: I like the old menu. It had more choices. B: Too bad the new one isn't **as varied**. *(It isn't as varied as the old menu.)*

2 Comparisons with *Than*

Use **comparative adjective + *than*** to show how people, places, or things are **different**.	The new room is **bigger than** the old room. The new waiters are **more professional than** the old waiters. The lunch menu is **less expensive than** the dinner menu.
You can add *even* before the comparison to make it stronger. *Even* expresses that something is surprising or unexpected.	The old waiters were very professional, but the new waiters are **even more professional than** the old waiters.
USAGE NOTE We usually do not use *less ... than* with one-syllable adjectives. Instead we use: • *not as ... as* • another adjective with the opposite meaning	 Our server isn't **as fast as** theirs. or Our server is **slower than** theirs. **NOT** Our server is ~~less fast than~~ theirs.
Remember that it is not necessary to mention the second part of the comparison when the meaning is clear.	The new tables are **smaller**. *(They are smaller than the old tables.)*

3 Forming Comparative Adjectives

There are several ways of forming comparative adjectives.

	ADJECTIVE	COMPARATIVE
For **short adjectives** (one syllable and two syllables ending in -*y*), use **adjective + -*er***.	loud friendly	loud**er** friendl**ier**
IN WRITING There are often **spelling changes** when you add -*er*.	late big early	lat**er** big**ger** earl**ier**
Some short adjectives have **irregular** comparative forms.	good bad far	**better** **worse** **farther**
For **long adjectives** (two or more syllables), use *more/less* + **adjective**. An exception is the short adjective *fun*. It forms the comparative in the same way as a long adjective.	expensive fun	**more** expensive **less** expensive **more** fun NOT ~~funner~~ **less** fun
For **some adjectives**, such as *lively, lovely, friendly,* and *quiet*, you can use -*er* or *more*. The -*er* form is more common.	The Inn is **livelier** than Joe's. *(more common)* The Inn is **more lively** than Joe's. *(less common)*	
BE CAREFUL! Do not use *more* or *less* with the comparative form of the adjective.	It's **louder than** Joe's. **NOT** It's ~~more louder~~. **NOT** It's ~~less noisier~~.	

4 To Show an Increase or Decrease

Repeat the **comparative adjective** to show an increase or a decrease.

comparative adjective + *and* + comparative adjective	The lines are getting **longer and longer**. *(Their length is increasing.)*
USAGE NOTE This form of comparison is common with the verbs *get*, *grow*, and *become*.	The food quality is getting **worse and worse**. *(The quality is decreasing.)*
BE CAREFUL! With **long adjectives**, repeat only *more* or *less*.	It's becoming **more and more popular**. NOT It's becoming more ~~popular~~ and more popular.

5 To Show Cause and Effect

Use **two comparative adjectives** to show cause and effect.

the + comparative adjective + *the* + comparative adjective	The **more crowded** the restaurant, **the slower** the service. *(The service is slower because the restaurant is more crowded.)*
USAGE NOTE When both comparative adjectives describe the same person, place, or thing, we often leave out the nouns.	A: The service is really fast here. B: **The faster, the better.** *(The faster the service, the better the service.)*

REFERENCE NOTES

For a list of **adjectives** that use **both forms of the comparative**, see Appendix 9 on page 325.
For a list of **irregular comparative adjectives**, see Appendix 10 on page 326.
For **spelling rules** for the **comparative form of adjectives**, see Appendix 23 on page 331.

EXERCISE 1   DISCOVER THE GRAMMAR

GRAMMAR NOTES 1–3   Read the information about two brands of frozen pizza. Then read each statement. Check (✓) *True* or *False*.

Size	Medium	Medium
Weight	765 grams	680 grams
Price	$6.99	$7.99
Calories*	364	292
Salt content*	731 milligrams	600 milligrams
Fat content*	11 grams	11 grams
Baking time	20 minutes	16 minutes
Taste	★ ★ ★	★ ★ ★ ★

* for one slice

	True	False
1. Maria's Pizza is bigger than John's Pizza.	☐	☑
2. John's Pizza is just as big as Maria's Pizza.	☐	☐
3. John's Pizza isn't as heavy as Maria's.	☐	☐
4. Maria's Pizza is just as expensive as John's.	☐	☐
5. John's is more expensive than Maria's.	☐	☐
6. Maria's is higher in calories than John's.	☐	☐
7. Maria's Pizza is saltier than John's.	☐	☐
8. John's Pizza is just as high in fat as Maria's Pizza.	☐	☐
9. The baking time for Maria's isn't as long as the baking time for John's.	☐	☐
10. John's Pizza tastes better than Maria's Pizza.	☐	☐

EXERCISE 2 COMPARISONS WITH AS ... AS

GRAMMAR NOTE 1 Look at the consumer magazine chart comparing three brands of pizza cheese. Complete the sentences. Use *(just) as ... as* or *not as ... as* and the correct form of the words in parentheses.

PIZZA CHEESE		Better ←→ Worse	
Brand	Price (per serving)	Taste	Smell
X	45¢	◐	●
Y	30¢	◐	◐
Z	30¢	○	◐

1. Brand Z ___*is as expensive as* or *is just as expensive as*___ Brand Y.
   (be / expensive)

2. Brand Y _____ Brand X.
   (be / expensive)

3. Brand X _____ Brand Y.
   (taste / good)

4. Brand Z _____ Brand Y.
   (taste / good)

5. Brand Y _____ Brand X.
   (smell / delicious)

6. Brand Y _____ Brand Z.
   (smell / delicious)

EXERCISE 3 COMPARISONS WITH THAN

GRAMMAR NOTES 2–3 Look at the menu on the next page. Then complete these sentences comparing items on the menu. Use the appropriate comparative form of the adjectives in parentheses and *than* where necessary.

1. The sweet-and-sour shrimp is ___*more expensive than*___ the steamed scallops.
   (expensive)

2. The beef with red pepper is _____ the beef with broccoli.
   (hot)

3. The pork with scallions is _____ the sweet-and-sour shrimp.
   (expensive)

4. The chicken with orange sauce is _____ the steamed scallops.
   (spicy)

5. The steamed vegetables are _____ the pork with scallions.
   (salty)

6. The steamed vegetables are _____ the beef with red pepper.
   (healthy)

7. The broccoli with garlic is _____ the chicken with broccoli.
   (cheap)

8. The shrimp dish is _____ the scallop dish.
   (sweet)

9. The restaurant's hours on Sunday are _____ on Saturday.
   (short)

10. The children's menu is _____ the adult's menu.
    (varied)

11. The children's menu is _____, too.
    (expensive)

12. The chicken wings are _____ the macaroni and cheese slices.
    (sweet)

The Golden Palace

TAKE-OUT MENU

2465 Mineral Springs Rd. • Tel: (401) 555-4923

Open 7 days a week
Mon-Thurs: 11 a.m.–10 p.m. • Fri-Sat: 11 a.m.–11 p.m. • Sunday: 12 noon–10 p.m.

Broccoli with Garlic Sauce	$7.25	
Beef with Broccoli	$8.75	Hot and Spicy
Beef with Dried Red Pepper	$8.25	No sugar, salt, or oil
Chicken with Broccoli	$8.75	
Chicken with Orange Sauce	$8.25	
Sweet-and-Sour Shrimp	$9.25	
Pork with Scallions	$7.25	
Steamed Mixed Vegetables	$6.50	
Steamed Scallops with Broccoli	$8.75	

Kids Corner

Honey Chicken Wings	$5.75
Pizza-Style Spring Roll	$4.50
Macaroni and Cheese Slices	$4.00

Place your order by phone and it will be ready when you arrive.

EXERCISE 4 INCREASE OR DECREASE; CAUSE AND EFFECT

GRAMMAR NOTES 4–5 Complete the conversations. Use the comparative form of the adjectives in parentheses to show an increase or decrease or a cause and effect.

1. A: Wow! The lines here are growing

   _____*longer and longer*_____.
              (long)

   B: Tell me about it. And, unfortunately,

   _____*the longer*_____ the wait,
           (long)

   _____*the hungrier*_____ I get.
           (hungry)

2. A: It's worth the wait. The food here is getting

   _____.
          (good)

   B: But _____ the food,
             (good)

   _____ the bill!
          (high)

3. A: Some of the servers look like they're not a day older

   than fifteen. They seem to be getting

   _____.
          (young)

   B: I know. And each time I come here, I feel _____!
                                (old)

4. A: It's now evident that the cook is really very creative. The menu is definitely becoming

   _____.
          (interesting)

   B: I know, but that means it's also _____ to choose something.
                (difficult)

5. A: There's Professor Lee. You know, his course is getting _____.
                (popular)

   B: It's absolutely amazing. _____ his classes are,
              (hard)

   _____ the course gets. He's an incredible teacher.
          (popular)

6. A: Is it the hot sauce, or has your cough been getting _____.
                (bad)

   B: It's the hot sauce, but I love it. For my taste, _____,
                (spicy)

   _____.
          (good)

7. A: The service used to be slow here, but it's getting _____.
                (fast)

   B: And that's good news. _____ the service,
              (fast)

   _____ the lines!
          (short)

EXERCISE 5 EDITING

GRAMMAR NOTES 1–5 **Read the student's essay. There are ten mistakes in the use of** *as...as* **and comparatives with** *than*. **The first mistake is already corrected. Find and correct nine more.**

Changing Tastes

When I was a teenager in the Philippines, I was an expert on snacks

and fast foods. I was growing fast, so the more I ate, the ~~hungry~~ *hungrier*

I felt. The street vendors in our town had the better snacks than

anyone else. In the morning, I used to buy rice muffins on the way

to school. They are even more sweeter that American muffins.

After school, I ate fish balls on a stick or *adidas* (chicken feet).

Snacks on a stick are small than traditional American hot dogs and

burgers, but they are much varied, and the food is much fresher. My

friend thought *banana-cue* (banana on a stick) was really incredible.

However, they weren't as sweet from *kamote-cue* (fried sweet

potatoes and brown sugar), my favorite snack.

When I came to the United States, I didn't like American fast

food at first. To me, it was interesting than my native food and less

tastier, too. Now I'm getting used to it, and in many ways it seems

just as good. In fact, it seems deliciouser and deliciouser.

UNIT 21

Adjectives: Superlatives
CITIES

OUTCOMES
- Form and use superlative adjectives
- Compare one person, place, or thing to others in a group
- Identify key details in an article about a city
- Identify places and locations by their descriptions in a conversation
- Describe and express opinions about places
- Write a description of one's hometown or city

STEP 1   **GRAMMAR IN CONTEXT**

BEFORE YOU READ

Look at the photo. Discuss the questions.

1. Do you recognize this city? Where do you think it is?

2. What are some important features for a city to have?

READ

▶ 21|01   Read this travel brochure.

The biggest! The best! The safest! The most exciting!

AFTER YOU READ

A VOCABULARY Choose the word or phrase that best completes each sentence.

1. A **financial** center has a lot of _____ .
   a. banks
   b. parks
   c. hospitals

2. A **multicultural** city has people from many different _____ .
   a. schools
   b. theaters
   c. countries

3. An important **feature** of Toronto is its _____ .
   a. city
   b. safety
   c. name

4. The transportation system is **public**. _____ can use it.
   a. Everyone
   b. No one
   c. Only rich people

5. A **dynamic** city is not _____ .
   a. interesting
   b. exciting
   c. boring

6. _____ is one of the seven **continents** of the world.
   a. Canada
   b. North America
   c. Toronto

A Superlative[1] City

TORONTO. It's the capital of the province of Ontario. It's also . . .

- the largest city in Canada
- the most important economic and financial center of the country
- one of the most multicultural places on earth[2] (Almost 50% of its population was born outside Canada, and over 100 languages are spoken in the city.)
- one of the easiest places to get around (It has the second largest public transportation system in North America.)
- the city that built the CN Tower, for many years the tallest free-standing structure in the world
- home to the Eaton Centre, a huge shopping mall (With more than fifty-two million visitors a year, it is one of the most popular tourist attractions in the city.)
- the safest city on the continent, and one of the most peaceful of all large, international cities on the planet

All of these features, and many more, make Toronto one of the most dynamic, exciting cities in the world and a major tourist destination.

---

1 *superlative:* excellent
2 *on earth:* on planet Earth (Earth is one of several planets, such as Mars or Jupiter, moving around the sun.)

B COMPREHENSION Read the statements. Check (✓) *True* or *False*.

	True	False
1. Some Canadian cities are larger than Toronto.	☐	☐
2. Some Canadian cities are more important financially than Toronto.	☐	☐
3. Many cities in the world aren't as multicultural as Toronto.	☐	☐
4. It's easy to get around Toronto.	☐	☐
5. Some cities on the North American continent are safer than Toronto.	☐	☐
6. The Eaton Centre attracts the most number of visitors in Toronto.	☐	☐

C DISCUSSION Work with a partner. Compare your answers in B. Why did you check *True* or *False*?

STEP 2 · GRAMMAR PRESENTATION

ADJECTIVES: SUPERLATIVES

Superlatives

	Superlative Adjective Form		
This is	the largest the busiest the best	city	*in* the world. *on* earth. *of* all. I've *ever* visited.
	the most interesting the least expensive		

GRAMMAR NOTES

1 Meaning of Superlative Adjectives

Use superlative adjectives to compare one person, place, or thing with other people, places, or things in a group.

• **people**	Canadians are **the friendliest** people I know. *(Canadians are friendlier than all other people I know.)*
• **places**	Toronto is **the largest** city in Canada. *(All other cities in Canada are smaller.)*
• **things**	The CN Tower is **the tallest** building in Canada. *(No other building in Canada is taller.)*

2 Forming Superlative Adjectives

There are several ways of forming superlative adjectives.

	ADJECTIVE	SUPERLATIVE
For **short adjectives** (one syllable and two syllables ending in -y), use *the* + **adjective** + *-est*.	tall	**the** tall**est**
	easy	**the** easi**est**

IN WRITING There are often **spelling changes** when you add *-est*.	large	**the** larg**est**
	big	**the** big**gest**
	early	**the** earli**est**

Some adjectives have **irregular** superlative forms.	good	**the best**
	bad	**the worst**
	far	**the farthest**

For **long adjectives** (two or more syllables), use *the most/the least* + **adjective**.	expensive	**the most** expensive
		the least expensive

An exception is the short adjective *fun*. It forms the superlative in the same way as a long adjective.	fun	**the most** fun NOT the ~~funnest~~

For **some adjectives**, such as *lively, lovely, friendly*, and *quiet*, you can use *the...-est* or *the most/the least*. The *-est* form is more common.	Rio is **the liveliest** city on earth. *(more common)*
	Rio is **the most lively** city on earth. *(less common)*

BE CAREFUL! Do not use *most* or *least* with the superlative form of the adjective.	It's **the tallest** building.
	NOT It's the ~~most~~ tallest building.

3 Superlative Adjectives with Other Words and Expressions

We often use superlative adjectives with other words and expressions.

• **phrases with** *in, on,* or *of*	It's **the greatest** city *in the world*.
	It's **the safest** place *on earth*.
	This was **the best** day *of our visit*.
• *one of* + **plural count noun**	Toronto is *one of* **the most dynamic** *cities* in the world.
• *some of* + **plural count noun** + **non-count noun**	*Some of* **the best** *cities* have large parks.
	Toronto has *some of* **the best** *food* in Canada.
• *second (third, fourth...)*	It has **the** *second* **largest** transportation system.
• *ever* + **present perfect**	This is **the biggest** building I*'ve ever seen*.

REFERENCE NOTES

For a list of **adjectives** that use **both forms of the superlative**, see Appendix 9 on page 325.

For a list of **irregular superlative adjectives**, see Appendix 10 on page 326.

For **spelling rules** for the **superlative form of adjectives**, see Appendix 23 on page 331.

EXERCISE 1
DISCOVER THE GRAMMAR

A GRAMMAR NOTES 1–3
Read more information about Toronto. Underline all the superlative adjectives.

What to Do and See in Toronto

- **Go to the CN Tower.** It's one of the tallest buildings in the world. From there, you can get the best view of the city and countryside.

- **Drive along Yonge Street.** At 1,200 miles (1,800 km), it's one of the longest streets in the world. For one weekend in July, it's one of the liveliest, too. Come and join one million others for the exciting Yonge Street Festival.

- **Visit PATH,** the world's largest underground shopping complex.

- **Explore the Old Town of York.** It has the most historic buildings in the whole city.

- **Take the Yuk Yuk's Comedy Tour** of the Entertainment District— you'll have a good time on the funniest bus ride in town.

- **Visit the Toronto Zoo.** There's always something new and fascinating going on. Local people call it the best family outing in Toronto.

B Check (✓) all the true statements.

☑ **1.** There are buildings taller than the CN Tower.

☐ **2.** There are better views of the city than the views from the CN Tower.

☐ **3.** There are longer streets than Yonge Street.

☐ **4.** Yonge Street is the liveliest street in the world.

☐ **5.** PATH is larger than all other underground shopping complexes.

☐ **6.** The Old Town of York has more historic buildings than other sections of Toronto.

☐ **7.** There is no funnier bus ride in town than the Yuk Yuk's Comedy Tour.

☐ **8.** There are better family outings than the zoo.

EXERCISE 2 SUPERLATIVE ADJECTIVES

GRAMMAR NOTES 1–2 Look at the chart. Complete the sentences. Use the superlative form of the correct adjectives in parentheses.

CITY STATISTICS[1]

		ISTANBUL	MEXICO CITY	SEOUL	TORONTO
👥	Population	14,377,019	8,693,387	10,388,055	2,791,140
⬠	Area	2,063 sq mi (5,343 sq km)	573 sq mi (1,485 sq km)	234 sq mi (605 sq km)	243 sq mi (630 sq km)
🌡	Average January Temperature	42°F (5.5°C)	54°F (12.2°C)	27°F (-2.7°C)	23.5°F (-4.7°C)
🌡	Average July Temperature	71°F (21.6°C)	63°F (17.22°C)	76.5°F (24.7°C)	69.5°F (20.83°C)
☂	Average Rainfall per Year	25.1 in (640 mm)	30 in (762 mm)	49 in (1,242 mm)	35.5 in (852.9 mm)
☕	Cost of a Cup of Coffee[2] ($US)	$3.92	$3.22	$4.54	$4.08
🚌	Cost of a Bus Ticket ($US)	$1.30	$0.27	$0.86[3]	$2.39

1 based on 2013–2015 statistics
2 based on the cost of Starbuck's "grande latte" (a large cup of strong coffee with steamed milk)
3 based on the cost of the "yellow" city bus

1. Of all four cities, Toronto is _____*the smallest*_____ city in population, but not
   (large / small)
   in area.

2. The _____ city in area is Seoul.
   (big / small)

3. Istanbul has _____ population of all four cities, and it is
   (large / small)
   _____ city in area.
   (big / small)

4. In January, _____ city is Toronto.
   (warm / cold)

5. Seoul has _____ July temperatures.
   (hot / cool)

6. After Seoul, Istanbul has _____ July temperatures.
   (warm / cool)

7. _____ city is Seoul. _____
   (dry / rainy)   (dry / rainy)
   city is Istanbul.

8. You'll find _____ cup of coffee in Mexico City, and you'll find
   (cheap / expensive)
   _____ in Seoul.
   (cheap / expensive)

9. The city with _____ public buses is Mexico City. Toronto has
   (cheap / expensive)
   _____ .
   (cheap / expensive)

EXERCISE 3 SUPERLATIVE ADJECTIVES

GRAMMAR NOTES 1–3 **Read about the CN Tower. Complete the information. Use the superlative form of the correct adjective from the box.**

| clear | famous | fast | heavy | long | popular | ~~tall~~ |

The CN Tower / *La Tour CN*

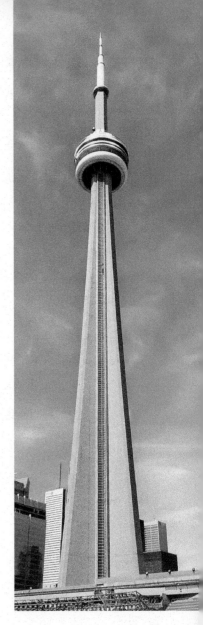

1. At 1,815 feet, 5 inches (553.33 m), the CN Tower is one of
   _____ *the tallest* _____ structures in the world.

2. Everyone recognizes Toronto's CN Tower. It is certainly
   _____ building in Canada.

3. At 130,000 tons (117,910 metric tonnes), the impressive CN Tower is
   one of _____ buildings on the planet.

4. With two million visitors every year, the CN Tower is one of
   _____ tourist attractions in the country.

5. Because of its very high antenna, the tower provides the people of
   Toronto with some of _____ radio and TV
   reception in North America.

6. Moving at 15 miles (22 km) per hour, the six elevators are among
   _____ in the world. The ride to the Look
   Out Level takes just 58 seconds.

7. If you don't want to take the elevator, you can try the stairs! The CN
   Tower has _____ metal staircase on earth.

EXERCISE 4 *THE MOST* AND *THE LEAST* + *EVER*

GRAMMAR NOTE 3 **Write superlative sentences about your own experiences. Use the words in parentheses with *the most* or *the least* + *ever* and the present perfect. Write two sentences for each item. See Appendix 1, page 453, for help with the irregular past participles.**

EXAMPLE: Toronto is the most multicultural city I've ever visited.
Meadville is the least multicultural city I've ever visited.

1. (multicultural / city / visit)

   _____

   _____

2. (comfortable / place / stay)

   _____

   _____

3. (friendly / people / meet)

_____

_____

4. (expensive / trip / take)

_____

_____

5. (interesting / place / see)

_____

_____

6. (exciting / team / watch)

_____

_____

EXERCISE 5 EDITING

GRAMMAR NOTES 1–3 **Read this email. There are eight mistakes in the use of superlative adjectives. The first mistake is already corrected. Find and correct seven more.**

● ● ●

Greetings from Toronto—the ~~beautifulest~~ _most beautiful_ city I've visited on the North American

continent. Yesterday, we went to the CN Tower—the more recognizable structure in

Canada. From there, you get the best view of the city—the different neighborhoods,

the harbor, the fast traffic. It made my head spin! This is one of most dynamic

places I've ever visited! The restaurant was the most expensivest I've ever seen, so

we just enjoyed the view and then went to Kensington Market to eat. This place has

the baddest crowds, but the cheapest and the goodest food we've had so far. We're

staying in East Toronto. It's not the closer place to downtown, but it has some of

most historic buildings. In fact, our bed-and-breakfast is called 1871 Historic House.

John Lennon slept here!

Love, Marissa

Adverbs: *As...as*, Comparatives, Superlatives

SPORTS

OUTCOMES
- Form and use comparative and superlative adverbs
- Express how two actions are similar or different
- Identify main ideas in an opinion article and in a debate
- Discuss issues in a debate, supporting opinions
- Describe and compare people's abilities
- Write arguments for and against a statement

STEP 1   **GRAMMAR IN CONTEXT**

BEFORE YOU READ

Look at the photo. Discuss the questions.

1. What sport is this?
2. Describe the pitcher (the person holding the ball).
3. Is there anything unusual about the pitcher? If yes, what?

READ

22|01   Read this newspaper opinion piece.

SPORTS

Separation of the Sexes?

Pitcher Eri Yoshida

Can women compete in sports as well as men? Can they run as fast as men or throw a ball as far? Should they be able to compete against men or play with men on the same team? These questions have been the source of debate for ages. And people on both sides of the debate are arguing more passionately[1] than ever.

Many sports require upper-body strength. The average man has more upper-body strength than the average female. But some women can use their strength more efficiently than men. In 1973, in a tennis

---

1 *passionately*: with strong feelings

match called the "Battle of the Sexes," Billie Jean King (female) beat Bobby Riggs (male) in front of 30,000 people. In more recent years, pitcher Eri Yoshida has been playing professionally on all-male baseball teams, and she has won several games.

Physical strength does not tell the whole story. Society does not value female athletes as much as male athletes. As a result, women have not had enough opportunity to play. They do not compete as frequently as men, and when they play, they aren't taken as seriously as men. Professional female athletes have even received insults from their male teammates and from spectators.[2] This attitude is changing, however, especially among younger people. As a result, women will have more opportunities to play. And the more they play, the better they'll be able to compete.

So, should women and men play on separate teams, or should women be allowed to play with men on the same teams? The answer is clear: If an athlete plays well enough to compete in a sport, that person, male or female, should be allowed to. On the other hand, if an athlete plays the best he or she can, but still cannot meet the qualifications[3] of the team, then that person should not be on the team. Sports should be an equal opportunity activity. It's that simple. No ifs, ands, or buts.[4]

---

2 *spectators:* people who watch sports events

3 *qualifications:* the skills necessary for a job or position
4 *no ifs, ands, or buts:* without any questions or doubts

AFTER YOU READ

A VOCABULARY **Complete the sentences with the words from the box.**

competes	debate	insults	requires	source	values

1. Tennis _____ a lot of upper-body strength.

2. The manager _____ her. He thinks she's an important member of the team.

3. The two sides in the TV _____ had very different opinions.

4. My school's baseball team often _____ against the Blues.

5. I think the _____ of the problem is that the team hasn't practiced enough.

6. The crowd shouted _____ at the losing players. It was terrible.

B COMPREHENSION **Read the statements. Check (✓) *True* or *False*.**

	True	False
1. People are not interested in the role of women athletes in sports.	☐	☐
2. Some women make more efficient use of their strength than men do.	☐	☐
3. Women need more opportunities to compete.	☐	☐
4. Society takes female athletes seriously.	☐	☐
5. All women should be allowed to compete against men.	☐	☐

C DISCUSSION **Work with a partner. Compare your answers in B. Why did you check *True* or *False*?**

ADVERBS: *AS . . . AS*, COMPARATIVES, SUPERLATIVES

As . . . as

		As	Adverb	*As*	
Women	play don't play	as	hard well aggressively consistently	as	men.

Comparatives

		Comparative Adverb Form	*Than*	
Alexis	played	harder better more aggressively less consistently	than	Tyler.

Superlatives

		Superlative Adverb Form	
The star player	played	the hardest the best the most aggressively the least consistently	*of* anyone in the game.

GRAMMAR NOTES

1 Comparisons with *As . . . As*

Use *as* + **adverb** + *as* to show how the actions of two people or things are **the same or equal**.	Gilbert plays **as well as** Miller. *(Gilbert and Miller play equally well.)*
You can add *just* before the comparison to make it stronger.	Gilbert plays *just* **as well as** Miller. *(Gilbert and Miller really play equally well.)*
Use *not as* + **adverb** + *as* to show how the actions of two people or things are **not the same or equal**.	Gilbert did**n't** play **as aggressively as** Jones. *(Gilbert and Jones didn't play the same. Jones played more aggressively.)*
Notice that *not* goes before the main verb.	**NOT** Gilbert played ~~not~~ as aggressively as Jones.
USAGE NOTE We often leave out the second part of the comparison when the meaning is clear.	A: Gilbert hit the ball as well as Miller. B: But she didn't run **as fast**. *(She didn't run as fast as Miller.)*

2 Comparisons with *Than*

Use **comparative adverbs** + *than* to show how the actions of two people or things are **different**.	The Mets played **better than** the Pirates. Clark played **more skillfully than** Brown. He played **less skillfully than** Rogers.
You can add *even* before the comparison to make it stronger. *Even* expresses that something is surprising or unexpected.	The Pirates played aggressively, but the Mets played **even more aggressively than** the Pirates.
USAGE NOTE We usually do not use *less . . . than* with one-syllable adverbs. Instead we use:	**NOT** Clark runs ~~less fast than~~ Brown.
• *not as . . . as*	Clark does**n't** run **as fast as** Brown. or
• another adverb with the opposite meaning	Clark runs **slower than** Brown.
Remember that it is not necessary to mention the second part of the comparison when the meaning is clear.	Brown didn't play as hard as Clark, but she hit the ball **more consistently**. *(. . . more consistently than he hit the ball)*

3 Superlative Adverbs

Use **superlative adverbs** to compare one action with the actions of other people or things in a group.	All the players worked hard, but Robins worked **the hardest**.
We often use a **phrase with** *of* after a superlative adverb.	She scored **the most frequently** *of any player* on the team.
USAGE NOTE We don't use superlative adverbs very often. Instead, we use a comparison with *than* to compare an action with the actions of a group.	Robins worked **the hardest** of anyone on the team. *(less common)* Robins worked **harder than** anyone on the team. *(more common)*

4 Forming Comparative and Superlative Adverbs

There are several ways of forming comparative and superlative adverbs.

	ADVERB	COMPARATIVE	SUPERLATIVE
For most **short adverbs** (one syllable), use **adverb + -er** or *the* + **adverb + -est**.	fast	fast**er**	**the** fast**est**
	hard	hard**er**	**the** hard**est**
Some short adverbs have **irregular** comparative and superlative forms.	well	**better**	**the best**
	badly	**worse**	**the worst**
	far	**farther**	**the farthest**
	much/a lot	**more**	**the most**
	little	**less**	**the least**
For **long adverbs** (two or more syllables), use *more/less* + **adverb** or *the most/the least* + **adverb**.	skillfully	**more/less** skillfully	**the most/the least** skillfully
Some **adverbs of manner** have two comparative and two superlative forms.	quickly	**more** quickly	**the most** quickly
		quicker	**the quickest**

IN WRITING In formal writing, the forms with *more/less* and *the most/the least* are more common. The *-er/-est* forms are more common in spoken English and informal writing.

> He got there **more quickly than** the ball. *(newspaper)*
> He got there **quicker than** the ball. *(conversation)*

BE CAREFUL! Do not put an **adverb of manner** between the verb and the object.

> She *threw the ball* **farther** than Tommy.
> NOT She ~~threw farther the ball~~ . . .

5 To Show an Increase or Decrease

Repeat the comparative adverb to show an increase or a decrease.

comparative adverb + *and* + comparative adverb	Yoshida is playing **better and better**. *(Her performance keeps getting better.)*

BE CAREFUL! With **long adverbs**, repeat only *more* or *less*.

> She's playing **more and more aggressively**.
> NOT She's playing more ~~aggressively~~ and more aggressively.

6 To Show Cause and Effect

Use **two comparative adverbs** to show cause and effect.

the + comparative adverb + *the* + comparative adverb	**The harder** she played, **the better** she got. *(When she played harder, she got better.)*

REFERENCE NOTES

For a list of **irregular comparative and superlative adverbs** see Appendix 10 on page 326.
For more information on **adverbs**, see Unit 19 on page 186.

EXERCISE 1 DISCOVER THE GRAMMAR

A GRAMMAR NOTES 1–6 Read this letter to the editor. Underline all the comparisons with *(not) as* + adverb + *as*, and all the comparative and superlative adverbs forms.

● ● ●

To the Editor:

I read with interest last week's article "Sports: Separation of the Sexes?" The author claims that female athletes can compete <u>as well as</u> males. I cannot disagree more strongly! Women are simply not as powerful as men. That's not an insult. It's a fact. And it's the source of the problem. Even the best female athlete cannot throw a ball as hard or run as fast as the average male athlete. It's true that in some sports that don't require great strength, some women can compete as effectively as men. But those are the exceptions, not the rule. There are many examples of women who play the best of anyone on their team, but still play worse than the average male athlete. Women are trying harder and harder to enter the sports world of men. And the harder they try, the more they will fail. Clearly, women can be great athletes. I just think that they should play with women against other women.

Mary Kennedy, Student
Bryant University, Smithfield, RI

B Which underlined words in the letter to the editor express...

1. equal ability: _as well as_ _____

2. unequal ability: _____

3. a comparative: _____

4. a superlative: _____

5. an increase: _____

6. cause and effect: _____

EXERCISE 2 COMPARISONS WITH AS ... AS

GRAMMAR NOTE 1 Read this chart comparing three brands of basketball shoes. Complete the sentences. Use *(not) as* + adverb + *as* and the words in parentheses.

SHOES				BETTER ●──────● ○ WORSE	
Brand	**Comfort**	**Support**	**Protection**	**Durability***	**Cost**
X	●	◐	●	◐	$98
Y	●	○	●	○	$72
Z	○	○	◐	◐	$72

* how long the product lasts

1. Brand X _____*fits as comfortably as*_____ Brand Y.
   (fit / comfortable)

2. Brand Z _____ Brand X or Y.
   (fit / comfortable)

3. Brand Y _____ Brand Z.
   (support / the ankles / good)

4. Brands Y and Z _____ Brand X.
   (support / the ankles / good)

5. Brand Z _____ Brand X or Y.
   (protect / the feet / effective)

6. Brand X _____ Brand Y.
   (protect / the feet / effective)

7. Brand X _____ Brand Z.
   (last / long)

8. Brand Y _____ Brand X or Z.
   (last / long)

9. Brands Y and Z _____ Brand X.
   (cost / much)

EXERCISE 3 AS ... AS, COMPARATIVE AND SUPERLATIVE ADVERBS

(A) GRAMMAR NOTES 1–6 Complete this conversation between sports commentator Carla Lobo and player Elena Bard. Change the adjectives in parentheses to adverbs. Use them with *as ... as* or with the comparative or superlative forms. Add *the* or *than*, and choose between *more* or *less* where necessary.

LOBO: Why do people still take female basketball players _____*less seriously than*_____
                                                              1. (serious)

male players? Do women really play _____ men?
                                           2. (aggressive)

BARD: Absolutely not! We play just _____. And when we fall, we
                                         3. (aggressive)

hit the floor just _____ the guys do.
                         4. (hard)

LOBO: You could sure see that in tonight's game. Jackson played _____
                                                                      5. (effective)

of all the players I've seen—male or female. She never let Cash anywhere near the basket.

BARD: Yes. And she performs like that much _____ a lot of men.
                                                          6. (consistent)

Jackson always gets the job done.

LOBO: Some people say women play _____ men.
                                              7. (cooperative)

BARD: I agree. I think we have better teamwork—we play _____
                                                                      8. (good)

on a team. We're also more patient. I've noticed that most women players are able to wait

_____ for a good chance to shoot.
        9. (long)

LOBO: Tickets for women's basketball games cost _____ tickets for
                                                            10. (little)

men's games. Does that bother you?

BARD: Sure. It shows that society doesn't value female athletes as much as they value males. But

_____ women players are able to attract fans,
        11. (fast)

_____ the women's leagues will make money.
        12. (fast)

▷22|02 **B** LISTEN AND CHECK **Listen to the conversation and check your answers in A.**

EXERCISE 4 COMPARATIVE AND SUPERLATIVE ADVERBS

GRAMMAR NOTES 2–4 Read this chart comparing the performances of four athletes. Then
complete the sentences. Use the comparative or superlative adverb form of the words
from the box. You will use some words more than once.

| bad | far | fast | good | high | slow |

	Broad Jump [distance]	**Pole Vaulting** [height]	**5-mile (8-km) Run** [speed]
Nolan	10.3 ft (3.14 m)	17.3 ft (5.27 m)	26 minutes
Smith	10.1 ft (3.08 m)	17.2 ft (5.24 m)	28 minutes
Costas	11.2 ft (3.42 m)	17.8 ft (5.43 m)	30 minutes
Olsson	11.4 ft (3.48 m)	18.2 ft (5.55 m)	25 minutes

1. Nolan jumped _____ *farther than* _____ Smith.

2. Olsson vaulted _____ *the highest* _____ of all.

3. Costas ran _____.

4. Smith ran _____ Olsson.

5. Olsson jumped _____.

6. Nolan ran _____ Smith.

7. Olsson vaulted _____ Smith.

8. All in all, Olsson did _____.

9. All in all, Smith did _____.

EXERCISE 5 EDITING

GRAMMAR NOTES 1–6 **Read this transcript of a TV sports program. There are eight mistakes in the use of adverbs. The first mistake is already corrected. Find and correct seven more.**

CINDY: What a game! Spero, have you ever seen two teams play more aggressively ~~than~~?

SPERO: No, I haven't, Cindy. Folks, we're in Bangkok, Thailand, watching the Australian and French teams battle for the Women's World Basketball Championship. It's halftime, and just listen to that crowd! I think the Australians cheer the most loudest of any fans in the game!

CINDY: Well, the court really belonged to France for the first part of the game, Spero. And without question, Maud Medenou of France was playing the better of all the players on both teams. But the Australian team recovered more quickly than I thought possible. They've scored almost as frequently than the French in the first half. The score is now 30-28, France, and no one can predict a winner at this point.

SPERO: I heard that Elizabeth Cambage, Australia's star player, injured her arm yesterday, but you can't tell from the way she's playing today. So far, she's scored the least of any player on her team. She's playing a great game.

CINDY: And with an injury, too! Spero, I have to say that's pretty amazing. But Medenou isn't that far behind. Did you notice that she's been playing more intensely and more intensely in this tournament? You can see that she really wants the ball, and she's getting it more consistently in every game.

SPERO: You're right, Cindy. And the more hard she plays, the more she scores. The spectators love her. They're cheering more and less enthusiastically.

CINDY: The Australians have really been playing a great defense tonight. They've been blocking Medenou more effectively than any other team this season. But can they stop her?

SPERO: We'll find out soon! The second half is ready to begin. See you again after the game.

Elizabeth
Cambage

Gerunds and Infinitives

PART 7

OUTCOMES
- Use gerunds as the subject or object of a verb
- Recognize main ideas in an article about a habit and trend
- Recognize whether an action is recommended or not recommended in a conversation
- Discuss health and exercise habits
- Discuss one's opinion on a controversial topic
- Write a short opinion essay on a controversial topic

OUTCOMES
- Use verbs that are followed by infinitives
- Identify statistics in a short article
- Evaluate speakers' attitudes in a conversation
- Discuss tendencies and preferences
- Give an opinion in response to a literary quote
- Write a paragraph on a personal topic, using transition words

OUTCOMES
- Express purpose with an infinitive or *in order to*
- Use adjectives/adverbs + infinitives
- Identify important details and opinions in a short text with quotes
- Identify key details in a TV ad
- Discuss the pros and cons of new technologies
- Write a paragraph describing the pros and cons of a smart device

OUTCOMES
- Use verbs that can be followed by gerunds or infinitives
- Use prepositions/phrasal verbs + gerunds
- Identify key points in an article and in an interview
- Discuss solutions to common problems
- Give an opinion in response to a literary quote
- Write several paragraphs about how to achieve one's goals

UNIT

23

Gerunds: Subject and Object

HEALTH ISSUES

OUTCOMES
• Use gerunds as the subject or object of a verb
• Recognize main ideas in an article about a habit and trend
• Recognize whether an action is recommended or not recommended in a conversation
• Discuss health and exercise habits
• Discuss one's opinion on a controversial topic
• Write a short opinion essay on a controversial topic

STEP 1   GRAMMAR IN CONTEXT

BEFORE YOU READ

Look at the cartoon. Discuss the questions.

1. Why are the people standing on the ledge of the building?

2. How do you think they feel about it?

3. How do *you* feel about it?

READ

▶23|01   Read this article about smoking regulations.

No Smoking: Around the World from **A** to **Z**

In the past few decades,[1] life has become more and more difficult for people who enjoy lighting up.[2] At the same time, it has become more comfortable for people who don't smoke. And for those who want to quit smoking, it has become easier as countries around the world introduce laws that limit or ban smoking in public, and sometimes even private spaces. Here are some examples, from **A** to **Z**:

• **AUSTRIA:** In Austria, the law prohibits smoking in many public places, including trains and train stations. It's also banned in offices unless all employees are in favor of permitting it. Large restaurants must provide areas for non-smokers, but smaller ones can choose between permitting smoking or being smoke-free.

• **JAPAN:** Smoking is illegal on the streets in some cities in Japan.

• **MEXICO:** In Mexico, smoking is not permitted at all in restaurants. The government has also banned advertising tobacco products on TV or radio.

• **UAE:** The United Arab Emirates has recently started banning cigarettes in shopping malls and other public places. Selling cigarettes to minors[3] has also become illegal.

• **ZAMBIA:** In Zambia, the law bans smoking in all public places. Not obeying the law can result in fines and even jail time.

---

1 *decades:* ten-year periods
2 *lighting up:* smoking
3 *minors:* people under the age of eighteen

By now, almost everyone agrees that smoking is bad for your health. But, although many people approve of the new laws, not everyone is in favor of prohibiting public smoking. "It's one thing to try to discourage the habit by putting a high tax on cigarettes," says one smoker, "but some of the new laws go too far." Smokers argue that the laws limit personal freedom. They say everyone today knows the dangers of lighting up. So, if someone won't quit smoking and wants to smoke outdoors in a park or on the beach, it is that person's choice. Those smokers are only hurting themselves. There are many things that people do that are not good for them, such as eating junk food[4] and not exercising. But there are no laws that regulate[5] those behaviors.

NO SMOKING

4 *junk food:* food that is bad for you (usually with a lot of sugar and fat)
5 *regulate:* control (with rules or laws)

AFTER YOU READ

Ⓐ VOCABULARY **Look at the words in the box. Which words can you use for something that is *OK to Do*? Something that is *Not OK to Do*? Write the words in the appropriate column.**

approve of	ban	illegal	in favor of	permit	prohibit

OK to Do   **Not OK to Do**

_____   _____

_____   _____

_____   _____

Ⓑ COMPREHENSION **Complete each statement with the name of the correct country.**

1. Smoking outside is illegal in some parts of _____.

2. In _____, workers can decide on permitting smoking in the workplace or not.

3. _____ bans smoking in shopping malls.

4. Breaking non-smoking laws is a very serious crime in _____.

5. In _____, people can choose between dining in a smoke-free restaurant or in a smaller cigarette-friendly place.

6. You won't see any cigarette ads on TV in _____.

7. _____ has recently banned selling cigarettes to young people.

Ⓒ DISCUSSION **Work with a partner. Compare your answers in B. Why did you choose each country?**

GERUNDS: SUBJECT AND OBJECT

Gerund as Subject

Gerund (Subject)	Verb	
Smoking	causes	health problems.
Not smoking	is	healthier.

Gerund as Object

Subject	Verb	Gerund (Object)
You	should quit	**smoking**.
We	suggest	**not smoking**.

Gerund as Object of a Preposition

	Preposition	Gerund	
Are you	**against**	**smoking**	in public?
I plan	**on**	**quitting**	next month.
I'm in favor	**of**	**permitting**	smoking.

GRAMMAR NOTES

1 Forming Gerunds

A gerund is **the base form of the verb + -ing**.	**Smoking** is bad for your health. I enjoy **having** a cigarette in the park. She's against **allowing** cigarettes in the office.

BASE FORM	GERUND
smoke	smok**ing**
permit	permit**ting**
die	d**ying**

IN WRITING There are often spelling changes when you add *-ing*.	
Form the **negative** by placing *not* before the gerund: *not* + **gerund**.	**Not exercising** is bad for you. The doctor suggested **not drinking** coffee. She's happy about **not working** today.
Do not confuse the gerund with the **progressive**. The progressive needs a form of the verb *be*.	GERUND **Drinking** a lot of coffee is unhealthy. PROGRESSIVE He **is drinking** coffee right now.

2 Gerunds as Subjects or Objects

A gerund is a verb form that you use **like a noun**—as a **subject** or an **object**.

A gerund can be the **subject** of a sentence. It is always singular. Use the third-person-singular form of the verb after gerunds.	**Eating** junk food *makes* me sick. **Advertising** cigarettes on TV *is* illegal.
A gerund can be the **object** of certain verbs. Use a gerund after these verbs:	

admit	can't stand	like	recommend	He *can't stand* seeing all the no smoking signs.
advise	consider	limit	resist	Have you *considered* quitting?
allow	deny	mind	risk	Do they *allow* smoking in malls?
appreciate	dislike	miss	start	I *dislike* sitting near smokers in cafés.
avoid	enjoy	permit	stop	She *stopped* smoking last year.
ban	finish	prohibit	suggest	Dr. Ho *suggested* not staying up late.
begin	keep	quit	support	She *kept* trying to quit.

USAGE NOTE We often use *go* + **gerund** to describe activities such as *shopping, dancing, fishing, skiing, swimming,* and *camping.*	Let's *go swimming* in the lake. I *went* shopping for running shoes at the mall.

3 Preposition + Gerund

A gerund can also be the **object of a preposition**.

Use a gerund **after prepositions** such as:

about	at	by	in	to	He spoke to the doctor *about* quitting.
after	before	for	of	with	She's *for* banning tobacco ads.
against	between	from	on	without	I'm *against* smoking in public places.

There are many **expressions with prepositions**. You can use a gerund after expressions with:	
• **verb + preposition** advise *against* believe *in* count *on*	I *believe in* taking care of my health.
• **adjective + preposition** afraid *of* bored *with* excited *about*	I'm *excited about* joining the health club.
BE CAREFUL! Use a **gerund**, not the base form of the verb, after expressions with the preposition *to*: look forward *to* be opposed *to* object *to*	I *look forward to* seeing you. NOT I look forward to ~~see~~ you.

REFERENCE NOTES

For **spelling rules for verb + *-ing***, see Appendix 21 on page 330.

For a list of **verbs followed by gerunds**, see Appendix 13 on page 327.

For a list of **adjectives followed by prepositions**, see Appendix 17 on page 327.

For a list of **verbs followed by prepositions**, see Appendix 18 on page 328.

EXERCISE 1 DISCOVER THE GRAMMAR

GRAMMAR NOTES 1–3 Read this online bulletin board about smoking. Underline all the gerunds.

Re: Can't Stand <u>Seeing</u> Those Signs!

Posted by Grofumeur on February 16, 2016 at 15:30:03

I can't stand seeing all the new No Smoking signs. It's getting harder and harder to have a good time. Next thing you know, they'll ban laughing! Eating in a restaurant or having an espresso in a café is just no fun anymore! Junk food is worse than smoking. But I bet the government won't prohibit people from ordering burgers and fries for lunch!

Reply posted by Nuffsed on February 17, 2016 at 12:15:22

Hey, Grofumeur—I'm against smoking in public places. I'm even in favor of banning smoking in apartment buildings. I don't get sick when my boyfriend has a Big Mac, but sitting in a room full of his cigarette smoke makes my hair and clothing stink. I'm really enjoying the new regulations.

Reply posted by Swissfriend on February 17, 2016 at 20:53:11

Hi, Smokers! I am a member of Freunde der Tabak, a Swiss group of smokers and non-smokers. We always suggest practicing courtesy to non-smokers and tolerance of smokers. I enjoy smoking, but I dislike inhaling secondhand smoke. I don't see a problem with people smoking outside, and I'm against banning it.

Reply posted by Cleanaire on February 18, 2016 at 9:53:11

Friend—Have you ever tried to stop smoking? If so, then you know you are addicted to nicotine. The younger you start smoking, the harder it is to quit. I definitely don't approve of advertising cigarettes or selling them to young people. That should be illegal!

EXERCISE 2 AFFIRMATIVE OR NEGATIVE GERUNDS

GRAMMAR NOTES 1–2 Complete this article with gerunds. Use the verbs from the box.
Choose between affirmative and negative.

drink	eat	exercise	go	increase	join	~~pay~~	smoke	start	stay

_____*Not paying*_____ attention to their health is a mistake a lot of college students make.
1.

_____ healthy will help you do well in school and help you enjoy your
2.

college experience. Here are some tips:

• Smokers have more colds and less energy. Quit _____ now or don't start.
3.

• _____ regularly reduces stress and brings more oxygen to your brain. If
4.

you don't exercise, I suggest _____ every day with a walk or run
5.

around campus.

• _____ breakfast is a common mistake. It's the most important meal of
6.

the day.

• Avoid _____ soda and other sugary beverages. Your body will thank you!
7.

• Health experts advise _____ the fruits and vegetables in your diet. You
8.

need at least four and a half cups a day, but more is better.

• _____ to the doctor when you're sick is another common mistake. Know
9.

where your school Health Service is, and use it when you need it.

• Better yet—consider _____ Healthy Campus—a program for
10.

staying healthy.

EXERCISE 3 GERUND AS OBJECT

GRAMMAR NOTE 2 Write a summary sentence for each conversation. Use the correct form
of the verbs from the box and the gerund form of the verbs in parentheses.

admit	avoid	deny	enjoy	go	keep	mind	~~stop~~

1. DANTE: Would you like a cigarette?
   MARTA: Oh, no, thanks. Since restaurants have banned cigarettes, I don't smoke anymore.

   Summary: Marta _____*has stopped smoking*_____.
   (smoke)

2. BRIAN: Where are the cookies I bought? You ate them, didn't you?
   LYDIA: No, I didn't.

   Summary: Lydia _____ the cookies.
   (eat)

3. ANGELA: Do you want to go running with me before work?
   SERGEY: Running? Are you kidding? I hate running!

   Summary: Jan doesn't _____.
   (run)

4. CHEN: What are you doing after work?
  AN-LING: I'm going to that new swimming pool. Would you like to go with me?

  Summary: An-ling is going to _____ .
  _____(swim)

5. LARA: You're lazy. You really need to exercise more.
  ROMAN: You're right. I *am* lazy.

  Summary: Roman _____ lazy.
  _____(be)

6. MONICA: Would you like a piece of chocolate cake?
  PAULO: No, thanks. I try to stay away from sweets.

  Summary: Paulo _____ sweets.
  _____(eat)

7. CRAIG: I know exercise is important, but I hate it. What about you?
  VILMA: Well, I don't *love* it, but it's OK.

  Summary: Vilma doesn't _____ .
  _____(exercise)

8. DORA: How's your new exercise program going?
  ERIK: Not great. But I won't give up!

  Summary: Erik is going to _____ .
  _____(try)

EXERCISE 4 GERUND AS OBJECT OF A PREPOSITION

GRAMMAR NOTE 3 Combine the pairs of sentences to make statements about the Healthy
Campus Program. Use the prepositions in parentheses plus a gerund.

Bo Yang

Bo's Tips for Freshmen

Many college freshmen develop unhealthy habits. It doesn't have to happen!

If <u>you're interested in staying healthy</u> _____ ,
  1. You're interested. You want to stay healthy. (in)

join **Healthy Campus**.

Read what members are saying about the program:

Lisa Suarez: _____ . I did, and
  2. You can improve your health. Quit smoking. (by)

  I feel great.

Omar Sisane: _____ . It's fun.
  3. I'm very happy. I'm starting an exercise program (about)

Zhang Feng: _____ .
  4. This program gives you great ideas. Those ideas solve health issues (for)

Mee-Yon Go: I *was* a couch potato! _____.
                                         5. Now I'm proud of myself. I swim a mile every day. (for)

Amy Kaplan: The doctors are great. _____.
                                         6. They can help. They listen to your concerns. (by)

Leon Zimmer: _____.
                        7. I ran my first 10 km race. I didn't stop. (without)

REMEMBER: _____.
                        8. You should ask a doctor. Then you can start an exercise program. (before)

EXERCISE 5 EDITING

GRAMMAR NOTES 1–3 **Read part of an ex-smoker's journal. There are fifteen mistakes in the use of gerunds. The first mistake is already corrected. Find and correct fourteen more. Remember to check for spelling mistakes.**

DAY 1: I quit ~~to smoke~~ *smoking*! This was the first day of the rest of my life as a non-smoker. Get through the day wasn't too difficult. I quit drinking coffee today, too, and I think that helped. I used to enjoy had a cigarette with a cup of coffee in the morning. But now I'm looking forward to get healthier.

DAY 3: Today was harder. I kept wanting a cigarette. I called Dinah. She told me to take deep breaths and stay busy. That worked. I have to resist eat too much. Gaining 5 pounds aren't a big deal, but I don't want to gain more than that.

DAY 5: I got through the workweek smoke free. My boss definitely approves of the new me. She keeps tells me, "You can do it." I really appreciate to have her support. I miss smokeing, but I DON'T miss to standing outside in the cold just to have a cigarette. I also don't mind don't burning holes in my clothes!

DAY 7: Dinah suggested to go out to dinner, but I can't risk be around smokers. Instead, we went shoping, and I bought a shirt with the money I saved during my first week as a non-smoker. Also, I'm happy about have clothes that smell fresh! Not smoking has advantages.

Infinitives After Certain Verbs

HAPPINESS

OUTCOMES
- Use verbs that are followed by infinitives
- Identify statistics in a short article
- Evaluate speakers' attitudes in a conversation
- Discuss tendencies and preferences
- Give an opinion in response to a literary quote
- Write a paragraph on a personal topic, using transition words

STEP 1 GRAMMAR IN CONTEXT

BEFORE YOU READ

Look at the photo. Discuss the questions.

1. What is the relationship of these people?
2. Do you think they are happy? Why?
3. What makes *you* feel happy?

READ

24|01 Read this magazine article about happiness.

Can People Learn to Be Happy?

WE ALL KNOW people who have problems in life, but who still seem to be happy most of the time. On the other hand, there are people who appear to have it all—money, health, good friends, and family, but still seem unhappy. What makes one person happy and another unhappy? According to psychologist[1] Martin Seligman, 50 percent of happiness is genetic—you are born with a certain disposition.[2] This means that you are "programmed" from birth to feel a certain way. Another 10 percent of happiness is situational—if bad things happen, people tend to feel bad; if good things happen, they feel good, at least for a while. Interestingly, research shows that after some time, people seem

1 *psychologist:* a person whose job it is to study the mind and how it works
2 *disposition:* the way a person usually feels or acts

Sources of Happiness

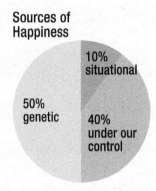

- 10% situational
- 50% genetic
- 40% under our control

to return to their pre-set genetic levels of happiness. But perhaps the most significant finding is that 40 percent of our feelings is under our control—we can choose to react to life's situations one way or another.

If 40 percent of happiness is under our control, what can we do to feel happier? Studies show that happy people tend to do the following:

- interact with friends and people they like
- stay healthy
- focus on goals
- participate in enjoyable activities
- do meaningful work
- show compassion[3] to themselves and others

Most people want to be happy. Life is not always easy, however, and it is appropriate to feel sad in reaction to a life-changing event such as illness, death, or other losses. We can, however, try to feel better even when we have problems. And it's good to know that although genetics play a large role in how we feel, there is still a lot we can do to increase our chances at happiness.

---

3 *compassion:* a strong feeling of sympathy for someone who feels bad or has problems

AFTER YOU READ

A VOCABULARY Match the underlined words with the words in **bold**.

_____ **1.** You'll feel better if you talk and work with other people.

_____ **2.** Don't keep your attention on your problems.

_____ **3.** Sometimes it is a normal reaction to feel sad.

_____ **4.** Good friends and family usually make people feel better.

_____ **5.** The research on happiness is important.

_____ **6.** People who do more enjoyable activities are happier.

a. focus

b. tend to

c. significant

d. appropriate

e. participate in

f. interact

B COMPREHENSION Read the statements. Check (✓) *True* or *False*.

	True	False
1. People who have money and health are always happy.	☐	☐
2. People always feel bad in reaction to bad events.	☐	☐
3. Participating in enjoyable activities usually increases happiness.	☐	☐
4. People's attitudes can affect their happiness.	☐	☐
5. Feeling good is one of life's goals.	☐	☐
6. People can't change the way they feel.	☐	☐

C DISCUSSION Work with a partner. Compare your answers in B. Why did you check *True* or *False*?

INFINITIVES AFTER CERTAIN VERBS

Statements

Subject	Verb	(Object)	Infinitive	
I	**decided**		**(not) to stay**	home.
You	**advised**	John	**(not) to change**	jobs.
He	**wanted**	(her)	**(not) to be**	happy.

GRAMMAR NOTES

1 Forming Infinitives

An infinitive is *to* + **the base form of the verb.**	She decided **to join** a health club.
Form the **negative** by placing *not* before the infinitive: *not to* + **base form.**	She decided **not to join** the math club.

2 Verb + Infinitive

An infinitive can directly **follow certain verbs.**

agree	fail	manage	seem
attempt	forget	offer	tend
begin	hope	plan	try
can't wait	learn	refuse	volunteer
choose	like	remember	wait
decide	love	rush	want

VERB + INFINITIVE
They **seemed to enjoy** it.
He **tends to be** happy.
She **tried not to arrive** late.
I **can't wait to see** you.
We **like to go** to the movies.
Did they **decide to take** a dance class?

BE CAREFUL! When there is **more than one infinitive** in a clause, **do not repeat** *to*.

He **wants to move** and **get** a job.
NOT He wants to move and ~~to~~ get a job.

3 Verb + Object + Infinitive

Some verbs need an **object (noun or pronoun)** before the infinitive.

advise	encourage	permit	tell
allow	force	persuade	urge
convince	invite	remind	warn

VERB + OBJECT + INFINITIVE
I **advised Jason to take** the train to the party.
Ana **persuaded me to try** the desert.
She **convinced me to take** another piece of cake.

The **object** can be a noun or a pronoun.

• **noun**

VERB + NOUN + INFINITIVE
We **invited *Marta* to have** dinner with us.

• **pronoun**

VERB + PRONOUN + INFINITIVE
We **invited *her* to have** dinner with us.

BE CAREFUL! Do not forget the object after these verbs.

Marta **persuaded us to go** dancing.
NOT Marta ~~persuaded to go~~ dancing.

An **infinitive** or an **object** + **infinitive** can follow some verbs.				
ask	*help*	*prefer*	*teach*	VERB + INFINITIVE She *wanted* **to take** dance lessons. VERB + OBJECT + INFINITIVE She *wanted Tomás* **to take** dance lessons.
choose	*need*	*promise*	*want*	
expect	*pay*	*remind*	*would like*	

USAGE NOTE After the verb *help*, you can use **the base form** of the verb **or the infinitive**.	He *helped* me **meet** new people. He *helped* me **to meet** new people.

PRONUNCIATION NOTE

24|02   **Pronunciation of *Want to***

In **informal conversation**, we often pronounce **want to** "wanna."	A: Do you **want to** go dancing Friday night?
	    (wanna)
	B: Sure. Where do you **want to** go?
	    (wanna)

IN WRITING Sometimes people use *wanna* in **informal notes**, **text messages**, and **email** to friends.	Hi, Lyn. I **wanna** ask you a question. *(email)*
BE CAREFUL! Do not use *wanna* when you write to people you have a formal relationship with. Also, do not use *wanna* in formal writing.	Professor, I **want to** ask you a question. *(email)* NOT Professor, I ~~wanna~~ ask you a question. Studies show that people **want to** be happy. *(paper)* NOT Studies show that people ~~wanna~~ be happy.

REFERENCE NOTES

For a list of **verbs followed by infinitives**, see Appendix 14 on page 327.

For a list of **verbs** followed by **object + infinitive**, see Appendix 16 on page 327.

EXERCISE 1 DISCOVER THE GRAMMAR

Ⓐ GRAMMAR NOTES 1–4 Read Alissa's journal entry. Underline all the verb + infinitive and the verb + object + infinitive combinations. Circle the objects.

I have been unhappy since I moved here. Dara advised (me) to join a club. I didn't know

anyone, and I wanted to make new friends. So, I finally did it! I decided to join the

school's Outdoor Adventure Club, and I went to my first meeting last night. I'm really

excited about this. The club is planning a hiking trip next weekend. I can't wait to go.

I hope it won't be too hard for my first adventure. Last night, they also decided to go

rafting in the spring. At first, I didn't want to sign up, but the leader was so nice.

He urged me not to miss this trip, so I put my name on the list. After the meeting,

a group of people asked me to go out with them. We went to a coffee shop and talked

for hours. Well, I hoped to make some new friends when I joined this club, but I didn't

expect everyone to be so friendly. I'm glad Dara persuaded me not to give up.

Ⓑ Read what people said to Alissa. Then find the words in her journal entry that describe the situation.

1. "We're going out for coffee. Why don't you come?" _A group of people asked me to go out with them._

2. "We're all going rafting in the spring." _____

3. "Don't miss this trip!" _____

4. "I'm happy that I listened to Dara. I didn't quit." _____

5. "You really should join a club." _____

6. "I'm really looking forward to going!" _____

7. "I'm going to join!" _____

8. "I'm surprised everyone is so friendly." _____

9. "I don't think I'll sign up." _____

10. "I'd like to make some new friends." _____

EXERCISE 2 VERB + INFINITIVE

GRAMMAR NOTES 1–2 Psychologist Martin Seligman advises people to make a list of things that went well during the day. Complete Lucas's list. Use the verbs in parentheses. Choose between affirmative and negative.

1. I've been feeling tired, so I _____ *refused to work* _____ late today. I needed the rest.
   (refuse / work)

2. I _____ on my problem with my co-worker. Instead, I
   (decide / focus)
   thought about her good qualities.

3. I _____ my aunt. Yesterday, I forgot.
   (remember / call)

4. I _____ to my friends so much. It's really not appropriate.
   (try / complain)

5. I _____ to Miguel's party. I need to have some fun.
   (agree / go)

6. Jon and I _____ to work today. It's better to walk.
   (choose / drive)

7. I _____ at the health fair. I think it's an important event.
   (volunteer / help)

EXERCISE 3 VERB + OBJECT + INFINITIVE

GRAMMAR NOTES 1, 3–4 Read these tips from Helen's Happiness Workshop. Rewrite each tip using an object + infinitive. Choose between affirmative and negative.

1. "Go outside every day. But don't stay out in the sun too long."

   Helen advised *us to go outside every day* _____ .

   But she warned *us not to stay out in the sun too long* _____ .

2. "Get enough sleep. Aim for at least six hours."

   She urged _____ .

   She told _____ .

3. "Stay healthy. Don't eat junk food."

   She told _____ .

   She urged _____ .

4. "Do something fun every day."

   She encouraged _____ .

5. "Don't spend too much time alone."

   She persuaded _____ .

6. "Don't give up! Be patient!"

   She urged _____

   and reminded _____ .

7. "Come to the next happiness workshop!"

   She invited _____ .

EXERCISE 4 OBJECT OR NO OBJECT

GRAMMAR NOTES 1–4 Write a summary sentence for each conversation. Use the correct form of a verb from the box followed by an infinitive or an object + infinitive.

| advise | ask | decide | encourage | forget | ~~invite~~ | remind |

1. **JASON:** You look a little down, Meghan. We're going out. Would you like to join us?
   MEGHAN: I'd love to.

   Summary: Jason _invited Meghan to join them_ .

2. **INA:** This math problem is too hard. I can't do it.
   TIM: Come on, Ina. I'm sure you can do it. Don't give up. Just keep trying!

   Summary: Tim _____ .

3. **SALLY:** Stop focusing on your problems. You'll only feel worse.
   DIEGO: You're probably right, but it's easier said than done.

   Summary: Sally _____ .

4. **ROBERTO:** Don't forget to go to the happiness workshop. It's tomorrow night.
   EMILIA: Oh, OK. Thanks! I'll be there.

   Summary: Roberto _____ .

5. **LYNN:** Can you help me plan a birthday party for Bill?
   LARRY: Sure. I'd be happy to. When's his birthday?

   Summary: Lynn _____ .

6. **LISA:** I'm finally going take a photography class.
   KYLE: Great. You need to have more fun.

   Summary: Lisa _____ .

7. **RITA:** So, did you go to the workshop?
   EMILIA: Oh, no! When was it?

   Summary: Emilia _____ .

GRAMMAR NOTES 1–4   Read this article on friendship and happiness. There are ten mistakes in the use of infinitives. The first mistake is already corrected. Find and correct nine more.

How to Make
New Friends
and Increase
Your **Happiness**

Studies show that happy people tend ~~having~~ *to have* more friends. You know from experience that friends are important for your happiness, and you'd like to make some new ones. Maybe you're at a new school or job, or, possibly, you have changed and the "new you" wants meet new people.

To begin with, psychologist Timothy Johnson strongly advises to turn off your computers. He says that "friending" people on Facebook just isn't the same as making real friends. You need go out and interact with real people. He says, "Decide right now to don't refuse invitations. When a classmate or co-worker invites you for coffee, just say *yes*." Join a club and volunteer to doing something. That responsibility will force you to attend the meetings. By doing these things, you will manage meeting a lot of new people. Dr. Johnson warns us, however, don't rush to become close friends with someone right away. Relationships take time. You have to learn to listen. It is important to encourage your new friend to talks by asking him or her questions. Allow each relationship develops naturally, and soon you'll have a group of people you are really comfortable interacting with. These types of friendships are important to happiness because they help you to feel connected, and feeling connected leads to increased happiness.

More Uses of Infinitives
SMART DEVICES

STEP 1 GRAMMAR IN CONTEXT

BEFORE YOU READ

Look at the photo and at the title of the article. Discuss the questions.

1. Why is the article called "The World in Your Hand—or on Your Wrist"?
2. What can you use a smartphone or smartwatch for?
3. Do you have a smartphone or a smartwatch? How do you use it?

READ

25|01 Read this article about smart devices.

The World in Your Hand—or on Your Wrist

No device has changed people's lives as much as the smartphone. When smartphones first came out, people used them for just three major purposes: to make calls, to check email, and to connect to the Internet. Today, people of all ages and walks of life[1] are using them for a lot more. In order to find out how people are using them, we conducted a survey. Here's what some happy users report:

"I use my smartphone to play games, listen to music, and watch videos. It's awesome!"—*Todd Miller, 16, high school student* ● "I use it to translate words I don't understand."—*Lia Chang, 21, nurse* ● "When I'm considering buying something in a store, I use it to look up reviews."—*Rosa Ortiz, 56, accountant* ● "When I'm on the road, I use it to avoid traffic jams. And if I get lost, I use it to get directions."—*Brad King, 32, reporter*

It's easy to see why these multipurpose devices are so popular. They combine the functions of a phone, GPS,[2] camera,

---

1 *walks of life:* occupations
2 *GPS:* Global Positioning System, a device that tells you where you are and gives you directions

computer, calculator, organizer, and much more. They have also become cheap enough for more people to afford.

And then came the smartwatch. At first, some people thought it was too big and unattractive to wear, but in time, it became smaller and more fashionable. It also has some benefits that the smartphone doesn't have. You can use it to check quickly for emails and text messages, without anyone noticing. Just a glance[3] at your wrist alerts[4] you to important information. (And, of course, you can check the time, too.)

What will come next? It's hard to predict. By the time you read this article, the smartwatch may be a thing of the past, or it may be so common that everyone is "wearing the world" on their wrists.

---

3 *glance:* a quick look
4 *alerts:* makes you notice something important

AFTER YOU READ

Ⓐ VOCABULARY Choose the word or phrase that best completes each sentence.

1. An **old-fashioned** idea is not _____.
   a. good   b. modern   c. interesting

2. A **device** is a small _____.
   a. phone   b. machine   c. video

3. If something is **multipurpose**, it has many _____.
   a. uses   b. pieces   c. meanings

4. If you **combine** several things, you _____.
   a. separate them   b. clean them   c. bring them together

5. Another word for **function** is _____.
   a. information   b. purpose   c. computer

6. A **benefit** is a _____ result.
   a. positive   b. surprising   c. negative

Ⓑ COMPREHENSION Read the statements. Check (✓) *True* or *False*.

	True	False
1. People mostly use smartphones to make calls.	☐	☐
2. Todd Miller uses one to have fun.	☐	☐
3. Rosa Ortiz uses one to write reviews.	☐	☐
4. It's surprising that smartphones are so popular.	☐	☐
5. They have become cheaper.	☐	☐
6. You can't check for emails with a smartwatch.	☐	☐
7. We can easily predict what the next device will be.	☐	☐

Ⓒ DISCUSSION Work with a partner. Compare your answers in B. Why did you check *True* or *False*?

INFINITIVES

Infinitives of Purpose

Affirmative
I use it **to call** my friends.
People use it **in order to perform** better.

Negative
I left at 9:00 **in order not to be** late.
Charge it daily **in order not to lose** power.

Infinitives After Adjectives and Adverbs

With *Too*				
	(Too)	Adjective/ Adverb	*(For* + Noun/ Object Pronoun)	Infinitive
It's	(too)	hard		to use.
It's not		expensive	for Todd	to buy.
She spoke	too	quickly	for him	to understand.
They worked		slowly		to finish.

With *Enough*				
	Adjective/ Adverb	*(Enough)*	*(For* + Noun/ Object Pronoun)	Infinitive
It's	easy	(enough)		to use.
It's	cheap		for Todd	to buy.
She spoke	slowly	enough	for him	to understand.
They didn't work	quickly			to finish.

GRAMMAR NOTES

1 Infinitives of Purpose

You can use an infinitive to explain the **purpose of an action**.

An infinitive (**to** + **base form** of the verb) can explain the purpose of an action. It often answers the question *Why?*	A: **Why** did you go to the mall? B: I went there **to buy** a new phone.
USAGE NOTE In **conversation**, you can answer the question *Why?* with an incomplete sentence beginning with **to**.	A: **Why** did you go to the mall? B: **To buy** a new phone.
USAGE NOTE We usually **do not repeat** *to* when we give more than one purpose.	I went to the mall **to buy** a phone, **eat** lunch, and **see** a movie. *(more common)* I went to the mall **to buy** a phone, **to eat** lunch, and **to see** a movie. *(less common)*

2 Infinitives of Purpose with *In order (not) to*

You can also use *in order (not) to* + **base form** of the verb to explain the **purpose of an action**.

In order to is quite **formal** and we use it mostly in **formal speech** and **formal writing**.	People use their devices **in order to perform** many everyday functions. *(magazine article)*
USAGE NOTE In everyday **conversation** and **informal writing**, we usually don't use *in order to* to explain a purpose. We just use the **infinitive**.	I use my smartphone **to check** email. *(blog)*
We use *in order not to* + **base form** of the verb to explain a **negative purpose**. Again, we use it mostly in **formal speech** and **formal writing**.	Users should back up all their files daily **in order not to lose** information. *(newspaper)*
USAGE NOTE In everyday **conversation** and **informal writing**, we usually express a **negative purpose** with *because* + **a reason** or *so that* + **a reason**.	I back up my files every day *because* **I don't want to lose information.** *(conversation)* I back up my files every day *so that* **I don't lose information.** *(email)*

3 Infinitives After Adjectives and Adverbs

You can use an infinitive after an adjective or an adverb.

• **adjective + infinitive**	ADJECTIVE It's *difficult* **to use.**
• **adverb + infinitive**	ADVERB We worked *hard* **to finish** on time.
Sometimes we use *for* + **noun/pronoun** before the infinitive.	It's **easy** *for Todd* **to use.** It's **easy** *for him* **to use.**
Use *too* before the adjective or adverb to show the reason something is **not possible**.	It was *too expensive* **to buy.** *(It was expensive, so I couldn't buy it.)*
Use *enough* after the adjective or adverb to show the reason something is **possible**.	It was *cheap enough* **to buy.** *(It was cheap, so I could buy it.)*
BE CAREFUL! *Enough* goes after the adjective or adverb.	It was **easy** *enough* to use. NOT It was ~~enough easy~~ to use.
Notice the word order in sentences with: • *too* + adj. + *for* + noun/pro. + infinitive • adj. + *enough* + *for* + noun/pro. + infinitive	It's **too hard** *for my son* **to understand.** It's **easy enough** *for Jana* **to use.**
USAGE NOTE We don't need the infinitive when the meaning is clear.	A: Did you buy a smartwatch? B: Yes. It's finally **cheap enough** *for me.* *(It's cheap enough for me to buy.)*

PHONE TALK The telephone has really changed a lot in less than a century. From the 1920s through the 1950s, there was the good old-fashioned rotary phone. It had just one function, but it wasn't that <u>convenient to use</u>. Callers had to turn a dial <u>to make</u> a call. And it was (too) big and heavy to move from place to place. (Besides, there was that annoying cord connecting it to the wall!) The 1960s introduced the touch-tone phone. It was much faster to place a call with it. You just pushed buttons in order to dial. With cordless phones, introduced in the 1970s, callers were free to move around their homes or offices while talking. Then came a really major change—hand-held cell phones. These were small enough to carry with you, and you didn't even have to be inside to talk to your friends. But it wasn't until the invention of the camera phone that people began to use the phone to do more than just talk. And that was nothing compared to today's multipurpose smartphones. People use them to do almost everything. What will the newest technology bring to the phone? It's hard to predict. But one thing is certain: It will be faster and cheaper. And, as always, people will find uses for it that are difficult to imagine today.

EXERCISE 1
DISCOVER THE GRAMMAR

GRAMMAR NOTES 1–3
Read about changes in the telephone. Underline once all the infinitives of purpose. Underline twice all the adjective + infinitive or adverb + infinitive combinations. Circle *too* and *enough*.

EXERCISE 2 AFFIRMATIVE AND NEGATIVE PURPOSES

Ⓐ GRAMMAR NOTES 1–2 Match the actions with their purposes.

Action	Purpose
_b_ **1.** She bought a smartphone because she	**a.** didn't want to get calls.
____ **2.** He took the bus because he	~~**b.**~~ wanted to check email.
____ **3.** We turned our phone off because we	**c.** wanted to buy a new phone.
____ **4.** She recorded her favorite TV show because she	**d.** didn't want to be late.
____ **5.** He went to Eli's Electronics because he	**e.** didn't want to miss it.

Ⓑ Now combine the sentences. Use infinitives of purpose.

1. _She bought a smartphone (in order) to check email._

2. _____

3. _____

4. _____

5. _____

EXERCISE 3 AFFIRMATIVE STATEMENTS

GRAMMAR NOTE 1 Look at these postings to a social media site. Complete the sentences with the correct phrases from the box. Use infinitives of purpose.

| buy fruits and vegetables | drive to Montreal | get more gas | pass it |
| communicate with her | exchange money | have coffee | ~~take a selfie~~[1] |

My Trip to Montreal

1. That's me! I used my phone *to take a selfie* _____.

2. We rented this car _____.

3. This truck was in front of us. We had to drive fast _____.

4. We stopped here _____.

5. We went to the bank _____.

6. We came here _____.

7. We stopped here _____.

8. This is Léa. We had to speak French _____.

[1] *selfie:* a picture someone takes of himself or herself, usually with a camera phone, to share on a social network site such as Facebook or Instagram

EXERCISE 4 INFINITIVES AFTER ADJECTIVES

GRAMMAR NOTE 3 Complete the responses to an online survey. Use the infinitive form of the verbs from the box.

| find out | ~~have~~ | own | remember | spend | use | watch |

2-10-2017   **SURVEY** **Are you going to buy the latest and greatest smartwatch?**

2-10-2017   **BobG:** Yes. I think it's important _____ *to have* _____ the latest technology. And
1.
it's cool!

2-10-2017   **Finefone:** I don't know. I'm always a little nervous about buying a new device. I hope it
isn't too difficult for me _____.
2.

2-10-2017   **YIKES:** No. I'm just not ready _____ the money on another new
3.
device. Besides, I'm happy with my current smartwatch. It does everything I want.

2-11-2017   **LilaX:** Definitely! I love the fact that it's not necessary _____ to take it
4.
with you when you go out or even go into another room. You can always wear it—even
when you sleep. It sure beats having to carry a phone everywhere you go! And you don't
have to search for it in your handbag or briefcase! Just look at your wrist!

2-11-2017   **Cat2:** Actually, I'm not sure. I really want a smart device for videos. But the screen on a
smartwatch is too small _____ them on. I think, for me, a tablet is still
5.
the better choice.

2-11-2017   **TimeOut:** Not yet. I think I'll wait until the next one comes out. It'll be interesting
_____ what new features it'll have—and how much it'll cost.
6.

2-12-2017   **Rosy:** No thanks! Call me old-fashioned, but I really don't think it's necessary
_____ all these multipurpose devices. Give me a cell phone, a digital
7.
watch, a laptop computer, a paperback book, a radio—and I'll be happy.

EXERCISE 5 INFINITIVES AFTER ADJECTIVES AND ADVERBS

Ⓐ GRAMMAR NOTE 3 Complete the conversations. Use the words in parentheses with *too* or *enough* and the infinitive.

1. A: Did you buy the new smartwatch?

   B: No. Right now it's still _____ *too expensive for me to buy* _____.
   (expensive / for me)

2. A: Can we call Alicia now?

   B: Sure. It's _____ her.
   (early)

3. **A:** What did Mrs. Johnson just say? I didn't understand her.

   B: Me neither. She always speaks _____ her.
   (quickly / for me)

4. **A:** Did you see Dan last night?

   B: No. Unfortunately, we got there _____ him.
   (late)

5. **A:** Does he have enough money to get that new device that he wants?

   B: It's only $150. I think it's _____ .
   (cheap / for him)

6. **A:** Do you want to go to the movies tonight?

   B: Sorry. I'm _____ tonight.
   (busy)

25|02 **B** LISTEN AND CHECK **Listen to the conversations and check your answers in A.**

EXERCISE 6 EDITING

GRAMMAR NOTES 1–3 **Read this online bulletin board about smart devices. There are thirteen mistakes in the use of infinitives of purpose and infinitives after adjectives or adverbs. The first mistake is already corrected. Find and correct twelve more.**

● ● ●

                    to tell
Click here <s>for telling</s> us how you've used your smartphone or smartwatch recently.

I was riding my bike when I saw an accident. A car hit a truck, but it didn't stop. I used my

smartphone take a picture of the car and the license plate number. Then I used it to call the

police. It was so fast and convenient to using!   **Jason Harvey, England**

I was at a great concert in Mexico City. I wanted to share the experience with my best friend

back home. I picked up my smartphone and used it to make a video and sending it to my friend.

Instantly my friend was "there" with me. Awesome!   **Emilia Leale, Italy**

I was at the mall and used my smartwatch for paying for my purchases. It's quick, easy, and safe.

I didn't have to take my wallet out of my pocket or hand my credit card to the store assistant. I

just held my watch near the store's "reader" and double clicked. Done!   **Bruno Neves, Brazil**

I'm really into health and fitness. In order monitor my health, I use my smartwatch to check my

heart rate when I run. I also use it to count my steps when I'm out and about. It's always on my

wrist, so I don't have to remember to take it with me.   **Clarisa Flores, Mexico**

I sell houses. I always use my smartphone in order no waste my customers' time. When I see an interesting house, I immediately send a photo. Then, if they are interested, I make an appointment for them. That way, they can see the house enough fast to make an offer before other people. Without a smartphone, my job would be to hard to do. **Andrea Cook, U.S.**

Last night, I used my phone to helping me make dinner. First, I searched online for a recipe. It was in ounces, so I used an app to converts it to grams. Then I used another app to create a shopping list. When I returned home from shopping, I set the phone's timer to reminded me when to take the food out of the oven. While dinner was baking, I used the phone to listen to my favorite songs. I love this thing! It combines functions for work and play, and it's enough smart to do almost everything. Too bad it can't do the dishes, too! **Kim Soo-Min, South Korea**

UNIT

26

Gerunds and
Infinitives

PROCRASTINATION

OUTCOMES
- Use verbs that can be followed by gerunds or infinitives
- Use prepositions/phrasal verbs + gerunds
- Identify key points in an article and in an interview
- Discuss solutions to common problems
- Give an opinion in response to a literary quote
- Write several paragraphs about how to achieve one's goals

STEP 1   GRAMMAR IN CONTEXT

BEFORE YOU READ

Look at the cartoon and at the title of the article. Discuss the questions.

1. What is procrastination?

2. What types of things do you put off doing?

3. Why do people procrastinate?

READ

26|01   Read this excerpt from a magazine article about procrastinating.

Stop Procrastinating—Now!

It's a beautiful day. Eva doesn't feel like studying for her test. She goes to the park instead. She keeps telling herself she'll work better the next day.

Todd planned to make an appointment with the dentist, but he decided to wait another week, or maybe two.

Procrastinating—putting off until tomorrow things you need to do today—is a universal problem. College students are famous for procrastinating, but we all do

it sometimes. Why do people put off important tasks? Read what the experts say.

Unpleasant Tasks It's not always fun to do a lot of the things on our "To Do" lists. Most people prefer to do enjoyable things.

Poor Time Management[1] Having too little time for a task is discouraging. It's hard to get started on a project when you feel that you can't finish it.

Did you finish writing your paper about procrastination?

No. I'll do it tomorrow.

---

1 *time management:* the skills for using your time well when you are trying to reach a goal

Fear An important test can make you feel so anxious that you put off studying.

Perfectionism The belief that you must do a perfect job can prevent you from starting or finishing a task.

As you can see, people often procrastinate because they want to avoid bad feelings. This tactic, however, usually fails because procrastinators end up feeling even worse as a result of their procrastination. It's a vicious cycle.[2] The only solution to the problem is to stop procrastinating—now!

----

2 *vicious cycle:* a situation where one problem causes another problem that then causes the first problem again

AFTER YOU READ

A VOCABULARY **Complete the sentences with the words from the box.**

anxious	discouraging	project	tactic	task	universal

1. Have you finished your class _____ yet?

2. Procrastination is a _____ problem. People all over the world do it.

3. I get very _____ before a test.

4. Shopping for dinner is my least favorite _____ on my "To Do" list.

5. The problem is _____, but I won't give up hope!

6. Do you know a good _____ for solving this problem?

B COMPREHENSION **Check (✓) the reasons the article gives for procrastination.**

☐ 1. being lazy

☐ 2. not enjoying the task

☐ 3. not understanding something

☐ 4. not having enough time

☐ 5. feeling anxious about the task

☐ 6. not getting enough sleep

☐ 7. feeling depressed

☐ 8. thinking your work has to be perfect

C DISCUSSION **Work with a partner. Compare your answers in B. Why did you or didn't you check each item?**

GERUNDS AND INFINITIVES

Gerunds
Eva **enjoys going** to the park.
She **prefers taking** long breaks.
She **stopped studying**.
Starting a project is hard.
She's worried **about finishing** her paper.

Infinitives
Eva **wants to go** to the park.
She **prefers to take** long breaks.
She **stopped to study**.
It's hard **to start** a project.

GRAMMAR NOTES

1 Verb + Gerund

Some verbs are followed by a **gerund** (base form + -*ing*).

These are some common verbs followed by a gerund:

avoid	*deny*	*keep*
consider	*enjoy*	*postpone*
delay	*finish*	*quit*

Eva *avoids* **doing** her work.
She *doesn't enjoy* **studying**.
She *delays* **getting** to work.

2 Verb + Infinitive

Some verbs are followed by an **infinitive** (*to* + base form).

These are some common verbs followed by an infinitive:

agree	*decide*	*need*★	*promise*★
arrange	*expect*★	*offer*	*want*★
choose★	*fail*	*plan*	*would like*★

Todd *decided* **not to work** late.
He *arranged* **to leave** early.
He *plans* **to meet** some friends.

★These verbs can also be followed by:
object + infinitive

We *expect* **to start** the project soon.
We *expect* **them to start** the project soon.

USAGE NOTE We usually do not repeat *to* when there is more than one infinitive.

He plans **to watch** TV, **read** the paper, and **call** his friends. *(more common)*
He plans **to watch** TV, **to read** the paper, and **to call** his friends. *(less common)*

3 Verb + Gerund or Infinitive

Some verbs are followed by **a gerund or an infinitive**. They have the same meaning.

These are some common verbs that are followed by a gerund or an infinitive:

begin	hate	prefer
can't stand	like	start
continue	love	try

Jeff *hates* **studying**. or Jeff *hates* **to study**.
He *likes* **reading**. or He *likes* **to read**.
He *loves* **dancing**. or He *loves* **to dance**.

USAGE NOTE When two or more verbs follow another verb, we use the same form of the verb. (In writing, this is called *parallel structure*.)

He *hates* **studying** and **doing** homework.
NOT He hates studying and ~~to do~~ homework.
He *hates* **to study** and **do** homework.
NOT He hates to study and ~~doing~~ homework.

BE CAREFUL! Some **verbs**, such as the ones below, can be **followed by a gerund or an infinitive**, but they have a very different meaning:

stop   remember   forget

Eva *stopped* **taking** breaks.
   (She doesn't take breaks anymore.)
Eva *stopped* **to take** a break.
   (She stopped an activity in order to take a break.)
Todd *remembered* **reading** the story.
   (First he read the story. Then he remembered that he did it.)
Todd *remembered* **to read** the story.
   (First he remembered. Then he read the story. He didn't forget.)
Jeff *forgot* **meeting** Dana.
   (Jeff met Dana, but afterwards he didn't remember the event.)
Jeff *forgot* **to meet** Dana.
   (Jeff had plans to meet Dana, but he didn't meet her because he forgot about the plans.)

4 Preposition or Phrasal Verb + Gerund

A **gerund** is the only verb form that can **follow a preposition or a phrasal verb**.

- **preposition + gerund**

   PREPOSITION
   He's worried *about* **writing** it.
   PREPOSITION
   He's looking forward *to* **finishing** it.
   PREPOSITION
   Jeff doesn't feel *like* **working** on his paper.

- **phrasal verb + gerund**

   PHRASAL VERB
   He won't *put off* **starting** it anymore.

5 For General Statements

To make **general statements**, you can use either:

- **gerund as subject**

   Writing a paper is hard.
   or
- ***it* + infinitive**

   It's hard **to write** a paper.

They have the **same meaning**.

REFERENCE NOTES

For a list of **verbs followed by a gerund**, see Appendix 13 on page 327.

For a list of **verbs followed by an infinitive**, see Appendix 14 on page 327.

For a list of **verbs followed by a gerund or an infinitive**, see Appendix 15 on page 327.

For more information on **gerunds after prepositions**, see Unit 23 on page 226, and Appendices 17 and 18 on pages 327 and 328.

| STEP 3 | FOCUSED PRACTICE |

EXERCISE 1
DISCOVER THE GRAMMAR

Ⓐ GRAMMAR NOTES 1–5
Read this paragraph.
Underline the gerunds.
Circle the infinitives.

Like many students, Eva is a procrastinator. She keeps <u>putting</u> off her schoolwork. When she studies, she often stops (to go) for a walk in the park. She wants to improve her study habits, but she isn't sure how. Eva decided to make a list every day of tasks she needs to do. She always remembers to make her list, but she often forgets to read it. It's very discouraging, and Eva is worried about getting bad grades. Last night, Eva remembered reading an article in the school newspaper about a support group for procrastinators. She thinks being in a group is a good idea. It's difficult to try to change on your own. She likes sharing ideas with other students. Maybe it will help.

Ⓑ Now read the statements. Check (✓) *True* or *False*. Correct the false statements.

		True	False
1.	Eva ~~never does~~ *puts off doing* her schoolwork.	☐	☑
2.	She quit going for walks in the park.	☐	☐
3.	She'd like to be a better student.	☐	☐
4.	Eva makes a list every day.	☐	☐
5.	She always reads her list.	☐	☐
6.	She read about a support group.	☐	☐
7.	She thinks it's good to be in a group.	☐	☐
8.	She doesn't like to share ideas with others.	☐	☐

EXERCISE 2 GERUND OR INFINITIVE

GRAMMAR NOTES 1–4
Read the quiz. Circle the correct form of the verbs. In some cases, both forms are correct.

Are You a Procrastinator?

☐ When I don't feel like to do / (doing) something, I often put off to start / starting it.
   <u>1.</u>   <u>2.</u>

☐ I sometimes start to study / studying the night before a test.
                       <u>3.</u>

☐ I sometimes start a job but then postpone to finish / finishing it.
                                              <u>4.</u>

☐ I often delay to make / making difficult decisions.
            <u>5.</u>

☐ I find excuses for not to do / doing things I dislike.
                       <u>6.</u>

☐ When a task seems too difficult, I often avoid to work / working on it.
                                              <u>7.</u>

☐ I prefer to do / doing easy tasks first.
         <u>8.</u>

☐ I often promise myself to work / working on a project but then fail to do / doing it.
                       <u>9.</u>   <u>10.</u>

☐ I worry about to make / making mistakes or about not to be / being perfect.
                <u>11.</u>   <u>12.</u>

☐ I often choose to do / doing other tasks instead of the most important one.
               <u>13.</u>

☐ I want to improve / improving, but I keep to put / putting it off.
        <u>14.</u>   <u>15.</u>

EXERCISE 3 GERUND OR INFINITIVE

GRAMMAR NOTES 1–4 Complete these tips from a website. Use the correct form of the verbs in parentheses.

● ● ●

Some Tips for ___*Stopping*___ Procrastination
          <u>1. (stop)</u>

■ If you have a large project to work on, break it into small tasks. Finish _____
                                                                  2. (do)

   one small task before _____ the next.
                      3. (start)

■ Choose _____ the hardest task first. You'll get it out of the way, and you'll feel
       4. (do)

   better about yourself.

■ Promise yourself _____ at least fifteen minutes on a task even if you don't really
                5. (spend)

   feel like _____ it. You'll be surprised. You can get a lot done in fifteen minutes—
          6. (do)

   and you'll often keep _____ even longer.
                      7. (work)

■ Stop _____ short breaks—but for no longer than ten minutes at a time.
     8. (take)

■ Arrange _____ yourself a reward when you succeed in _____ a
        9. (give)   10. (finish)

   task. Do something you enjoy _____ .
                              11. (do)

■ Consider _____ a support group for procrastinators.
         12. (join)

EXERCISE 4 GENERAL STATEMENTS

Ⓐ GRAMMAR NOTE 5 Complete these conversations. The people talking agree on everything. Read one person's opinion and write the other's. If the first person uses a gerund, use an infinitive. If the first person uses an infinitive, use a gerund.

1. EVA: It's hard to start a new project.

   TODD: I agree. *Starting a new project is hard.*

2. PAT: Taking short breaks is helpful.

   LEE: You're right. *It's helpful to take short breaks.*

3. UTA: It's difficult to work on a long project.

   KAY: That's true. _____

4. LEV: Completing a job on time feels great.

   JEFF: You're right. _____

5. PAT: Rewarding yourself for finishing a project is a good idea.

   LEE: I agree. _____

6. UTA: Being in a support group is very helpful.

   KAY: Yes. _____

7. EVA: It's good to meet people with the same problem.

   TODD: I feel the same way. _____

▶26|02 Ⓑ LISTEN AND CHECK Listen to the conversations and check your answers in A.

EXERCISE 5 GERUND OR INFINITIVE

GRAMMAR NOTES 1–3 Read these conversations that took place at a procrastinators' support group meeting. Complete the summary statements. Use a gerund or an infinitive.

1. SARA: Hi, Todd. Did you bring the soda?
   TODD: Yes. Here it is.

   Summary: Todd remembered *to bring the soda* _____.

2. CHO: Eva, do you remember Todd?
   EVA: Oh, yes. We met last year.

   Summary: Eva remembers _____.

3. EVA: Todd, will Miriam be here tonight? I haven't seen her in ages!
   TODD: Yes, she's coming later.

   Summary: Todd expects Miriam _____.

4. SARA: You take too many breaks.
   TODD: No, I don't!

   Summary: Todd denied _____.

5. EVA: What do you do in your free time, Aki?
AKI: I listen to music a lot.

Summary: Aki likes _____.

6. UTA: I'm tired. Let's go home.
AKI: OK. Just five more minutes.

Summary: Uta wants _____.

7. UTA: Eva, can we give you a ride home?
EVA: Thanks, but I think I'll stay a little longer.

Summary: Uta offered _____.

Eva decided _____.

8. DAN: Good night. Please drive carefully.
UTA: Don't worry. I will.

Summary: Uta promised Dan _____.

EXERCISE 6 EDITING

GRAMMAR NOTES 1–5 Read Eva's blog entry. There are eight mistakes in the use of gerunds and infinitives. The first mistake is already corrected. Find and correct seven more.

Eva's Blog

The Test of Time

For months I was thinking about ~~to go~~ *going* to a support group for procrastinators, but I

kept putting it off! Last night, I finally decided going, and I'm glad I did. I'm not alone!

There were a lot of people there with the same problem as me. I expected them being

boring, but they were really quite interesting—and helpful. I even knew some of the

other students there. I remembered to meet a few of them at a school party last year. I

really enjoyed to talk to Todd, and before I left I promised coming again.

I have a math test tomorrow, so I really should stop to write now and start studying.

See, I've already learned some helpful tactics from to be in this group! I have to stop

making excuses and start my work! NOW!

Pronouns and Phrasal Verbs

PART 8

OUTCOMES

- Use *each other*, *one another*, and reflexive pronouns
- Identify the subject of a description in an article
- Identify important information in a conversation
- Complete a questionnaire and discuss the results
- Write an email or letter, giving advice

OUTCOMES

- Use a range of phrasal verbs
- Use phrasal verbs with separated objects
- Identify key details in an article and a conversation
- Discuss illustrations, using phrasal verbs
- Conduct an online search and share results with the class
- Write a paragraph about animal intelligence

Reflexive and Reciprocal Pronouns

SELF-TALK

OUTCOMES
- Use *each other*, *one another*, and reflexive pronouns
- Identify the subject of a description in an article
- Identify important information in a conversation
- Complete a questionnaire and discuss the results
- Write an email or letter, giving advice

STEP 1   GRAMMAR IN CONTEXT

BEFORE YOU READ

Look at the photos and at the examples of self-talk. Discuss the questions.

1. What do you think *self-talk* is?
2. Is the man's self-talk positive or negative?
3. What about the woman's self-talk? Is it positive or negative?

READ

▶ 27|01   Read this article from a psychology magazine.

Self-Talk

SELF-TALK is the way we explain a problem to ourselves. It can impact how we feel and how we act. Take the case of Tom and Sara. They both got laid off[1] from their jobs at the same company, but their reactions were totally different. Sara maintained her normal life. She frequently talked on the phone with her friends, continued her usual activities, and kept herself fit.

Tom, on the other hand, spent all of his time at home by himself, didn't allow himself to have a good time, and gained 10 pounds (4.5 kilograms).

Why were their reactions so very different from one another? They both lost their jobs, so the situation itself can't explain

It was all my fault.

I'll never find another job.

---

1 *got laid off*: lost their jobs because their employer didn't have enough money to keep them or because there wasn't enough work

I'll find a better job soon.

I'm the best worker they had.

Tom's problems. The main difference was the way Tom and Sara explained the problem to themselves.

Sara told herself that the problem was temporary and that she herself could change it. Tom saw himself as completely helpless and likely[2] to be unemployed forever.

Tom and Sara both got their jobs back. Their reactions when they talked to each other were, again, very different. For his part, Tom grumbled,[3] "Oh, I guess they were really desperate." Sara, on the other hand, smiled and said, "Well! They finally realized that they need me!"

---

2 *likely:* probably
3 *grumbled:* complained in a quiet but slightly angry way

AFTER YOU READ

A VOCABULARY **Complete the sentences with the words from the box.**

fault	impact	maintain	reaction	realize	temporary

1. What was Tom's _____ when he heard the news? Was he surprised?

2. At first, they didn't _____ that the problem at work was so serious.

3. It wasn't the workers' _____. They didn't do anything wrong.

4. Sara believed that the problem was just _____. She expected to find another job.

5. The layoffs didn't _____ their boss's job. She's still at the company.

6. Sara exercised and saw friends in order to _____ her health and positive attitude.

B COMPREHENSION **Read the questions. Check (✓) *Tom*, *Sara*, or *Tom and Sara*.**

	Tom	Sara	Tom and Sara
1. Who stayed in good physical condition?	☐	☐	☐
2. Who spent a lot of time alone?	☐	☐	☐
3. Who thought the problem was temporary?	☐	☐	☐
4. Who felt helpless?	☐	☐	☐
5. Who had a conversation back at work?	☐	☐	☐

C DISCUSSION **Work with a partner. Compare your answers in B. Why did you check *Tom*, *Sara*, or *Tom and Sara*?**

REFLEXIVE AND RECIPROCAL PRONOUNS

Reflexive Pronouns			
Subject Pronoun		Reflexive Pronoun	
I		myself	
You		yourself	
He		himself	
She	looked at	herself	in the mirror.
It		itself	
We		ourselves	
You		yourselves	
They		themselves	

Reciprocal Pronouns		
Subject Pronoun		Reciprocal Pronoun
We You They	looked at	each other. one another.

GRAMMAR NOTES

1 Reflexive Pronouns

Use a **reflexive pronoun** when the **subject and object** refer to the **same people or things**.

• same people	SUBJECT = OBJECT **Sara** looked at **herself** in the mirror. *(Sara looked at her own face.)*
• same things	SUBJECT = OBJECT My **office light** turns **itself** off. *(It turns off automatically.)*

2 Reflexive Pronouns for Emphasis

You can also use a reflexive pronoun to **emphasize a noun** or **a pronoun**.

The reflexive pronoun usually **follows** the noun or pronoun **directly**.	Tom was upset when he lost his job. The **job itself** wasn't important to him, but he needed the money. Tom believed that **he himself** was at fault for losing his job.
USAGE NOTE When we use a reflexive pronoun for emphasis, we often stress the identity of the person or thing the pronoun is referring to in **comparison to other people or things**.	**Sara herself** didn't get depressed, but her co-workers felt terrible. *(This compares Sara to her co-workers.)*

3 Reflexive Pronouns in Imperative Sentences

Imperative sentences can have reflexive pronouns.

• *yourself* when the subject is singular	"Don't push **yourself** so hard, **Tom**," Sara said. *(talking to one person)*
• *yourselves* when the subject is plural	"Don't push **yourselves** so hard, **guys**," Sara said. *(talking to several people)*

4 Reflexive Pronouns in Common Expressions

Some **common expressions** use reflexive pronouns.

• *by* + reflexive pronoun *(alone or without help)*	Sara lives **by herself**. *(Sara lives alone.)* We finished the job **by ourselves**. *(No one helped us.)*
• *be* + reflexive pronoun *(act in the usual way)*	Just **be yourself** at your interview. *(Act like you usually act.)*

5 Reciprocal Pronouns

Use a **reciprocal pronoun** when the **subject and object** of a sentence refer to the **same people**, and these people have a **two-way relationship**.

• *each other* for two people	SUBJECT = OBJECT **Tom and Sara** met **each other** at work. *(Tom met Sara, and Sara met Tom.)*
• *one another* for more than two people	SUBJECT = OBJECT **We all** told **one another** about our jobs. *(Each person exchanged news with every other person.)*
USAGE NOTE In conversation, many people use *each other* and *one another* in the **same way**.	**Sara and Tom** saw **each other**. or **Sara and Tom** saw **one another**. **All six men** knew **each other**. or **All six men** knew **one another**.
BE CAREFUL! Reciprocal pronouns and plural reflexive pronouns have different meanings.	Fred and Jane blamed **each other**. *(Fred blamed Jane, and Jane blamed Fred.)* Fred and Jane blamed **themselves**. *(Fred blamed himself, and Jane blamed herself.)*
Reciprocal pronouns have **possessive forms**: *each other's, one another's.*	Tom and Sara took **each other's** numbers. *(Tom took Sara's number, and Sara took Tom's.)*

REFERENCE NOTE

For a list of **verbs and expressions that often take reflexive pronouns**, see Appendix 3 on page 322.

EXERCISE 1 DISCOVER THE GRAMMAR

GRAMMAR NOTES 1–3, 5 Read this article about positive self-talk. Underline the reflexive pronouns once and the reciprocal pronouns twice. Draw an arrow to the words that the pronouns refer to.

Positive Self-Talk and Athletes

POSITIVE SELF-TALK can affect our thoughts, feelings, and actions. It can even make the difference between winning and losing. Top athletes not only compete against one another, they also compete against themselves when they try to improve their performances. Many athletes use self-talk to maintain their self-confidence and help themselves reach new goals. If you've asked yourself how Korean Olympic gold and silver winner Yuna Kim can do those perfect jumps under so much stress, now you know it's probably because she's telling herself, "Yuna! You can! You will! You are!"

One sports psychologist believes that Olympic athletes are not very different from one another—they are all the best in their sports. When two top athletes compete against each other, the winner is the one with the most powerful positive "mental movies." According to many psychologists, ordinary people themselves can use these techniques, too. (And they can do it by themselves, without getting professional help.) They can create "mental movies" to help themselves succeed in difficult situations. So, when you are feeling discouraged about something, picture yourself succeeding and tell yourself, "You can do it!"

Yuna Kim

EXERCISE 2 REFLEXIVE OR RECIPROCAL PRONOUNS

Ⓐ GRAMMAR NOTES 1–5 **Tom and Sara's company had an office party. Circle the correct pronouns to complete the conversations.**

1. **A:** Listen, guys! The food and drinks are over here. Don't be shy. Please come and help (yourselves) / themselves.

   B: Thanks. We will.

2. **A:** Isn't that the new head of the accounting department over there?

   B: I think so. Let's go over and introduce himself / ourselves.

3. **A:** I'm really nervous about my date with Nicole after the party. I actually cut herself / myself twice while shaving, and then I lost my car keys.

   B: Come on. This is a party, Tom. Just relax and be yourself / yourselves. You'll do just fine.

4. **A:** What are you giving your boss for the holidays this year?

   B: We always give ourselves / each other the same holiday gifts. Every year, I give him a book, and he gives me a box of candy. I realize that this doesn't sound very exciting, but I myself / ourselves am quite happy with the arrangement. It makes things easy that way.

5. **A:** What's your department's reaction to the new computer program?

   B: I'm not sure. We're still teaching ourselves / themselves how to use it.

6. **A:** Jessica looks upset. Didn't she get a promotion?

   B: No, and she keeps blaming herself / himself. She thinks it's all her fault. Of course it isn't.

7. **A:** The Aguayos are finally going to Japan on vacation this year.

   B: That's wonderful. They really need one. Are they going by each other / themselves or with a tour group?

8. **A:** This was a great party.

   B: Yeah. We really enjoyed ourselves / myself.

27|02 **Ⓑ** LISTEN AND CHECK **Listen to the conversations and check your answers in A.**

EXERCISE 3 REFLEXIVE OR RECIPROCAL PRONOUNS

GRAMMAR NOTES 1–5 **Read the interview with George Prudeau, a high school French teacher. Complete the interview. Use the correct reflexive or reciprocal pronouns.**

INTERVIEWER: How did you become a teacher?

GEORGE: When I got laid off from my sales job, I told _____*myself*_____, "Here's your
1.
chance to finally do what you really want." One of the great things about teaching is
the freedom I have. I run the class by _____—just the way I want to.
2.

I also like the way my students and I learn from _____. My teaching

                                     3.

impacts my students' lives, but they teach me a lot, too.

INTERVIEWER: What about maintaining discipline? Is that a problem?

GEORGE: We have just a few rules. I tell my students, "Keep _____ busy.

                                                              4.

Discuss the lessons, but don't interfere with _____'s work."

                                                                5.

INTERVIEWER: What do you like to teach best?

GEORGE: I love French, but the subject _____ really isn't all that important. A

                                                6.

good teacher helps students learn by _____ and encourages them

                                                  7.

not to give up when they have problems. For instance, John, one of my students, just

taught _____ how to bake French bread. The first few loaves were

                                8.

failures. His first reaction was to give up, but I encouraged him to use positive self-

talk, and in the end he succeeded.

INTERVIEWER: What teaching materials do you use?

GEORGE: Very simple ones. I pride _____ on the fact that I can teach

                                                9.

anywhere, even on a street corner.

INTERVIEWER: What do you like least about your job?

GEORGE: The salary. I teach French culture, but I can't afford to travel to France. I have to

satisfy _____ with trips to French restaurants!

                                10.

EXERCISE 4 VERBS WITH REFLEXIVE OR RECIPROCAL PRONOUNS

GRAMMAR NOTES 1, 4–5 Sara and Tom went to an office party. Look at each picture and write a sentence describing what happened. Use the correct form of a verb from the box with a reflexive or reciprocal pronoun. You will use one verb more than once.

buy	cut	drive	greet	introduce	smile at	talk to

1. *Sara bought herself a new dress.*   2. _____

3. _____

4. _____

5. _____

6. _____

7. _____

8. _____

EXERCISE 5 EDITING

GRAMMAR NOTES 1–5 **Read this woman's diary. There are seven mistakes in the use of reflexive and reciprocal pronouns. The first mistake is already corrected. Find and correct six more.**

Jan's birthday was Wednesday, and I forgot to call him. I reminded ~~me~~ *myself* all day, and then I forgot

anyway! I felt terrible. My sister Anna said, "Don't be so hard on yourselves." But I myself didn't

believe her. She prides herself on remembering everything. Then I finally remembered the article

on self-talk. It said that people can change the way they explain problems to theirselves. Well, I

listened to the way I talked to me, and I realized it sounded really insulting—like the way our high

school math teacher used to talk to us. I thought, Jan and I are good friends, and we treat each

other's well. One mistake shouldn't impact our friendship that much. In fact, he forgave myself for

my mistake right away. And I forgave him for forgetting our dinner date two weeks ago. Friends can

forgive themselves, so I guess I can forgive myself.

28

Phrasal Verbs
SCIENCE

OUTCOMES
- Use a range of phrasal verbs
- Use phrasal verbs with separated objects
- Identify key details in an article and a conversation
- Discuss illustrations, using phrasal verbs
- Conduct an online search and share results with the class
- Write a paragraph about animal intelligence

STEP 1   GRAMMAR IN CONTEXT

BEFORE YOU READ

Look at the photos. Discuss the questions.

1. What kind of work do you think Dr. Eloy Rodriguez does?
2. Where do you think he is in the photo below?
3. What is he doing?

READ

28|01   Read this article about Dr. Eloy Rodriguez.

Planting Ideas

As a child, Eloy Rodriguez picked cotton to help support his family. He also picked up an interest in plants. Dr. Rodriguez is now a famous scientist, but he is still interested in plants. Every summer, he takes off his lab coat, puts on his mosquito repellent,[1] and travels to the Amazon region of Venezuela with his students. There, they search for medicinal plants.

Dr. Rodriguez grew up in Texas. The adults in his very large family (sixty-seven cousins lived nearby) brought their children up to be honest, fair, and *vivo*, or quick-thinking. Rodriguez did well in high school, especially in chemistry, and he went on to college. He took a job there cleaning a laboratory. He became a science major and then went on to graduate school. Soon he was managing the lab.

Eloy Rodriguez and anthropologist[2] Richard Wrangham once noticed that sick animals often pick out certain plants to eat. They turned their observations into a new area of science—zoopharmacognosy (the study of how animals use plants as medicine). Today, Rodriguez is one of the most brilliant scientists in the United

Dr. Eloy Rodriguez

States. Rodriguez thanks his family. He points out that sixty-four of his cousins graduated from college, eleven with advanced degrees. "Although poverty was there, family was what helped us get by in life."

---

1 *mosquito repellent:* a chemical that keeps mosquitoes (small flying insects that bite) away from people
2 *anthropologist:* a scientist who studies people and their societies

AFTER YOU READ

A VOCABULARY Match the phrasal verbs with their meanings.

_____ 1. take off   **a.** to continue

_____ 2. grow up   **b.** to choose

_____ 3. go on   **c.** to get

_____ 4. pick out   **d.** to remove

_____ 5. get by   **e.** to become an adult

_____ 6. pick up   **f.** to survive

B COMPREHENSION Read the statements. Check (✓) *True* or *False*.

	True	False
1. Dr. Rodriguez became interested in plants when he was a child.	☐	☐
2. Rodriguez's family helped him survive.	☐	☐
3. After high school, Rodriguez quit school.	☐	☐
4. He doesn't wear his lab coat in the Amazon.	☐	☐
5. He doesn't do anything to prevent mosquito bites in the Amazon.	☐	☐
6. Sick animals often choose special plants to eat.	☐	☐

C DISCUSSION Work with a partner. Compare your answers in B. Why did you check *True* or *False*?

PHRASAL VERBS: TRANSITIVE AND INTRANSITIVE

Transitive Phrasal Verbs

Subject	Verb	Particle	Object (Noun)
He	put	on	his lab coat.
	helped	out	his students.

Subject	Verb	Object (Noun/Pronoun)	Particle
He	put	his lab coat	on.
		it	
	helped	his students	out.
		them	

Intransitive Phrasal Verbs

Subject	Verb	Particle	
She	started	over.	
He	grew	up	in Texas.
They	got	back	early.

GRAMMAR NOTES

1 Form of Phrasal Verbs

Phrasal verbs (also called *two-word verbs*) are made up of a **verb + particle**.

- phrasal verb = verb + particle

VERB + PARTICLE
He **put on** his lab coat.

These are some **common particles** that combine with verbs to form a phrasal verb:

- *on* (go on, put on, turn on)   She **turned on** the light.
- *off* (call off, take off, turn off)   He **turned off** the TV.
- *up* (bring up, grow up, look up)   They **looked up** the word.
- *down* (sit down, turn down, write down)   She **wrote down** the address.
- *out* (help out, pick out, point out)   He **helps out** a lot.

Prepositions and **particles** look the same. However, **particles** are part of the verb phrase, and they often **change the meaning** of the verb.

VERB + PREPOSITION
She's **looking up** at the sky.
   (She's looking in the direction of the sky.)
VERB + PARTICLE
She's **looking up** the word.
   (She's searching for the word in the dictionary.)

Many **phrasal verbs** and **one-word verbs** have **similar meanings**.

To the right are some **common phrasal verbs** and one-word verbs with similar meanings.

USAGE NOTE Phrasal verbs are often **less formal** than one-word verbs.

PHRASAL VERB	ONE-WORD VERB
(less formal)	(more formal)
figure out	solve
give up	quit
hand in	submit
help out	assist
keep on	continue

3 Transitive and Intransitive Phrasal Verbs

Phrasal verbs can be **transitive** or **intransitive**.

Transitive phrasal verbs have **objects**.

<pre>
       VERB + OBJECT
He took off his lab coat.
</pre>

Most transitive phrasal verbs are **separable**. This means that the **object** can come:

- **after** the verb + particle

- **between** the verb + particle

<pre>
    VERB + PARTICLE + OBJECT
He helped out the students.
or
    VERB + OBJECT + PARTICLE
He helped the students out.
</pre>

BE CAREFUL! When the **object is a pronoun**, it must come **between** the verb and the particle.

He helped *them* out.
NOT He ~~helped out them~~.

A few phrasal verbs can have a **gerund** (verb + -*ing*) as an **object**. The gerund always comes **after** the particle.

She **kept on** *learning*.
He **didn't put off** *applying* to school.

Intransitive phrasal verbs do not have objects.

Eloy Rodriguez **grew up** in Texas.
He never **gives up**.

USAGE NOTE Intransitive phrasal verbs are often action verbs and they occur frequently in the **imperative**.

Please, **sit down**.
Don't get up.

IN WRITING Transitive phrasal verbs are common in conversation and formal writing. **Intransitive phrasal verbs** are very common in conversation, but they are rare in formal writing.

They **carried out** *experiments*. (conversation and formal report)
He **went on** with his studies. (conversation)
He **continued** with his studies. (formal report)

REFERENCE NOTES

For a list of **transitive phrasal verbs** and their meanings, see Appendix 4 on page 323.
For a list of **intransitive phrasal verbs** and their meanings, see Appendix 5 on page 324.

EXERCISE 1 DISCOVER THE GRAMMAR

A GRAMMAR NOTES 1–3 Read this article. Underline the phrasal verbs. Circle the objects of the transitive phrasal verbs.

Eloy Rodriguez grew up in Edinburg, Texas, where his elementary school teachers passed Chicano[1] students over for special honors classes. They also punished them for speaking Spanish. Before Rodriguez went on to become the first U.S.-born Chicano biology instructor at his university, he worked eighteen hours a day and slept in his lab, getting by on very little sleep. "I was very aware that I was the first this, and the first that, and I knew that some people were waiting for me to slip up." Rodriguez didn't slip up. However, he knows that when students feel teachers don't treat them fairly, it turns them off education. Many of them just give up.

Today, Dr. Rodriguez is passing his own success on. When he became a professor at Cornell University, he set out to find Latino[2] graduate students. He takes these students with him on many of his trips and works hard to turn them into top scientists. In 1990, he set up KIDS (Kids Investigating and Discovering Science)—a science program for minority elementary school children. They put on white lab coats and investigate science with university teachers who treat them like research scientists. They observe nature and figure out problems. In interviews, Rodriguez always brings up role models. "I saw my first snowflake before I saw my first Chicano scientist," he says. Because of Rodriguez's efforts, many students will not face the same problem.

1 *Chicano:* Mexican-American
2 *Latino:* from a Spanish-speaking country in Central or South America

B Read the statements. Check (✓) *True* or *False*.

	True	False
1. In Eloy Rodriguez's elementary school, teachers chose Chicano students for honors classes.	☐	☑
2. When Rodriguez became a biology instructor, some people expected him to fail.	☐	☐
3. Unfair treatment makes students less interested in education.	☐	☐
4. Today, Dr. Rodriguez wants to forget his own success.	☐	☐

	True	False
5. He searches for Latino graduate students for his program at Cornell.	☐	☐
6. In 1990, Rodriguez visited a program called KIDS.	☐	☐
7. Children in KIDS wear the same lab clothes as the scientists.	☐	☐
8. Rodriguez rarely mentions role models.	☐	☐

EXERCISE 2 MEANING

GRAMMAR NOTE 2 Complete this advertisement for a field trip to the Amazon. Choose the phrasal verb from the box that is closest in meaning to the verb in parentheses. Use the correct form of the phrasal verb. See Appendices 4 and 5 on pages 323 and 324 for help.

fill out	get up	keep on	pick up	sign up	try out
find out	hand in	pass up	~~set up~~	talk over	work out

Two Weeks in the Amazon! Sign Up Now!

The Biology Department is now _____*setting up*_____ its summer field trip to the Amazonian
                                    1. (prepare)

rain forest in Venezuela. If you want to _____, _____ your
                                          2. (register)   **3.** (get)

application from the Department Office (Room 215), and _____ it

_____ right away. _____ it _____ by May 1.
4. (complete)   **5.** (submit)

Last summer, we collected plants and identified them. This summer, we plan to talk to

local people and _____ how they use plants in traditional medicine. This trip is
                   6. (learn)

extremely challenging. We travel to our camp by canoe. When there are problems, we

_____ them _____ by ourselves. We _____ very
                     7. (solve)   **8.** (get out of bed)

early, and we _____ working until dark. There is
               9. (continue)

also some danger, so please _____ the trip

_____ with your families before you decide.
10. (discuss)

This is a wonderful chance to _____ your
                              11. (use)

research skills and make a real contribution. We really

hope you won't _____ this
                12. (decide not to use)

opportunity to do important

"hands-on" science.

EXERCISE 3 PARTICLES

GRAMMAR NOTES 1–2 Circle the correct particle to complete each phrasal verb. See Appendices 4 and 5 on pages 455 and 456 for help.

Eat Some Leaves and Call Me in the Morning

In 1972, Richard Wrangham of Harvard University set (out) / up to study
1.
chimpanzees in Tanzania. He observed that these chimps get by / up
2.
at dawn to eat the leaves of *Aspilia*. They clearly hate the taste. This
brought back / up a question: Why do chimpanzees pick out / over this
3.   **4.**
plant but pass out / up delicious fruit nearby? Wrangham thought this
5.
question over / up for several years. He then asked Eloy Rodriguez to
6.
help him in / out with the analysis. Together, they worked over / out the
7.   **8.**
puzzle: *Aspilia* contains an antibiotic. Zoopharmacognosy—the study of
how animals "doctor" themselves with plants—was born.

EXERCISE 4 SEPARABLE PHRASAL VERBS AND PRONOUNS

Ⓐ GRAMMAR NOTE 3 Complete the conversations. Use phrasal verbs and pronouns.

1. A: Don't forget to put on your mosquito repellent!

   B: Don't worry! I _____ *put it on* _____ as soon as we got here.

2. A: Can we take off our hats? It's really hot.

   B: Don't _____. They protect you from the sun.

3. A: How do you turn on the generator?

   B: It's easy. You _____ with this switch.

4. A: Did you cover up the leftover food? We don't want the ants to get at it.

   B: Don't worry. We'll _____.

5. A: Is Dr. Rodriguez going to call off the field trip tomorrow?

   B: He'll only _____ if someone gets sick.

6. A: Good night. Oh, can someone wake Mike up tomorrow morning?

   B: No problem. I'll _____.

28|02 Ⓑ LISTEN AND CHECK Listen to the conversations and check your answers in A.

EXERCISE 5 WORD ORDER

GRAMMAR NOTE 3 Unscramble the words to make sentences. If more than one answer is possible, give both.

1. on / put / your lab coats   *Put on your lab coats.* or *Put your lab coats on.*

2. the experiment / set / up _____

3. out / it / carry _____

4. down / sit / when you're done _____

5. to page 26 / on / go _____

6. up / your reports / write _____

7. in / them / hand _____

8. off / take / your lab coats _____

9. them / put / away _____

10. the lab / clean / up _____

EXERCISE 6 EDITING

GRAMMAR NOTES 1–3 Read these notes from a student's journal. There are nine mistakes in the use of phrasal verbs. The first mistake is already corrected. Find and correct eight more.

---

got back
I just ~~got~~ from Venezuela ~~back~~! I spent two weeks in the Amazon rain forest with Dr. Rodriguez. We carried out research there on plants that the Piaroa people use as medicine. We made down a list of these plants, and we're going to analyze them when we get back to school next week.

We set down camp near the Orinoco River, hundreds of miles from any major city. Life there is hard. You get very early up every morning. You must always watch up and never touch a new insect or plant. If you pick up it, you can get a bad skin rash. But plants can also cure. One day, I felt sick. One of the Piaroa gave me the stem of a certain plant to chew. It worked! Later, I found up that the same plant helps cure insect bites. And believe me, insects are a big problem in the rain forest. I used up many bottles of repellent. But even when I put on it, it didn't totally keep the insects away.

This trip changed my life! I'm now thinking about switching my major to pharmacology. I want to find over more about how people can use the same plants that animals use as medicine.

More Modals and Similar Expressions

9

OUTCOMES

- Express necessity or absence of necessity
- Identify key ideas in an article about travel rules
- Identify details in a conversation about driving regulations
- Recognize and discuss the meaning of common signs
- Discuss rules, regulations, and future plans
- Write a paragraph explaining procedures for obtaining an official document

OUTCOMES

- Express expectations with *be supposed to*
- Identify key points in an article about manners
- Identify details in a conversation about manners
- Discuss customs and life events from one's culture
- Describe an illustration, discussing polite and impolite behavior
- Write a paragraph about a life event in a specific culture

OUTCOMES

- Express likelihood of future events
- Distinguish between possibility and certainty of a future event
- Identify key details in a transcript
- Identify the probability of a situation in a report
- Describe future plans and intentions in detail, giving degrees of probability
- Write an email or short letter that expresses the probability of future plans

OUTCOMES

- Come to conclusions about present situations
- Express varying degrees of certainty about the present
- Identify main ideas in a short story
- Identify the certainty of speakers about events
- Draw conclusions about everyday objects and situations
- Write a paragraph about a short story, drawing possible conclusions

Necessity: *Have (got) to, Must, Can't*

RULES AND REGULATIONS

OUTCOMES
- Express necessity or absence of necessity
- Identify key ideas in an article about travel rules
- Identify details in a conversation about driving regulations
- Recognize and discuss the meaning of common signs
- Discuss rules, regulations, and future plans
- Write a paragraph explaining procedures for obtaining an official document

---

STEP 1   GRAMMAR IN CONTEXT

BEFORE YOU READ

Look at the title and the photo. Discuss the questions.

1. Have you ever traveled to a different country?

2. How did you prepare for your trip?

3. What did you need to know before you went?

READ

▶29|01   Read this article about some rules for international travel.

Know Before You Go

What do international travelers have to know before they go? This week's column answers some questions from our readers.

Q My passport is going to expire in three months. Can I use it for a short trip to Asia next month?

A For many countries, your passport must be valid for at least six months after you enter the country. Renew your passport before you leave, or you'll have to check the rules of each country you plan to visit.

Q I'm a French citizen. Last month, I visited the United States, and I brought some gifts for friends. Why did U.S. Customs agents take the cheese?

A You can't bring most types of soft cheese into the U.S. Many governments have strict rules about bringing food into their countries. To avoid problems, don't bring gifts of fresh food, and eat your snacks on the plane.

Q Do I have to put my laptop computer through the X-ray machine at airport security?[1] I'm worried that the machine will damage it.

A You don't have to put your laptop through the X-ray machine as long as it is in a "checkpoint-friendly" bag.[2] If it isn't, then you must remove it for X-ray inspection. But don't worry. This particular X-ray won't hurt your equipment.

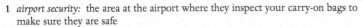

1 *airport security:* the area at the airport where they inspect your carry-on bags to make sure they are safe

2 *checkpoint-friendly bag:* a special bag without zippers or pockets that allows you to keep your laptop in it while you go through airport security

Q I'm from Australia. My family and I are planning a trip to Europe and North America. We'd like to rent cars in a few places. Do I have to get an International Driver's Permit (IDP)?

A Regulations differ: In Italy, for example, you must not drive without an IDP (unless you have a European Union driving license); in Canada, you don't have to have one for a short trip, but it's recommended. For a world tour, you really should get an IDP to avoid problems and disappointment. And remember, you still have to carry a valid driver's license from home in addition to the IDP.

Q I'm planning a trip from Toronto to Hong Kong. There's a new nonstop flight, but it's more expensive, and it's more than fifteen hours long! What do you recommend?

A Several airlines are now offering super-long flights. They provide more comfortable seats, Wi-Fi, and lots of entertainment. They cost a bit more, but you won't have to make as many connecting flights. That saves you time and hassles. But remember: To stay healthy on long flights, you've got to get up and move around. You also must drink plenty of water. On a long flight, these are "musts," not "shoulds"!

AFTER YOU READ

A VOCABULARY Cross out the one word that does not belong in each category.

1. They must be **valid**:	passports	licenses	computers
2. Agents **inspect** them at airports:	rules	luggage	tickets
3. They can be **hassles**:	cars	flights	movies
4. There are **regulations** for them:	sleeping	driving	traveling
5. They can be **strict**:	books	laws	agents
6. They are **equipment**:	cameras	X-ray machines	bags

B COMPREHENSION Read the statements. Check (✓) *True* or *False*.

	True	False
1. Passengers must put computers through security X-ray equipment.	☐	☐
2. A passport is always valid.	☐	☐
3. Travelers are not allowed to bring some types of cheese into the United States.	☐	☐
4. You can't eat cheese on the plane.	☐	☐
5. Non-European Union visitors need an IDP to drive in Italy.	☐	☐
6. It isn't necessary to have an IDP to drive in Canada.	☐	☐
7. To stay healthy on long flights, passengers must stay in their seats.	☐	☐

C DISCUSSION Work with a partner. Compare your answers in B. Why did you check *True* or *False*?

NECESSITY: *HAVE (GOT) TO, NOT HAVE TO*

Affirmative Statements

Subject	Have to/ Have got to	Base Form of Verb	
I You We They	**have to have got to**		
		leave	now.
He She It	**has to has got to**		

Negative Statements*

Subject	Do not	Have to	Base Form of Verb	
I You We They	**don't**			
		have to	**leave**	now.
He She It	**doesn't**			

*There is no negative form for *have got to*.

Contractions*

have got to	=	**'ve got to**
has got to	=	**'s got to**

*There are no contractions for *have to* and *has to*.

Yes/No Questions

Do	Subject	Have to	Base Form of Verb
Do	I you we they		
		have to	**leave?**
Does	he she it		

Short Answers

Affirmative				Negative			
Yes,	you I/we you they	**do.**		**No,**	you I/we you they	**don't.**	
	he she it	**does.**			he she it	**doesn't.**	

Wh- Questions

Wh- Word	Do	Subject	Have to	Base Form of Verb
When	**do**	I you we they		
			have to	**leave?**
	does	he she it		

NECESSITY: *MUST, MUST NOT, CAN'T*

Must*			
Subject	*Must (not)*	Base Form of Verb	
I You He She	**must**	**leave**	very early.
It We They	**must not**	**arrive**	too late.

Contraction
must not = **mustn't**

Can't*			
Subject	*Can't*	Base Form of Verb	
You He They	**can't**	**sit**	over there.

* *Must* and *can't* are modals. Modals have only one form.
They do not have *-s* in the third-person singular.

GRAMMAR NOTES

1 Have to, Have got to, Must

Use *have to*, *have got to*, or the modal *must* to show that something is **necessary**.

• *have to*	You **have to carry** your passport when you travel to most countries.
• *have got to*	I**'ve got to apply** for a new passport right away!
• *must*	All passengers **must show** their passports when they check in.

USAGE NOTE *Have to* is the **most common** expression in conversation and writing. You can also use *have got to* in conversation and **informal** writing.	A: We **have to check in** now. B: OK. But I**'ve got to make** a quick call first.
USAGE NOTE *Must* is much **stronger** than *have to* and *have got to* and is not very common in conversation. Usually only people with power use it (government leaders, police officers, customs agents, teachers, parents).	A: You **must put on** your seat belt. B: Yes, Officer. A: Lia, honey. You really **must pack** tonight. B: OK, Mom.
IN WRITING You will see *must* in **formal writing** and in official forms, signs, and notices that describe **rules and regulations**.	Passengers **must have** their passports out and ready to show the agent before boarding the plane. *(sign)*

2 For Present, Future, and Past Necessity

Use a form of *have (got) to* or *must* to express a **present or future** necessity.	
• **present necessity**	He **has (got) to travel** a lot for his job. You **must turn off** your phone now.
• **future necessity**	We **have (got) to leave** tomorrow. We**'re going to have to leave** at 2:00. We**'ll have to visit** them soon. We **must meet** the new clients tomorrow.
Use a past form of *have to* to express a **past** necessity.	
• **past necessity**	He **had to travel** a lot last year.
BE CAREFUL! *Have got to* and *must* have no past forms. Use only *have to* for the past.	We **had to** work last night. NOT We ~~had got to~~ work last night. NOT We ~~must~~ work last night.

3 Questions

Use *have to* for most questions. Again, it can refer to a **present**, **future**, or **past** necessity.	
• **present necessity**	**Do** you **have to check** your bags?
• **future necessity**	When **do** we **have to get** to the airport? **Are** we **going to have to check** this bag? When **will** we **have to show** our passports?
• **past necessity**	**Did** you **have to renew** your passport?
USAGE NOTE We almost never use *must* in questions.	**Must** I leave right now? *(not common)*
BE CAREFUL! Do not use *have got to* in questions.	**Do** I **have to** leave right now? NOT ~~Have I got to~~ leave right now?

4 Negative Statements

Use a form of *not have to* to show that something is **not necessary**. There is a **choice**.	
• **no present necessity**	Tourists **don't have to have** an IDP in Canada.
• **no future necessity**	We **don't have to get** there before 7:00 p.m. You **won't have to go** through customs.
• **no past necessity**	We **didn't have to show** our passport.
BE CAREFUL! There is no negative form of *have got to*. Use *don't have to*.	Tourists **don't have to** have an IDP in Canada. NOT Tourists ~~haven't got to~~ have an IDP in Canada.

CONTINUED ▶

Use *must not* to express **prohibition** (to say something is **against the rules**). There is **no choice**.	You **must not drive** without a license. It's against the law.
Must not can refer to the **present** or the **future**.	You **must not smoke** on the plane. *(present)* You **must not get up** until the "fasten your seat belt" sign is turned off. *(future)*
The contraction *mustn't* is less formal than *must not*.	You **mustn't forget** to renew your license, Tommy!
BE CAREFUL! In the affirmative, *have (got) to* and *must* have similar meanings. However, *not have to* and *must not* have very **different meanings**.	Passengers **don't have to board** now. *(They can board now, but it isn't necessary.)* Passengers **must not board** now. *(They can't board now. It's against the rules.)*
USAGE NOTE In **conversation**, we often use *can't* instead of *must not* to express prohibition.	You **can't drive** without a license. *(very common)*

PRONUNCIATION NOTE

29|02

Pronunciation of *Have to, Has to, Have got to,* and *Mustn't*

In **informal conversation**, we often pronounce *have to* "hafta" and *has to* "hasta."	A: What time do we **have to** be at the airport? *(hafta)* B: Eight o'clock. But John still **has to** pack. *(hasta)*
For *have got to*, we often pronounce *got to* "gotta," and we sometimes leave out *have*.	We'**ve got to** leave now. *('ve gotta)* or *(gotta)*
We always pronounce the contraction for *must not* "musnt." We never pronounce the first -t in *mustn't*.	You **mustn't** forget to take your passport. *(musnt)*
IN WRITING Sometimes people use *hafta, hasta,* and *gotta* in **informal notes**, **text messages**, and **emails** to friends.	I **gotta** go now. See you later. *(text to friend)*
BE CAREFUL! Do not use *hafta, hasta,* and *gotta* when you write to people you have a formal relationship with.	Dear Professor Chin, I **have to** take my parents to the airport today, so I'll be late for class. *(email)* **NOT** Dear Professor Chin, I ~~hafta~~ take...

REFERENCE NOTES

For general information on **modals**, see Unit 13, Grammar Notes 1–2, on page 125.

For *have (got) to, must,* and *can't* for **present conclusions**, see Unit 32 on page 310.

For *can't* for **ability and possibility** (see Unit 13), for **permission** (see Unit 14), or for **requests** (see Unit 15).

For a list of **modals and their functions**, see Appendix 19 on page 328.

EXERCISE 1 DISCOVER THE GRAMMAR

A GRAMMAR NOTES 1–4 Read Ben Leonard's telephone conversation with a clerk from the Italian consulate. Underline the words that show that something is *necessary*, *not necessary*, or *against the rules*.

BEN: Hello. I'm Australian, and I'm planning to spend several weeks in Europe with my family. I have some questions. First, <u>do we have to get</u> visas to visit Italy?

CLERK: No. Australians don't have to have a visa to enter Italy, but you can't stay for longer than ninety days without one. And, of course, you must have a valid passport to enter the country.

BEN: Can my wife and I use our Australian driver's licenses in Italy?

CLERK: You have to carry your Australian license, but you must also have a valid International Driver's Permit. And you've got to be at least eighteen years old.

BEN: When do we have to get the IDPs? Is it possible to apply for them when we get to Europe?

CLERK: No, you must apply before you leave. The Australian Automobile Association can help you. You'll also have to purchase accident insurance, but you can do this at the car rental agency in Italy.

BEN: We'll be in Italy in January. We don't have a set schedule, so we haven't made any reservations. Is that going to be a problem?

CLERK: Yes. You've really got to have reservations, even in January—especially in major cities like Rome, Florence, or Venice.

BEN: One more question. What about travel insurance? Is it necessary?

CLERK: You don't have to get travel insurance, but we strongly recommend it. That way, if something goes wrong, you can save yourselves a lot of money and hassles.

BEN: You're right. Better safe than sorry! Thanks a lot. You've been very helpful.

B Read the instructions. Check (✓) *Necessary*, *Not Necessary*, or *Against the Rules*.

	Necessary	Not Necessary	Against the Rules
1. Get a visa for a two-week visit.	☐	✓	☐
2. Have a valid passport to enter Italy.	☐	☐	☐
3. Use only an Australian driver's license.	☐	☐	☐
4. Be at least eighteen years old to rent a car.	☐	☐	☐
5. Apply for an IDP in Italy.	☐	☐	☐
6. Buy accident insurance.	☐	☐	☐
7. Buy travel insurance.	☐	☐	☐
8. Make hotel reservations.	☐	☐	☐

EXERCISE 2 AFFIRMATIVE AND NEGATIVE STATEMENTS WITH *HAVE TO*

GRAMMAR NOTES 1, 4 The Leonards have checked off the things they've already done to get ready for their trip. Read the lists and write sentences about what the Leonards still *have to do* and what they *don't have to do*.

BEN
✓ make copies of passports and IDPs

buy euros

give the house keys to Nora

ANN
buy phone cards online

✓ call Pet Care

buy batteries for the camera

✓ stop the mail for two weeks

SEAN AND MAYA
✓ pack clothes

download music for the trip

say good-bye to friends

Ben doesn't have to make copies of passports and IDPs.

He has to buy euros, and he . . .

Ann . . .

_____

_____

_____

_____

_____

_____

_____

EXERCISE 3 QUESTIONS AND STATEMENTS WITH *HAVE (GOT) TO* AND *CAN'T*

GRAMMAR NOTES 1–4 Ben's family is traveling from Australia to Italy. Complete the conversations. Use the correct form of *have to*, *have got to*, or *can't* and the verbs in parentheses. Use short answers.

1. BEN: What time ___*do*___ we ___*have to leave*___ tomorrow?
      a. (leave)

   ANN: We _____ later than 5:30. We _____ with
      b. (leave)   c. (check in)

   the airline by 7:00.

   SEAN: Our flight leaves at 10:00. We've got plenty of time before then. _____ we really

   _____ there so early?
      d. (get)

   ANN: Yes, _____. It takes a long time to check in and get through
      e.

   airport security these days. They're very strict, and they inspect everything. It's a hassle,

   but they _____ it!
      f. (do)

   MAYA: And Mom _____ the car. That takes some time, too!
      g. (park)

2. BEN: Maya, this bag _____ over 50 pounds (23 kilograms), or we
      a. (weigh)

   _____ extra. _____ you _____ so
      b. (pay)   c. (bring)

   many clothes?

   MAYA: Yes, _____. I _____ all my stuff! We'll be
      d.   e. (have)

   gone for weeks.

   ANN: Put some in my bag. And hurry. We _____!
      f. (go)

3. BEN: I'm tired. Why _____ we _____ so long to check in?
      a. (wait)

   ANN: Relax. We _____ much longer. We're next.
      b. (not wait)

4. SEAN: This is exciting! I _____ Randy when we take off. I promised him!
      a. (call)

   BEN: We _____ our phone on this plane. Sorry.
      b. (use)

5. ANN: We _____ around again. Come on, everybody, let's go.
      a. (walk)

   SEAN: Why _____ we _____ all the time?
      b. (get up)

   BEN: Remember our rules? We _____ for more than three hours.
      c. (sit)

   It's unhealthy.

6. MAYA: Are we there yet? This flight is endless!

   ANN: We _____ in here much longer. We're landing in an hour.
      a. (not be)

EXERCISE 4 *MUST* OR *MUST NOT*

GRAMMAR NOTES 1, 4 Complete the rules for airline travel. Use *must* or *must not*.

1. Passengers _____*must arrive*_____ three hours before an international flight.
    (arrive)

2. They _____ their bags with them at all times.
    (keep)

3. Carry-on bags _____ bigger than 45 inches (115 centimeters).
    (be)

4. They _____ under the seat or in the overhead compartment
    (fit)
   of the airplane.

5. They _____ knives, scissors, or other dangerous items.
    (contain)

6. Checked bags _____ labels with the passenger's name.
    (have)

7. They _____ more than 50 pounds (23 kilograms), or there will be
    (weigh)
   additional charges.

8. Travelers _____ identification when they check in with the airline.
    (show)

9. Everyone _____ a ticket in order to go through security.
    (have)

10. On board, passengers _____ when the seat belt sign is on.
    (get up)

11. On many flights, passengers _____ cell phones when the plane is
    (use)
   in the air.

EXERCISE 5
MUST NOT OR
DON'T HAVE TO

GRAMMAR NOTE 4
Read the sign at the
Casa Luciani swimming
pool. Complete each
statement. Use *must not*
or *don't have to*.

Swimming Pool Rules and Regulations

Pool Hours 10:00 a.m.–10:00 p.m.

Children under twelve years NOT
ALLOWED in pool without an adult.

Towels available at front desk.

- NO radio
- NO diving
- NO ball playing
- NO glass bottles
- NO alcoholic beverages

1. Children under age twelve ____*must not (or mustn't) swim*____ without an adult.
    (swim)

2. You _____ your own towel.
    (bring)

3. You _____ ball in or around the pool.
    (play)

4. You _____ into the pool.
    (dive)

5. Teenagers _____ with an adult.
    (swim)

6. You _____ the pool before 10:00 a.m.
    (enter)

7. You _____ the swimming pool at 8:00 p.m.
    (leave)

8. You _____ in the pool past 10:00 p.m.
    (stay)

EXERCISE 6 *HAVE TO* OR *HAFTA*, *GOT TO* OR *GOTTA*

▶29|03 PRONUNCIATION NOTE Listen to the conversations. Check (✓) *More Formal* if you hear *have to*, *got to*, or *must not*. Check (✓) *Less Formal* if you hear *hafta*, *hasta*, *gotta*, or *mustn't*.

		More Formal	Less Formal
1.	A: John has to renew his passport. What about you? B: I don't have to renew mine yet. It's valid for another year.	✓	☐
2.	A: My passport expires next May. B: Oh. You must not forget to renew it. You'll need it when we go to Italy.	☐	☐
3.	A: When does he have to be at the airport? B: He has to be there by 8:00.	☐	☐
4.	A: He's got to leave now. Is he ready? B: Almost. He's got to bring his bags downstairs, that's all.	☐	☐
5.	A: Will we have to show our tickets before we board? B: Yes. And you'll have to show your passports, too.	☐	☐
6.	A: We've got to hurry. B: Relax. We still have plenty of time.	☐	☐
7.	A: Sir, you must not use your phone during take off. B: Oh, sorry. I forgot. I'll turn it off right away.	☐	☐
8.	A: You've got to turn right here. B: No. I have to turn left. Look at the sign.	☐	☐
9.	A: It's 9:00. I've got to go. B: OK. See you later.	☐	☐

EXERCISE 7 EDITING

GRAMMAR NOTES 1–4 **Read Sean's email to his friend. There are six mistakes in expressing necessity. The first mistake is already corrected. Find and correct five more.**

Hi Randy,

                                       had

We're on our way back to Australia. We ~~have~~ to leave the hotel at 5:30 this morning, and then we had got to wait in line at the airport for hours. What a hassle! This flight is great, though. There are TVs at every seat and hundreds of movies to watch. But Mom says we can't sit for more than three hours at a time because it's unhealthy, and we must to drink water every hour when we're not sleeping. This flight is fourteen hours long, so we have to taking care of ourselves. Thanks for the camping knife. I used it a lot in Italy, but before we left, I has to put it in my checked suitcase because of the safety regulations. You don't have to bring knives in carry-on bags. Well, I've got to get up and walk around again. Email me. We'll be on this plane for ten more hours!   —Sean

Expectations:
Be supposed to
MANNERS

STEP 1   GRAMMAR IN CONTEXT

BEFORE YOU READ

Look at the cartoon. Discuss the questions.

1. Who are the people? What is their relationship?

2. Are they having a nice evening? How are they feeling?

3. What is the problem?

READ

30|01   Read this article about manners.

It Was Supposed to Be a Nice Evening

Last week, my friend (let's call her Anna) invited her new boyfriend (we'll call him Andy) home to meet her family for the very first time. It was supposed to be a nice evening, but it didn't exactly turn out as expected. To begin with, Andy came late. He was supposed to arrive at 7:00, but didn't get there until 7:20. Anna was upset. In her family, people always arrive exactly on time. Being even ten minutes late is considered rude. Then, when Anna introduced Andy to her mother, he tried to give her a kiss on the cheek. Her mother was shocked. In her culture, men aren't supposed to kiss women they don't know.

The evening went from bad to worse. When they sat down to eat, Andy put his elbows on the table—a definite no-no[1] in Anna's house, but the norm in Andy's more relaxed home. Andy thought the food was delicious, but when he helped himself to a second serving of potatoes, Anna kicked him under the table. He was supposed to wait until someone offered him more food. Andy sensed there was something wrong, but he didn't know what it was. He tried to break the ice[2] by asking some questions. He asked Anna's father about the nice, new car he saw in the driveway and got a polite answer. But when he asked about the price, there was a very uncomfortable silence around the table. Andy didn't realize that in many families, you aren't supposed to discuss money issues with strangers.

---

1 *no-no:* something people are not supposed to do because it is wrong or dangerous
2 *break the ice:* to say something to make someone you just met feel more comfortable

The details can vary, but the general story probably sounds familiar. Different cultures and even different families often have different rules of behavior. What are good manners for one group may be impolite for another group. For example, in some cultures you're not supposed to make any noise while eating, but in other cultures, such as Japan, slurping[3] is a way of showing that you like the food.

If good manners vary from place to place, how is a person supposed to know what to do? The Internet can provide a lot of helpful information about manners. Even better, you should try to discuss these issues with someone familiar with the situation you are going to be in. Andy needed to talk to Anna about her and her family's expectations before showing up at Anna's home. The evening was a disaster, and Andy and Anna are not seeing each other anymore. Andy feels bad, but he won't make the same mistakes twice. Sometimes experience is the best teacher.

---

3 *slurping:* making noise while you are eating or drinking something like noodles or soup

AFTER YOU READ

A VOCABULARY **Choose the word or phrase that best completes each sentence.**

1. Our plans are **definite**. We won't _____ them.
   a. change   **b.** enjoy   **c.** explain

2. A **rude** person is not _____.
   a. right   **b.** polite   **c.** late

3. The **norm** is the _____ way of doing something.
   a. wrong   **b.** new   **c.** usual

4. Andy **sensed** there was a problem, but he wasn't completely _____ about it.
   a. certain   **b.** unhappy   **c.** comfortable

5. An **issue** is a _____ or problem that people discuss.
   a. magazine   **b.** story   **c.** topic

6. If you are **familiar** with a custom, you _____ something about it.
   a. like   **b.** know   **c.** ask

B COMPREHENSION **Read the statements. Check (✓) *True* or *False*. If there isn't enough information in the reading to answer, check *Don't Know*.**

	True	False	Don't Know
1. Andy and Anna expected to have a nice evening.	☐	☐	☐
2. Andy arrived on time.	☐	☐	☐
3. He kissed Anna's mother.	☐	☐	☐
4. Anna's father wanted to discuss the price of the family car.	☐	☐	☐
5. Andy made noises while he was eating.	☐	☐	☐
6. It was OK for Andy to take more potatoes.	☐	☐	☐

C DISCUSSION **Work with a partner. Compare your answers in B. Why did you check *True, False,* or *Don't Know*?**

EXPECTATIONS: *BE SUPPOSED TO*

Statements

Subject	Be	(Not)	Supposed to	Base Form of Verb	
I	am was				
You We They	are were	(not)	supposed to	arrive	at 7:00.
He She It	is was				

Yes/No Questions

Be	Subject	Supposed to	Base Form of Verb
Am Was	I		
Are Were	you	supposed to	call?
Is Was	she		

Short Answers

Affirmative				Negative		
Yes,	you	are. were.		No,	you	aren't. weren't.
	I	am. was.			I	'm not. wasn't.
	she	is. was.			she	isn't. wasn't.

Wh- Questions

Wh- Word	Be	Subject	Supposed to	Base Form of Verb
Where	am was	I	supposed to	sit?
	are were	you		
	is was	she		

GRAMMAR NOTES

1 Be supposed to for Different Kinds of Expectations

Use the expression **be supposed to** + **base form** of the verb to express different kinds of expectations.

• **rules**	You**'re supposed to turn** right here. You can't turn left.
• **customs** (usual ways of doing things)	You**'re supposed to bring** a small gift.
• **predictions**	The forecast says it**'s supposed to rain** tonight.
• **hearsay** (something you have heard from other people, but don't know to be true)	Anna **is supposed to be** very nice. Everyone says so.
• **plans** or **arrangements**	Let's hurry. We**'re supposed to be** there at 7:00. They're expecting us then.

IN WRITING **Be supposed to** is common in conversation, informal writing (emails, text messages), and in journalistic writing (newspapers, magazines). However, in formal writing, it is more common to use other expressions, such as: *It is customary to.*	You**'re supposed to bring** a gift. *(conversation)* What time **are** we **supposed to get** there? *(email)* In the past, people **were supposed to write** a thank-you note to their dinner host. *(magazine)* **It is customary to** bring a gift. *(formal writing)*

2 Be supposed to for Present, Future, and Past Expectations

You can use a form of **be supposed to** to express a **present**, **future**, or **past** expectation.

• **present expectation**	You**'re supposed to wait** until someone offers you more food. *(simple present)*
• **future expectation**	It**'s supposed to be** nice tomorrow. *(simple present)*
• **past expectation**	They **were supposed to get** there by 6:00 p.m. yesterday, so they took a taxi. *(simple past)*

USAGE NOTE We often use *was/were supposed to* when something we expected to happen did not happen.	Andy **was supposed to arrive** at 7:00, but he came late.
BE CAREFUL! For future expectations, do not use *will* with *be supposed to.*	We**'re supposed to** help out tomorrow. NOT We ~~will be~~ supposed to help out tomorrow.

3 Word Order in Negative Statements

Use this word order in negative statements: **subject** + *be not* + *supposed to* + **base form** of the verb	You**'re not supposed to arrive** late.
BE CAREFUL! *Not* goes directly **before** *supposed*. Do not use *not* after *supposed*.	You**'re not supposed to kiss** her mother. NOT You're ~~supposed not to~~ kiss her mother. NOT You're ~~supposed to not~~ kiss her mother.

EXERCISE 1 DISCOVER THE GRAMMAR

Ⓐ GRAMMAR NOTES 1–3 Read this article about manners. Underline the phrases that express expectations.

Manners

THE GOOD,
THE BAD,
AND THE CONFUSING

THE DICTIONARY defines *manners* as polite ways of behaving in social situations. Manners are governed by rules (called *etiquette*). They tell us what we <u>are supposed to do</u> and, just as important, what we are not supposed to do. Manners are like the oil in a machine. They are supposed to make things run more smoothly.

Some examples of "good" manners seem very logical and easy to understand. You are supposed to hold the door open for the person behind you. If you don't, the door can hit the person in the face. In some cultures, you are not supposed to keep your street shoes on when you enter someone's home. Leaving your shoes on is considered "bad" manners. It's rude because they bring dirt into the home. Again, the reason for the custom is clear. But why in many cultures are you supposed to shake hands when you meet someone for the first time? Many historians believe that in the past, the handshake was supposed to prove that people were not hiding weapons (knives, for example) up their sleeve.

Many customs, such as the handshake, have complicated rules connected to them. Who is supposed to offer their hand first? How firmly and for how long are you supposed to hold the other person's hand? If you are wearing gloves, are you supposed to remove your glove before shaking hands? The answers to these and other questions vary from culture to culture. It can be confusing, and it is not always easy to know the right thing to do.

B Read each sentence. Then write a sentence based on the information from A that has a similar meaning.

1. The rules of etiquette give us information about what is OK behavior.

   They tell us what we are supposed to do.

2. The purpose of manners is to help make social interactions easier.

   _____

3. Holding the door open for the person behind you is an example of good manners.

   _____

4. Leaving your street shoes on when you enter someone's home is an example of bad manners.

   _____

5. Shaking hands used to show that you didn't have a weapon up your sleeve.

   _____

6. How long should you hold the other person's hand?

   _____

EXERCISE 2 AFFIRMATIVE AND NEGATIVE STATEMENTS

GRAMMAR NOTES 1–3 Read about manners in different countries. Complete the sentences with the correct form of *be supposed to* and the words in parentheses. Choose between affirmative and negative.

In the United States   You _____ *'re supposed to stand up* _____ when you're introduced
                                        1. (stand up)
to an older person. It's rude to stay seated.

In China   You _____ white or black to a wedding.
                                 2. (wear)
These colors are connected to death.

In Turkey   You _____ the bottom of your shoes when
                                 3. (show)
you are sitting. It's impolite because they aren't clean.

In Argentina   You _____ at a party thirty to sixty
                                 4. (arrive)
minutes later than the "starting" time. It's the norm.

In Japan   You _____ gifts in front of the gift giver. It's
                                 5. (open)
not polite.

In Brazil   You _____ gifts immediately. Don't wait
                                 6. (open)
until later.

In Jordan   You _____ a little food on your plate when
                                 7. (leave)
you are finished eating. This shows your host that he or she gave you enough to eat.

EXERCISE 3 AFFIRMATIVE AND NEGATIVE STATEMENTS

GRAMMAR NOTES 1–3 Read about table manners in the United States. Rewrite the rules with *be supposed to*. Choose between affirmative and negative.

1. Don't put your elbows on the table.

   You're not supposed to put your elbows on the table.

2. Chew with your mouth closed.

   _____

3. Don't reach across the table for food. Ask someone to pass it.

   _____

4. Eat quietly.

   _____

5. Use your napkin to clean your fingers and mouth.

   _____

6. Keep your napkin on your lap when you are not using it.

   _____

7. Do not start eating before your host.

   _____

8. Do not comb your hair at the table.

   _____

9. Don't put your napkin on the chair when you are finished eating.

   _____

10. Say "Excuse me" if you leave the table before the end of a meal.

   _____

EXERCISE 4 QUESTIONS AND STATEMENTS

Ⓐ GRAMMAR NOTES 1–3 Complete the conversations. Use the verbs in parentheses and the correct form of *be supposed to*. Choose between the simple present and simple past.

1. A: Carlos invited me to dinner at his parents' home tonight.

   B: Oh, that's nice. What time ____are____ you ____supposed to get____ there?

a. (get)

   A: He said 7:00. Tell me, _____ I _____ something? I'm

b. (bring)

   not familiar with the customs here.

   B: Why don't you bring flowers?

2. A: Last time I met Mia's mother, I shook her hand. I sensed that something was wrong. She

   seemed a little uncomfortable. _____ I _____ that?

a. (do)

B: I'm not sure. I think you _____ until the woman offers her
   b. (wait)

   hand first.

3. A: It _____ tonight, so don't forget your umbrella.
      a. (rain)

   B: I'm driving, so it won't be a problem. But I'm a little nervous about going to a formal dinner.

   A: Don't worry. The Chandlers _____ very nice. Everyone
      b. (be)

   likes them.

4. A: What _____ I _____ Miguel's mother?
      a. (call)

   B: Call her *Mrs. Gomez*, unless she tells you to use her first name.

5. A: Are you going to the party alone?

   B: Yes. I _____ with Teresa, but she's sick.
      a. (go)

6. A: What _____ I _____ when I meet Ina's parents?
      a. (say)

   B: Just say, "It's nice to meet you." And try to relax. You'll meet a lot of nice people there. It's a

   party. It _____ fun!
      b. (be)

30|02 **B** LISTEN AND CHECK **Listen to the conversations and check your answers in A.**

EXERCISE 5 EDITING

GRAMMAR NOTES 1–3 **Read this Q & A on etiquette and manners. Find and correct eight mistakes in the use of *be supposed to*. The first mistake is already corrected. Find and correct seven more.**

● ● ●

 # What's the Right Thing to Do?

Q: I had dinner at a friend's house last week. The first course was soup and it was already on the table. When

I sat down, I began to eat it. My friend's mother looked a little surprised. Did I do something wrong? ~~Am~~ I
                                                                                                    Was

supposed to wait before starting to eat?

A: Yes. In this country, you supposed to wait until your host begins or says, "Please begin." You are supposed

not to start first.

Q: My friend is getting married, and he chose me to be his "best man." What does this mean? As the best

man, what I am supposed to do?

A: First of all, you should feel very good. It is an honor to be the best man. In general, the best man's job is

to help the groom. You can find online lists with all your tasks (and there are many!). Perhaps one of the most important ones is that you are supposed to keep the ring for your friend until he needs it during the ceremony. (Nervous grooms are famous for forgetting or losing the ring.)

Q: We supposed to get married, but we just decided to cancel the wedding. We've already received some wedding gifts. What do we do with them? Do we supposed to return them to our friends and relatives now that the wedding is canceled?

A: Yes, unfortunately you are supposed to return all the gifts you received—unless you have already used them.

Q: I was in line at the supermarket waiting to pay. It was the "express" line, but the woman in front of me had a shopping cart filled with food and beverages. I had just one item. I said to the woman, "Sorry, but you are supposed to not be on this line if you have more than ten items." She got very angry at me. Was I wrong to say something?

A: No, you weren't wrong, the woman was wrong. First, for being in the wrong line, and then for getting angry at you. People are supposing to follow the rules, and her behavior was a definite violation of the rules. You were right to say something—as long as you did it politely.

Future Possibility:
May, Might, Could
WEATHER

OUTCOMES
- Express likelihood of future events
- Distinguish between possibility and certainty of a future event
- Identify key details in a transcript
- Identify the probability of a situation in a report
- Describe future plans and intentions in detail, giving degrees of probability
- Write an email or short letter that expresses the probability of future plans

---

STEP 1   GRAMMAR IN CONTEXT

BEFORE YOU READ

Look at the weather map for Europe. Discuss the questions.

1. Are the temperatures in Celsius or Fahrenheit?

2. What are the possible high and low temperatures for Ankara?

3. What's the weather forecast for Moscow? For London?

READ

31|01   Read this transcript of a weather report on British TV.

Weather Watch

CAROL: Good morning. I'm Carol Johnson, and here's the local forecast for tomorrow, Wednesday, January 10. The cold front that has been affecting much of northern Europe is moving quickly toward Great Britain. Temperatures may drop as much

as 11 degrees by late tomorrow afternoon. In London, expect a high of only 2 and a low of –4 degrees. We might even see some snow flurries[1] later on in the day. By evening, winds could exceed 40 miles per hour. So, bundle up;[2] it's going to be a cold one! And now it's time for our travelers' forecast with Ethan Harvey. Ethan?

ETHAN: Thank you, Carol. Take your umbrella if you're traveling to Paris. Stormy conditions may move into France by tomorrow morning. Rain could turn into snow by evening when temperatures fall to near or below freezing in the region. But look at the forecast for Italy! You may not need your coat at all if you plan to be in Rome, where we'll see partly cloudy skies with early morning temperatures around only 10 degrees on Wednesday. But later in the day, temperatures could climb to above 20 as skies clear up in the afternoon. The warming trend could reach the rest of western Europe by Thursday. But if not, it still looks like it will turn out to be a beautiful, sunny weekend in central Italy, Carol.

CAROL: Italy sounds great! Will you join me on a Roman holiday, Ethan?

ETHAN: I might!

---

1 *flurries:* small amounts of light snow that fall and blow around
2 *bundle up:* wear warm clothes

AFTER YOU READ

A VOCABULARY **Choose the word or phrase that best completes each sentence.**

1. A weather **forecast** tells you about _____ weather.
   a. foreign   b. yesterday's   c. tomorrow's

2. **Local** news gives you information about places that are _____ you.
   a. near   b. far from   c. interesting to

3. When the weather **affects** people, they always feel _____.
   a. better   b. worse   c. different

4. A **region** is a(n) _____.
   a. area   b. ocean   c. city

5. If winds **exceed** 30 miles per hour, they will be _____ 30 miles per hour.
   a. exactly   b. less than   c. more than

B COMPREHENSION **Read the statements. Check (✓) *True* or *False*.**

	True	False
1. Temperatures will definitely drop 11 degrees in Great Britain.	☐	☐
2. Snow is possible in London.	☐	☐
3. There will definitely be stormy weather in France.	☐	☐
4. Snow is possible in Paris.	☐	☐
5. Western Europe is going to get colder.	☐	☐
6. Temperatures will definitely be above 20 degrees Celsius in Rome.	☐	☐

C DISCUSSION **Work with a partner. Compare your answers in B. Why did you check *True* or *False*?**

FUTURE POSSIBILITY: *MAY, MIGHT, COULD*

Statements

Subject	Modal*	Base Form of Verb	
You It They	**may** (not) **might** (not) **could**	**get**	cold.

* *May, might,* and *could* are modals. Modals have only one form. They do not have *-s* in the third-person singular.

Yes/No Questions

Are you going to fly to Paris? Are you leaving on Monday?		
Are you going to Will you Is it possible you'll	**be**	there long?

Short Answers

I	**may** (not).* **might** (not).* **could**.	
We	**may** (not)* **might** (not)* **could**	**(be)**.

* *May not* and *might not* are not contracted.

Wh- Questions

When are you **going** to Paris?
How long are you going to **be** there?

Answers

I	**may**	**go**	next week.
We	**could**	**be**	there a week.

GRAMMAR NOTES

1 Affirmative Statements

Use the modals *may*, *might*, and *could* to express the **possibility** that something **will happen** in the future.

May, *might*, and *could* have very similar meanings. You can use any one to express **future possibility**.

- *may*
- *might*
- *could*

It **may rain** tonight. *(It's possible.)*
It **might rain** tonight. *(It's possible.)*
It **could rain** tonight. *(It's possible.)*

Remember that we use a **form of the future** (*be going to* or *will*) when we are **certain** that something **will happen**. (See Unit 6.)

It**'s going to rain** tonight. *(It's certain.)*

BE CAREFUL! *May be* and *maybe* both express possibility. Notice these differences:

May be is a modal + *be*. It is always two words.

Demetrios **may be** late today.

Maybe is an adverb. It is always one word, and it usually comes at the beginning of the sentence.

Maybe he'll take the train.
NOT He'll maybe take the train.

2 Negative Statements

Use *may not* and *might not* to express the **possibility** that something **will not happen** in the future.

• *may not*	There are a lot of clouds, but it **may not rain**.
• *might not*	There are a lot of clouds, but it **might not rain**.
	(It's possible that it won't rain, but we're not certain.)

Remember that we use a **form of the future** (*not be going to* or *won't*) when we are **certain** that something **will not happen**. (See Unit 6.)	You **won't need** a coat.
	(I'm certain that you will not need a coat.)

BE CAREFUL! We **never contract** *may not*, and we rarely contract *might not*.	You **may not** need a coat.
	NOT You ~~mayn't~~ need a coat.

3 Questions and Answers

Questions about future possibility do not usually use *may*, *might*, or *could*, but **answers** to these questions often **use *may*, *might*, or *could*.**

Questions about future possibility usually use *will*, *be going to*, the present progressive, or the simple present. They rarely use *may*, *might*, or *could*.	When **will** it **start** snowing?
	When **might** it **start** snowing? *(rare)*

Answers to questions about future possibility often use *may*, *might*, or *could*.	A: **Are** you **going to drive** to work?
	B: I don't know. I **may take** the bus.
	A: When **are** you **leaving**?
	B: I **might leave** in a few minutes.
	A: Do you think it**'ll snow** tomorrow?
	B: It **could stop** tonight.

In **short answers** to *yes/no* questions, we usually use *may*, *might*, or *could* alone. We do not repeat the main verb in the question.	A: **Will** your office **close** early?
	B: It **may**. **or** It **may not**.
	NOT It may not ~~close~~.

USAGE NOTE If *be* is the main verb, it is common to include *be* in the short answer.	A: **Will** our flight **be** on time?
	B: It **might be**. **or** It **might**.
	It **might not be**. **or** It **might not**.

REFERENCE NOTES

For general information on **modals**, see Unit 13, Grammar Notes 1–2, on page 125.

For *may* for **permission**, see Unit 14 on page 133.

For *might* for **present conclusions**, see Unit 32 on page 310.

For *could* for **ability and possibility** (see Unit 13), for **permission** (see Unit 14), for **requests** (see Unit 15), and for **present conclusions** (see Unit 32).

For a list of **modals and their functions**, see Appendix 19 on page 328.

EXERCISE 1 DISCOVER THE GRAMMAR

Ⓐ GRAMMAR NOTES 1–3 Anna is a college student who works part-time; Cody is her husband. Read their conversation. Underline the words that express future possibility.

ANNA: Are you going to drive to work tomorrow?

CODY: I don't know. I <u>might</u>. Why?

ANNA: I just heard the local weather report. A cold front is moving into the region. It may snow tonight.

CODY: Oh, then I may have to shovel snow before I leave. You know, on second thought, I might just take the 7:30 train instead of driving. I have a 9:00 meeting, and I don't want to miss it. Do you have a class tomorrow morning?

ANNA: No, but I'm going to the library to work on my paper. Maybe I'll bundle up and take the train with you in the morning. And let's try to go home together, too. Maybe we could meet at the train station at 6:00, OK? I'm taking the 6:30 train home.

CODY: I might not be able to catch the 6:30 train. My boss said something about working late tomorrow. I may be stuck there until 8:00. I'll call you tomorrow afternoon and let you know what I'm doing.

ANNA: OK. I'll get some takeout on the way home. Do you mind eating late?

CODY: No. I definitely want to have dinner together.

ANNA: Me too. Definitely.

Ⓑ Read the conversation again. Check (✓) *Certain* or *Possible* for each activity that they discuss.

CODY	Certain	Possible
1. drive to work		✓
2. shovel snow		
3. take 7:30 a.m. train		
4. 9:00 meeting		
5. work until 8:00 p.m.		
6. call Anna		
7. dinner with Anna		

ANNA	Certain	Possible
1. go to library	✓	
2. work on paper		
3. take train with Cody		
4. 6:00 p.m.—meet Cody		
5. take 6:30 train home		
6. buy takeout for dinner		
7. dinner with Cody		

EXERCISE 2 AFFIRMATIVE AND NEGATIVE STATEMENTS

GRAMMAR NOTES 1–2 Anna is graduating from college with a degree in meteorology.[1]
Circle the correct words to complete her journal entry.

I just got the notice from my school. I might not / (I'm going to) graduate in June, but I still
                                                   1.

don't know what I'm going to do after graduation. Some TV stations hire students to help

out their meteorologists, so I could / may not apply for a job next month. On the other hand,
                                      2.

I might / might not apply to graduate school and get my master's degree in atmospheric
         3.

science. I'm just not sure, though—these past two years have been really hard, and I

may / may not be ready to study for two more years. At least I am sure about my career.
    4.

I'm going to / I might forecast the weather—that's certain. I made an appointment to discuss
          5.

my grades with my advisor, Mrs. Humphrey, tomorrow. I maybe / may talk about my plans
                                                         6.

with her. She won't / might have an idea about what I should do.
         7.

---

1 meteorology: the scientific study of weather

EXERCISE 3
STATEMENTS WITH MAY, MIGHT, BE GOING TO

GRAMMAR NOTE 1 Look at Anna's
schedule for Monday. She put a
question mark (?) next to each
item she wasn't sure about. Write
sentences about Anna's plans for
Monday. Use may or might (for
things that are possible) and be
going to (for things that are certain).

MONDAY

1. call Cody at 9:00
2. buy some notebooks before class ?
3. go to the meeting with Mrs. Humphrey at 11:00
4. have coffee with Sue after class ?
5. go to work at 1:00
6. go shopping for snow boots after work ?
7. take the 7:00 train ?

1. Anna is going to call Cody at 9:00.

2. _____

3. _____

4. _____

5. _____

6. _____

7. _____

EXERCISE 4 SHORT ANSWERS

Ⓐ GRAMMAR NOTE 3 Complete the conversations with short answers. Use *could* (for things that are possible) or *won't* (for things that are certain). Use *be* when possible.

1. A: Do you think the roads will be dangerous? It's snowing really hard.

   B: _They could be._ _____ It's a big storm.

2. A: Will the schools stay open?

   B: I'm sure _____. It's too dangerous for school buses.

3. A: Will it be very windy?

   B: _____ The winds are very strong already. They might even exceed 40 miles per hour. So, bundle up!

4. A: Will it get warmer later today?

   B: _____, unfortunately. The temperature in Centerville is already below zero.

5. A: Is it possible that the storm will be over by tomorrow?

   B: _____ It's moving pretty quickly across the region now.

6. A: Do you think it will be warmer on Tuesday?

   B: _____ There seems to be a warming trend. It's stopped snowing already.

31|02 **Ⓑ** LISTEN AND CHECK Listen to the conversations and check your answers in A.

EXERCISE 5 EDITING

GRAMMAR NOTES 1–3 Read this student's report about El Niño. There are seven mistakes in the use of *may*, *might*, and *could*. The first mistake is already corrected. Find and correct six more.

Every few years, the ocean near Peru becomes warmer. This change is called El Niño. El Niño
~~maybe~~ cause big weather changes all over the world. The west coasts of North and South America

might have very heavy rains. On the other side of the Pacific, New Guinea might becomes very

dry. Northern regions could have warmer, wetter winters, and southern areas maybe become

much colder. These weather changes affect plants and animals. Some fish mayn't survive in

warmer waters. They may die or swim to colder places. In addition, dry conditions could causing

crops to die. When that happens, food may get very expensive. El Niño does not happen regularly.

It may happen every two years, or it might not come for seven years. Will El Niño get worse in

the future? It could be. Pollution will increase the effects of El Niño, but no one is sure yet.

Present Conclusions:
Must, Have (got) to, May, Might, Could, Can't
MYSTERIES

OUTCOMES
- Come to conclusions about present situations
- Express varying degrees of certainty about the present
- Identify main ideas in a short story
- Identify the certainty of speakers about events
- Draw conclusions about everyday objects and situations
- Write a paragraph about a short story, drawing possible conclusions

STEP 1	GRAMMAR IN CONTEXT

BEFORE YOU READ

Look at the photo. Discuss the questions.

1. Who is Sherlock Holmes?
2. Have you ever read or watched a Sherlock Holmes mystery?
3. Do you like mystery stories? Why?

READ

▶ 32|01 Read the first part of this Sherlock Holmes story.

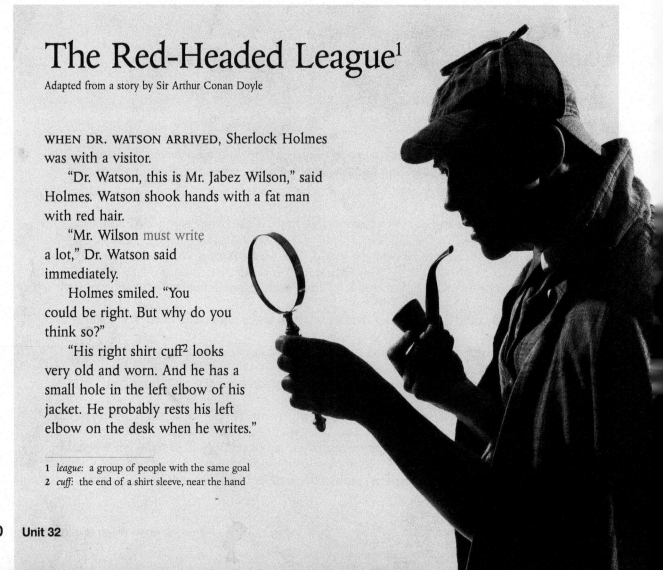

The Red-Headed League¹

Adapted from a story by Sir Arthur Conan Doyle

WHEN DR. WATSON ARRIVED, Sherlock Holmes was with a visitor.

"Dr. Watson, this is Mr. Jabez Wilson," said Holmes. Watson shook hands with a fat man with red hair.

"Mr. Wilson must write a lot," Dr. Watson said immediately.

Holmes smiled. "You could be right. But why do you think so?"

"His right shirt cuff² looks very old and worn. And he has a small hole in the left elbow of his jacket. He probably rests his left elbow on the desk when he writes."

---

1 *league:* a group of people with the same goal
2 *cuff:* the end of a shirt sleeve, near the hand

Wilson looked amazed. "Dr. Watson is correct," he told Holmes. "Your methods may be useful after all."

"Please tell Dr. Watson your story," said Holmes. Dr. Watson looked very interested.

"I have a small shop," began the red-headed man.

"I don't have many customers, so I was very interested in this advertisement. My clerk, Vincent, showed it to me." He showed Watson a newspaper ad that said:

> An American millionaire started the Red-Headed League to help red-headed men. The League now has one position open. The salary is £4 per week for four hours of work every day. The job is to copy the encyclopedia in our offices.

"They couldn't pay someone just for having red hair and copying the encyclopedia," Watson laughed. "This has to be a joke."

"It might not be," said Holmes. "Listen to Wilson tell the rest of his story."

"I got the job, and I worked at the League for two months. Then this morning I found a note on the door." Wilson gave Holmes the note...

(to be continued)

AFTER YOU READ

A VOCABULARY **Complete the sentences with the words from the box.**

advertisement	amazed	method	position	salary

1. Dr. Watson read the newspaper _____.

2. It's strange. The job is very easy, but the _____ is high.

3. Dr. Watson uses a special _____ to solve mysteries.

4. Mr. Wilson took the _____ at the Red-Headed League.

5. Mr. Wilson was _____. How did Dr. Watson know that he writes a lot?

B COMPREHENSION **Circle the correct information to complete each statement.**

1. Dr. Watson is <u>very sure</u> / <u>thinks it is possible</u> that Mr. Wilson writes a lot.

2. Holmes thinks Watson is <u>definitely</u> / <u>possibly</u> right.

3. Wilson thinks Watson's methods will <u>definitely</u> / <u>possibly</u> work.

4. Watson <u>believes</u> / <u>doesn't believe</u> the League pays people just to copy the encyclopedia.

5. Watson thinks the ad <u>is</u> / <u>is not</u> a joke.

6. Holmes thinks the ad is <u>definitely</u> / <u>possibly</u> not a joke.

C DISCUSSION **Work with a partner. Compare your answers in B. Why did you choose each answer?**

PRESENT CONCLUSIONS: *MUST, HAVE (GOT) TO, MAY, MIGHT, COULD, CAN'T*

Affirmative Statements

Subject	Modal*	Base Form of Verb	
I You He It They	must may might could	be	wrong.

Negative Statements

Subject	Modal + *Not*	Base Form of Verb	
I You He It They	must not may not might not couldn't can't	be	right.

*Must, may, might, could, and *can't* are modals. Modals have only one form. They do not have *-s* in the third-person singular.

Affirmative Statements with *Have (got) to*

Subject	*Have (got) to*	Base Form	
I You They	have (got) to	be	right.
He It	has (got) to		

Yes/No Questions

Can/Could	Subject	Base Form	
Could Can	he	know	that?

Do	Subject	Base Form	
Does	he	know	that?

Short Answers

Subject	Modal
He	must (not). may (not). might (not). could(n't). has (got) to. can't.

Yes/No Questions with *Be*

Can/Could	Subject	Be	
Could Can	he	be	a detective?

Be	Subject	
Is	he	a detective?

Short Answers

Subject	Modal	Be
He	must (not) may (not) might (not) could(n't) has (got) to can't	be.

Wh- Questions with *Can* and *Could*

Wh- Word	Can/Could	Subject	Base Form
Who What	can could	it they	be? want?

GRAMMAR NOTES

1 Conclusions and Degrees of Certainty

We often make guesses and come to **conclusions** about present situations using the facts we have.

We use **modals** and similar expressions to show how **certain or uncertain** we are about our conclusions.

Affirmative		Negative
must	**VERY CERTAIN**	*can't, couldn't*
have (got) to		*must not*
may, might, could	**LESS CERTAIN**	*may not, might not*

FACT	CONCLUSION
He has only one clerk.	His shop **must be** very small.
I just saw him.	He **can't be** dead!
The lights are on.	He **has to be** there.
The shop is dark.	He **must not be** there.
His sleeve has a hole.	He **may write** a lot.
He seems calm.	He **may not know** the news.

Use **the simple present** when you are **completely certain** about something.

He**'s** a detective. He **investigates** crimes.

2 Affirmative Conclusions About Present Situations

Use **affirmative modals** to show that you think something is **probable** or **possible** because of the facts you have.

Use *must*, *have to*, or *have got to* if you are **very certain** about your conclusion and you think something is **probable**.

• *must*	Wilson has only one clerk. His shop **must be** very small. *(His shop is probably very small.)*
• *have to*	Wilson applied for a position. He **has to need** money. *(He probably needs money.)*
• *have got to*	They pay men for having red hair. It**'s got to be** a joke. *(It's probably a joke.)*

Use *may*, *might*, or *could* if you are **less certain** about your conclusions and you think something is **possible**.

• *may*	Wilson has a hole in his sleeve. He **may write** a lot. *(It's possible that he writes a lot.)*
• *might*	Vincent knows a lot about cameras. He **might be** a photographer. *(It's possible he's a photographer.)*
• *could*	Holmes solves a lot of crimes. His method **could be** a good one. *(It's possible his method is a good one.)*

Use **negative modals** to show that you think something is **impossible** because of the facts you have.

Use *can't* and *couldn't* when you are **almost 100 percent certain** that something is impossible. Use *must not* when you are **slightly less certain**.	
• *can't*	He **can't be** dead! I just saw him. *(It's impossible that he's dead.)*
• *couldn't*	Vincent **couldn't be** dishonest. He works for half-pay. *(I'm almost certain that he is not dishonest.)*
• *must not*	He **must not earn** a good salary. He always needs money. *(He probably doesn't earn a good salary.)*
BE CAREFUL! Do not use the contraction *mustn't* for a conclusion about a present situation.	He **must not** be at work. NOT He ~~mustn't~~ be at work.
Use *may not* and *might not* when you are **even less certain**.	
• *may not*	He **may not know** about the plan. He seems very calm. *(It's possible that he doesn't know about the plan.)*
• *might not*	His boss **might not tell** him everything. She doesn't trust him. *(It's possible that his boss doesn't tell him everything.)*
BE CAREFUL! Do not use *have to* and *have got to* for negative conclusions.	It **can't** be true! NOT It ~~doesn't have to~~ be true!

Use *can* and *could* in **questions**.	Someone's coming. Who **can** it be? **Could** Vincent **be** in the shop?
In **short answers**, use a modal alone.	A: *Does* she still *work* at Wilson's? B: She **may not**. I saw a new clerk there. NOT She may not ~~work~~.
BE CAREFUL! Use *be* in short answers to questions with *be*.	A: *Is* Ron still with City Bank? B: I'm not sure. He **might not be**.

REFERENCE NOTES

For *may*, *can*, and *could* for **permission**, see Unit 14 on page 133.

For *must*, *have to*, and *have got to* for **necessity**, see Unit 29 on page 271.

For *may*, *might*, and *could* for **future possibility**, see Unit 31 on page 303.

For a list of **modals and their functions**, see Appendix 19 on page 328.

For the **pronunciation and usage** of *have to* and *have got to*, see Unit 29 on page 282.

EXERCISE 1 DISCOVER THE GRAMMAR

Ⓐ GRAMMAR NOTES 1-4 Read the next part of "The Red-Headed League." Underline the verbs that express conclusions.

The Red-Headed League *(continued)*

Sherlock Holmes studied the note: *The Red-Headed League does not exist anymore.*

"This <u>could be</u> serious," Holmes told Wilson. "What can you tell us about your clerk Vincent?"

"Vincent couldn't be dishonest," replied Wilson. "In fact, he took this job for half the usual salary because he wanted to learn the business. His only fault is photography."

"Photography?" Holmes and Watson asked together.

"Yes," replied Wilson. "He's always running down to the basement to work with his cameras."

Wilson left soon after that.

"Wilson's clerk might be the key to this mystery," Holmes told Watson. "Let's go see him." An hour later, Holmes and Watson walked into Wilson's shop. The clerk was a man of about thirty, with a scar on his forehead.

Holmes asked him for directions. Then he and Watson left the shop.

"My dear Watson," Holmes began. "It's very unusual for a thirty-year-old man to work for half-pay. This clerk has to have a very special reason for working here."

"Could it have something to do with the Red-Headed League?" Watson asked.

"Yes. Perhaps the clerk placed that ad in the newspaper. He may want to be alone in the shop. Did you look at his legs?"

"No, I didn't."

"He has holes in his trouser knees. He must spend his time digging a tunnel from Wilson's basement. But where is it?"

Holmes hit the ground sharply with his walking stick. "The ground isn't hollow, so the tunnel can't be here in front of the shop. Let's walk to the street in back of Wilson's shop."

B Read the second part of the story again. How certain is Sherlock Holmes about each of the statements? Check (✓) *Very Certain* or *Less Certain* for each statement.

	Very Certain	Less Certain
1. Something serious is happening.	☐	☑
2. The clerk is the key to the mystery.	☐	☐
3. The clerk has a special reason for working in Mr. Wilson's shop.	☐	☐
4. He wants to be alone in the shop.	☐	☐
5. He's digging a tunnel from Wilson's basement.	☐	☐
6. The tunnel isn't in front of the shop.	☐	☐

EXERCISE 2 AFFIRMATIVE AND NEGATIVE STATEMENTS

GRAMMAR NOTES 1–3 Read each statement and look at the illustration for the story "The Red-Headed League." Come to a conclusion and circle the appropriate modal.

1. It (must) / could be very late.

2. It must / must not be hot outside.

3. Number 27 might / can't be a bank.

4. The delivery couldn't / might be for the bank.

5. The box could / must not contain gold.

6. The two men on the sidewalk must not / could notice the delivery.

7. The manager might not / must want people to know about this delivery.

8. Robbers may / can't know about it.

EXERCISE 3 *MUST* AND *MUST NOT*

GRAMMAR NOTES 1–3 Look at the poster and the map of Mr. Wilson's neighborhood. Read each statement of fact. Write a conclusion. Use the words in parentheses with *must* and *must not*.

1. Wilson's clerk is the man on the poster.

He must be a criminal.
(he / be a criminal)

2. The man on the poster is named John Clay.

_____
(Vincent / be the clerk's real name)

3. Wilson trusts Vincent.

_____
(he / know about the poster)

4. Clay has committed a lot of crimes, but the police haven't caught him.

_____
(he / be very clever)

5. The address of the bank on the map and the address in the picture for Exercise 2 are the same.

_____
(number 27 Carlisle Street / be City Bank)

6. The hat shop and the drugstore don't make much money.

_____
(Vincent's tunnel / lead to those shops)

7. There's a lot of money in the bank, and it's very close to Wilson's shop.

_____
(Vincent's tunnel / lead to the bank)

8. The bank is expecting a shipment of gold.

_____
(the tunnel / be almost finished)

EXERCISE 4 *HAVE GOT TO* AND *CAN'T*

(A) GRAMMAR NOTES 1–3 Ann and Marie are buying hats in the shop on Carlisle Street. Read their conversation. Rewrite each underlined sentence. Use *have got to* or *can't* and the word in parentheses. Use contractions.

ANN: Look at this hat, Marie. What do you think?

MARIE: Oh, come on. That's got to be a joke.

You can't be serious.
                                                                            1. (serious)

        It's much too expensive. Look at the price tag. I mean, I'm not a millionaire!

ANN: It's $100! That can't be right.

_____
                                                                            2. (wrong)

MARIE: I know. It can't cost more than $50.

_____
                                                                            3. (less)

        Anyway, let's talk about it over lunch. I'm getting hungry.

ANN: It's too early for lunch. It has to be before 11:00.

_____
                                                                            4. (after)

MARIE: Look at the time. I'm amazed! It's already 12:30.

ANN: Then let's go to the café on Jones Street. It can't be far.

_____
                                                                            5. (nearby)

MARIE: Let's go home after lunch. I need a nap.

ANN: Oh, come on. You're fine. You're just hungry.

_____
                                                                            6. (tired)

▶32|02 (B) LISTEN AND CHECK Listen to the conversation and check your answers in A.

EXERCISE 5 SHORT ANSWERS WITH *MIGHT (NOT)* OR *MUST (NOT)*

(A) GRAMMAR NOTE 4 Sherlock Holmes and Dr. Watson have been discussing the mystery all evening. Complete their conversation. Write a short answer to each question. Use *might (not)* or *must (not)* and include *be* where necessary.

WATSON: You sound terrible, Holmes. Are you sick?

HOLMES: I _____*must be*_____. I have a headache, and my throat is starting to hurt. I'm sure
                        1.
         I'm sick. There's no other explanation!

WATSON: Hmm. This bottle is empty. Do you have more cough syrup?

HOLMES: I _____. I think it's the last bottle.
                    2.

WATSON: I'll have to go get some. My patients like Pure Drops Cough Medicine. Does that work for you, Holmes?

HOLMES: It _____. It's worth a try.
                3.

WATSON: I forgot to go to the bank today. Do you have any money?

HOLMES: I _____. Look in my wallet. It's on the table downstairs.
              4.

WATSON: I found it. It's 6:45. Is Drake Drugstore still open?

HOLMES: It _____. Their advertisement says, "Open 'til 7."
                5.

WATSON: Do you think they sell chicken soup? Some drugstores carry food.

HOLMES: They _____. It's a very small store.
                  6.

WATSON: What about the café on Jones Street? Do they have soup?

HOLMES: They _____. They've got everything.
                  7.

32|03 **B** LISTEN AND CHECK **Listen to the conversation and check your answers in A.**

EXERCISE 6 QUESTIONS AND STATEMENTS WITH *BE*

GRAMMAR NOTES 1–4 **Mr. and Mrs. Wilson are trying to get to sleep. Complete their conversation. Write questions and answers. Use *could be*, *couldn't be*, or *can't be*. Choose between affirmative and negative.**

MRS. WILSON: Shh! I hear someone at the door. It's 9:30. Who _____*could*_____ it _____*be*_____?
                                                                                     1.

MR. WILSON: It _____ a late customer. Mrs. Simms said she was going to stop by
                        2.
this evening.

MRS. WILSON: No, it _____ her. It's much too late. Maybe it's the cat.
                          3.

MR. WILSON: It _____. The cat is sleeping in the living room.
                        4.

MRS. WILSON: _____ it _____ Vincent? He's always down in the
                                            5.
basement with his camera.

MR. WILSON: No, Vincent went out an hour ago. He _____ back this early. Wait a
                                                                    6.
minute. It _____ Sherlock Holmes and Dr. Watson. They said they
                    7.
wanted to talk to me.

MRS. WILSON: _____ they really _____ here so late?
                                                              8.

MR. WILSON: No. You're right. It _____ them.
                                          9.

MRS. WILSON: What _____ it _____ then?
                                                    10.

MR. WILSON: That door rattles whenever the wind blows. It _____ the wind.
                                                                          11.

MRS. WILSON: That must be it. Let's go to sleep.

EXERCISE 7 EDITING

GRAMMAR NOTES 1–4 Read this student's reading journal for a mystery novel. There are six mistakes in the use of *must*, *have (got) to*, *may*, *might*, *could*, and *can't*. The first mistake is already corrected. Find and correct five more.

The main character, Molly Smith, is a college ESL teacher. She is trying to find her dead grandparents'

first home in the United States. It may ~~being~~ *be* in a nearby town. The townspeople there seem scared.

They could be have a secret, or they must just hate strangers. Molly found some letters hidden in

an old encyclopedia that might lead her to the place. They got to be important because the author

mentions them right away. The letters might contain family secrets. I'm almost certain of it. Who is

the bad guy? It couldn't be the student because he wants to help. It must be the newspaper editor in

the town. That's a possibility.

Appendices

1 Irregular Verbs

When two forms are listed, the more common form is listed first.

BASE FORM	SIMPLE PAST	PAST PARTICIPLE
arise	arose	arisen
awake	awoke	awoken
be	was or were	been
beat	beat	beaten/beat
become	became	become
begin	began	begun
bend	bent	bent
bet	bet	bet
bite	bit	bitten
bleed	bled	bled
blow	blew	blown
break	broke	broken
bring	brought	brought
build	built	built
burn	burned/burnt	burnt/burned
burst	burst	burst
buy	bought	bought
catch	caught	caught
choose	chose	chosen
cling	clung	clung
come	came	come
cost	cost	cost
creep	crept	crept
cut	cut	cut
deal	dealt	dealt
dig	dug	dug
dive	dove/dived	dived
do	did	done
draw	drew	drawn
dream	dreamed/dreamt	dreamed/dreamt
drink	drank	drunk
drive	drove	driven
eat	ate	eaten
fall	fell	fallen
feed	fed	fed
feel	felt	felt
fight	fought	fought
find	found	found
fit	fit/fitted	fit
flee	fled	fled
fling	flung	flung
fly	flew	flown
forbid	forbid/forbade	forbidden
forget	forgot	forgotten
forgive	forgave	forgiven
freeze	froze	frozen
get	got	gotten/got
give	gave	given
go	went	gone
grind	ground	ground
grow	grew	grown

BASE FORM	SIMPLE PAST	PAST PARTICIPLE
hang	hung	hung
have	had	had
hear	heard	heard
hide	hid	hidden
hit	hit	hit
hold	held	held
hurt	hurt	hurt
keep	kept	kept
kneel	knelt/kneeled	knelt/kneeled
knit	knit/knitted	knit/knitted
know	knew	known
lay	laid	laid
lead	led	led
leap	leaped/leapt	leaped/leapt
leave	left	left
lend	lent	lent
let	let	let
lie (lie down)	lay	lain
light	lit/lighted	lit/lighted
lose	lost	lost
make	made	made
mean	meant	meant
meet	met	met
pay	paid	paid
prove	proved	proven/proved
put	put	put
quit	quit	quit
read /rid/	read /rɛd/	read /rɛd/
ride	rode	ridden
ring	rang	rung
rise	rose	risen
run	ran	run
say	said	said
see	saw	seen
seek	sought	sought
sell	sold	sold
send	sent	sent
set	set	set
sew	sewed	sewn/sewed
shake	shook	shaken
shave	shaved	shaved/shaven
shine (intransitive)	shone/shined	shone/shined
shoot	shot	shot
show	showed	shown
shrink	shrank/shrunk	shrunk/shrunken
shut	shut	shut
sing	sang	sung
sink	sank/sunk	sunk
sit	sat	sat
sleep	slept	slept
slide	slid	slid

BASE FORM	SIMPLE PAST	PAST PARTICIPLE	BASE FORM	SIMPLE PAST	PAST PARTICIPLE
speak	spoke	spoken	swing	swung	swung
speed	sped/speeded	sped/speeded	take	took	taken
spend	spent	spent	teach	taught	taught
spill	spilled/spilt	spilled/spilt	tear	tore	torn
spin	spun	spun	tell	told	told
spit	spit/spat	spat	think	thought	thought
split	split	split	throw	threw	thrown
spread	spread	spread	understand	understood	understood
spring	sprang	sprung	upset	upset	upset
stand	stood	stood	wake	woke	woken
steal	stole	stolen	wear	wore	worn
stick	stuck	stuck	weave	wove/weaved	woven/weaved
sting	stung	stung	weep	wept	wept
stink	stank/stunk	stunk	win	won	won
strike	struck	struck/stricken	wind	wound	wound
swear	swore	sworn	withdraw	withdrew	withdrawn
sweep	swept	swept	wring	wrung	wrung
swim	swam	swum	write	wrote	written

2 Non-Action Verbs

APPEARANCE	EMOTIONS	MENTAL STATES		POSSESSION AND RELATIONSHIP	SENSES AND PERCEPTIONS	WANTS AND PREFERENCES
appear	admire	agree	imagine	belong	feel	desire
be	adore	assume	know	come from (origin)	hear	hope
look (seem)	appreciate	believe	mean	contain	hurt	need
represent	care	consider	mind	have	notice	prefer
resemble	detest	disagree	presume	own	observe	want
seem	dislike	disbelieve	realize	possess	perceive	wish
signify	doubt	estimate	recognize		recognize	
	envy	expect	remember		see	
VALUE	fear	feel (believe)	see (understand)		seem	
cost	forgive	find (believe)	suppose		smell	
equal	hate	forget	suspect		sound	
weigh	like	guess	think (believe)		taste	
	love	hesitate	understand			
	miss	hope	wonder			
	regret					
	respect					
	trust					

3 Verbs and Expressions Used Reflexively

allow yourself
amuse yourself
ask yourself
avail yourself of
be hard on yourself
be pleased with yourself
be proud of yourself
be yourself

behave yourself
believe in yourself
blame yourself
buy yourself
cut yourself
deprive yourself of
dry yourself
enjoy yourself

feel proud of yourself
feel sorry for yourself
forgive yourself
help yourself
hurt yourself
imagine yourself
introduce yourself
keep yourself (busy)

kill yourself
look after yourself
look at yourself
prepare yourself
pride yourself on
push yourself
remind yourself

see yourself
take care of yourself
talk to yourself
teach yourself
tell yourself
treat yourself
wash yourself

(s.o. = someone   s.t. = something)

PHRASAL VERB	MEANING
ask s.o. **over**	invite to one's home
blow s.t. **out**	stop burning by blowing air on it
blow s.t. **up**	make explode
bring s.o. **or** s.t. **back**	return
bring s.o. **up**	raise (a child)
bring s.t. **up**	bring attention to
burn s.t. **down**	burn completely
call s.o. **back**	return a phone call
call s.t. **off**	cancel
call s.o. **up**	contact by phone
calm s.o. **down**	make less excited
carry s.t. **out**	complete (a plan)
clean s.o. **or** s.t. **up**	clean completely
clear s.t. **up**	explain
close s.t. **down**	close by force
count on s.t. **or** s.o.	depend on
cover s.o. **or** s.t. **up**	cover completely
cross s.t. **out**	draw a line through
do s.t. **over**	do again
drink s.t. **up**	drink completely
drop s.o. **or** s.t. **off**	take someplace in a car and leave there
empty s.t. **out**	empty completely
end up doing s.t.	do something you didn't plan to do
figure s.o. **out**	understand (the behavior)
figure s.t. **out**	solve, understand after thinking about it
fill s.t. **in**	complete with information
fill s.t. **out**	complete (a form)
find s.t. **out**	learn information
get off s.t.	leave (a bus, a couch)
get over s.t.	recover from
give s.t. **back**	return
give s.t. **up**	quit, abandon
give up doing s.t.	quit, stop
go on doing s.t.	continue
hand s.t. **in**	give work (to a boss/teacher), submit
hand s.t. **out**	distribute
hand s.t. **over**	give
help s.o. **out**	assist
keep s.o. **or** s.t. **away**	cause to stay at a distance
keep s.t. **on**	not remove (a piece of clothing/ jewelry)
keep on doing s.t.	continue
keep s.o. **or** s.t. **out**	not allow to enter
lay s.o. **off**	end employment
leave s.t. **on**	1. not turn off (a light/radio)
	2. not remove (a piece of clothing/ jewelry)
leave s.t. **out**	not include, omit
let s.o. **down**	disappoint
let s.o. **or** s.t. **in**	allow to enter
let s.o. **off**	allow to leave (from a bus/car)
light s.t. **up**	illuminate
look for s.o. **or** s.t.	try to find
look s.o. **or** s.t. **over**	examine

PHRASAL VERB	MEANING
look s.t. **up**	try to find (in a book/on the Internet)
make s.t. **up**	create
pass s.t. **on**	give to others
pass s.t. **out**	distribute
pass s.o. **or** s.t. **over**	decide not to use
pass s.o. **or** s.t. **up**	decide not to use, reject
pay s.o. **or** s.t. **back**	repay
pick s.o. **or** s.t. **out**	choose
pick s.o. **or** s.t. **up**	1. lift
	2. go get someone or something
pick s.t. **up**	1. get (an idea/a new book)
	2. answer the phone
point s.o. **or** s.t. **out**	indicate
put s.t. **away**	put in an appropriate place
put s.t. **back**	return to its original place
put s.o. **or** s.t. **down**	stop holding
put s.t. **off**	delay
put off doing s.t.	delay
put s.t. **on**	cover the body (with clothes/lotion)
put s.t. **together**	assemble
put s.t. **up**	erect
set s.t. **up**	1. prepare for use
	2. establish (a business)
shut s.t. **off**	stop (a machine/light)
straighten s.o. **out**	change bad behavior
straighten s.t. **up**	make neat
switch s.t. **on**	start (a machine/light)
take s.o. **or** s.t. **back**	return
take s.t. **off/out**	remove
take over s.t.	get control of
talk s.o. **into**	persuade
talk s.t. **over**	discuss
tear s.t. **down**	destroy
tear s.t. **off**	remove by tearing
tear s.t. **up**	tear into small pieces
think about doing s.t.	consider
think s.t. **over**	consider
think s.t. **up**	invent
throw s.t. **away/out**	put in the trash, discard
try s.t. **on**	put clothing on to see if it fits
try s.t. **out**	use to see if it works
turn s.t. **around**	make it work well
turn s.o. **or** s.t. **down**	reject
turn s.t. **down**	lower the volume (a TV/radio)
turn s.t. **in**	give work (to a boss/teacher), submit
turn s.o. **or** s.t. **into**	change from one form to another
turn s.o. **off**	[slang] destroy interest in
turn s.t. **off**	stop (a machine/light), extinguish
turn s.t. **on**	start (a machine/light)
turn s.t. **up**	make louder (a TV/radio)
use s.t. **up**	use completely, consume
wake s.o. **up**	awaken
work s.t. **out**	solve, find a solution to a problem
write s.t. **down**	write on a piece of paper
write s.t. **up**	write in a finished form

5 Intransitive Phrasal Verbs

PHRASAL VERB	MEANING
blow up	explode
break down	stop working (a machine)
burn down	burn completely
call back	return a phone call
calm down	become less excited
catch on	1. begin to understand 2. become popular
clear up	become clear
close down	stop operating
come about	happen
come along	come with, accompany
come by	visit
come back	return
come in	enter
come off	become unattached
come on	1. do as I say 2. let's go
come out	appear
come up	arise
dress up	wear special clothes
drop in	visit by surprise
drop out	quit
eat out	eat in a restaurant
empty out	empty completely
find out	learn information

PHRASAL VERB	MEANING
fit in	be accepted in a group
follow through	complete
fool around	act playful
get ahead	make progress, succeed
get along	have a good relationship
get away	go on vacation
get back	return
get by	survive
get through	finish
get together	meet
get up	1. get out of bed 2. stand
give up	quit
go ahead	begin or continue to do something
go away	leave
go on	continue
grow up	become an adult
hang up	end a phone call
help out	assist
keep away	stay at a distance
keep on	continue
keep out	not enter
keep up	go as fast
lie down	recline

PHRASAL VERB	MEANING
light up	illuminate
look out	be careful
make up	end a disagreement, reconcile
pass away	die
play around	have fun
run out	not have enough
set out	begin an activity or a project
show up	appear
sign up	register
sit down	take a seat
slip up	make a mistake
stand up	rise
start over	start again
stay up	remain awake
straighten up	make neat
take off	depart (a plane)
tune in	1. watch or listen to (a show) 2. pay attention
turn up	appear
wake up	stop sleeping
watch out	be careful
work out	1. be resolved 2. exercise

6 Irregular Plural Nouns

SINGULAR	PLURAL
analysis	analyses
basis	bases
crisis	crises
hypothesis	hypotheses

SINGULAR	PLURAL
half	halves
knife	knives
leaf	leaves
life	lives
loaf	loaves
shelf	shelves
wife	wives

SINGULAR	PLURAL
man	men
woman	women
child	children
foot	feet
tooth	teeth
goose	geese
mouse	mice
person	people

SINGULAR	PLURAL
deer	deer
fish	fish
sheep	sheep

7 Non-Count Nouns

Non-count nouns are singular.

ACTIVITIES	COURSES OF STUDY	FOOD		IDEAS AND FEELINGS	LIQUIDS AND GASES	MATERIALS	VERY SMALL THINGS	WEATHER
baseball	archeology	bread	fruit	anger	air	ash	dust	fog
biking	art	broccoli	ice cream	beauty	blood	clay	pepper	ice
exploring	economics	butter	lettuce	fear	gasoline	cotton	rice	rain
farming	English	cake	meat	freedom	ink	glass	salt	snow
football	geography	cheese	pasta	friendship	milk	gold	sand	wind
golf	history	chicken	pizza	happiness	oil	leather	sugar	
hiking	mathematics	chocolate	salad	hate	oxygen	paper		
running	music	coffee	soup	hope	paint	silk		
sailing	photography	corn	spaghetti	loneliness	smoke	silver		
soccer	psychology	fat	spinach	love	soda	stone		
swimming	science	fish	tea	truth	water	wood		
tennis		flour	yogurt			wool		

NAMES OF CATEGORIES

clothing (BUT: coats, hats, shoes ...)
equipment (BUT: computers, phones, TVs ...)
food (BUT: bananas, eggs, vegetables ...)
furniture (BUT: beds, chairs, lamps, tables ...)
homework (BUT: assignments, pages, problems ...)
jewelry (BUT: bracelets, earrings, necklaces ...)
mail (BUT: letters, packages, postcards ...)
money (BUT: dinars, dollars, euros, pounds ...)
time (BUT: minutes, months, years ...)
work (BUT: jobs, projects, tasks ...)

OTHER

Some non-count nouns don't fit into any list.
You must memorize these non-count nouns.

advice
garbage/trash
help
information
luggage
news
traffic

8 Proper Nouns

Write proper nouns with a capital letter. Notice that some proper nouns use the definite article *the*.

PEOPLE

* first names — Anne, Eduardo, Mehmet, Olga, Shao-fen
* family names — Chen, García, Haddad, Smith
* family groups — the Chens, the Garcias, the Haddads, the Smiths
* titles — Doctor, Grandma, President, Professor
* title + names — Mr. García, Professor Smith, Uncle Steve

PLACES

* continents — Africa, Asia, Australia, Europe, South America
* countries — Argentina, China, France, Nigeria, Turkey, the United States
* provinces/states — Brittany, Ontario, Szechwan, Texas
* cities — Beijing, Istanbul, Rio de Janeiro, Toronto
* streets — the Champs-Elysées, Fifth Avenue
* structures — Harrods, the Louvre, the Petronas Towers
* schools — Midwood High School, Oxford University
* parks — Central Park, the Tivoli Gardens
* mountains — the Andes, the Himalayas, the Pyrenees
* oceans — the Atlantic, the Indian Ocean, the Pacific
* rivers — the Amazon, the Ganges, the Seine
* lakes — Baikal, Erie, Tanganyika, Titicaca
* canals — the Suez Canal, the Panama Canal
* deserts — the Gobi, the Kalahari, the Sahara

DOCUMENTS

the Bible, the Koran, the Constitution

LANGUAGES

Arabic, Chinese, Portuguese, Russian, Spanish

NATIONALITIES

Brazilian, Japanese, Mexican, Saudi, Turkish

RELIGIONS

Buddhism, Christianity, Hinduism, Islam, Judaism

COURSES

Introduction to Computer Sciences, Math 201

PRODUCT BRANDS

Adidas, Dell, Kleenex, Mercedes, Samsung

TIME

* months — January, March, December
* days — Monday, Wednesday, Saturday
* holidays — Bastille Day, Buddha Day, Christmas, Hanukah, New Year's Day, Ramadan

9 Adjectives That Form the Comparative and Superlative in Two Ways

The more common form of the comparative and the superlative is listed first.

ADJECTIVE	COMPARATIVE	SUPERLATIVE
cruel	crueler/more cruel	cruelest/most cruel
deadly	deadlier/more deadly	deadliest/most deadly
friendly	more friendly/friendlier	most friendly/friendliest
handsome	more handsome/handsomer	most handsome/handsomest
happy	happier/more happy	happiest/most happy
lively	livelier/more lively	liveliest/most lively
lonely	lonelier/more lonely	loneliest/most lonely
lovely	lovelier/more lovely	loveliest/most lovely
narrow	narrower/more narrow	narrowest/most narrow
pleasant	more pleasant/pleasanter	most pleasant/pleasantest
polite	more polite/politer	most polite/politest
quiet	quieter/more quiet	quietest/most quiet
shallow	shallower/more shallow	shallowest/most shallow
sincere	more sincere/sincerer	most sincere/sincerest
stupid	stupider/more stupid	stupidest/most stupid
true	truer/more true	truest/most true

10 Irregular Comparisons of Adjectives, Adverbs, and Quantifiers

ADJECTIVE	ADVERB	COMPARATIVE	SUPERLATIVE
bad	badly	worse	the worst
far	far	farther/further	the farthest/furthest
good	well	better	the best
little	little	less	the least
many/a lot of	—	more	the most
much*/a lot of	much*/a lot	more	the most

* *Much* is usually only used in questions and negative statements.

11 Participial Adjectives

-ED	-ING	-ED	-ING	-ED	-ING
alarmed	alarming	disturbed	disturbing	moved	moving
amazed	amazing	embarrassed	embarrassing	paralyzed	paralyzing
amused	amusing	entertained	entertaining	pleased	pleasing
annoyed	annoying	excited	exciting	relaxed	relaxing
astonished	astonishing	exhausted	exhausting	satisfied	satisfying
bored	boring	fascinated	fascinating	shocked	shocking
confused	confusing	frightened	frightening	surprised	surprising
depressed	depressing	horrified	horrifying	terrified	terrifying
disappointed	disappointing	inspired	inspiring	tired	tiring
disgusted	disgusting	interested	interesting	touched	touching
distressed	distressing	irritated	irritating	troubled	troubling

12 Order of Adjectives Before a Noun

1 When **adjectives from different categories** are used before a noun, they usually go in the order as displayed in the chart below. Do not use a comma between these adjectives. Remember that we do not usually use more than three adjectives before a noun.

EXAMPLES:
I bought an **antique Greek flower** vase.   NOT a ~~Greek antique~~ flower vase
She took some **easy college** courses.   NOT some ~~college easy~~ courses
We sat at an **enormous round wooden** table.   NOT a ~~wooden enormous round~~ table

OPINION	SIZE*	AGE	SHAPE	COLOR	ORIGIN	MATERIAL	NOUNS USED AS ADJECTIVES	
beautiful	enormous	antique	flat	blue	Asian	cotton	college	
comfortable	huge	modern	oval	gray	European	gold	flower	
cozy	little	new	rectangular	green	Greek	plastic	kitchen	**+ NOUN**
easy	tall	old	round	purple	Pacific	stone	mountain	
expensive	tiny	young	square	red	Southern	wooden	vacation	

***EXCEPTION:** *Big* and *small* usually go first in a series of adjectives: *a small comfortable apartment.*

2 When **adjectives from the same category** are used before a noun, they do not follow a specific order. Use a comma between these adjectives.

EXAMPLES:
We rented a **beautiful, comfortable, cozy** apartment. or
We rented a **cozy, comfortable, beautiful** apartment. or
We rented a **comfortable, cozy, beautiful** apartment.

13 Verbs Followed by Gerunds (Base Form of Verb + -ing)

acknowledge	consider	enjoy	go on*	permit	report
admit	delay	escape	imagine	postpone	resent
advise	deny	excuse	justify	practice	resist
allow	detest	explain	keep *(continue)*	prevent	risk
appreciate	discontinue	feel like	keep on*	prohibit	suggest
avoid	discuss	finish	limit	put off*	support
ban	dislike	forgive	mention	quit	think about*
can't help	end up*	give up*	mind *(object to)*	recall	tolerate
celebrate	endure	go	miss	recommend	understand

*A few phrasal verbs like these are followed by a gerund.

14 Verbs Followed by Infinitives (*To* + Base Form of Verb)

agree	can't wait	fail	manage	prepare	struggle
aim	claim	help*	mean *(intend)*	pretend	threaten
appear	choose	hesitate	need	promise	volunteer
arrange	consent	hope	neglect	refuse	wait
ask	decide	hurry	offer	request	want
attempt	deserve	intend	pay	rush	wish
can('t) afford	expect	learn	plan	seem	would like

* *Help* is often followed by the base form of the verb (example: *I helped paint the kitchen*).

15 Verbs Followed by Gerunds or Infinitives

begin	forget*	like	prefer	regret*	stop*
can't stand	hate	love	remember*	start	try
continue					

*These verbs can be followed by either a gerund or an infinitive, but there is a big difference in meaning *(see Unit 26)*.

16 Verbs Followed by Object + Infinitive

advise	choose*	get	order	promise*	tell
allow	convince	help**	pay*	remind	urge
ask*	encourage	hire	permit	request	want*
beg*	expect*	instruct	persuade	require	warn
cause	forbid	invite	prefer*	teach	would like*
challenge	force	need*			

*These verbs can also be followed by an infinitive without an object (example: *ask to leave* or *ask someone to leave*).
** *Help* is often followed by the base form of the verb, with or without an object (example: *I helped (her) paint the kitchen*).

17 Adjective + Preposition Combinations

accustomed to	bad at	curious about	good at	responsible for	sorry for/about
afraid of	bored with/by	different from	happy about	sad about	surprised at/
amazed at/by	capable of	disappointed with	interested in	safe from	about/by
angry at	careful of	excited about	nervous about	satisfied with	terrible at
ashamed of	certain about	famous for	opposed to	shocked at/by	tired of
aware of	concerned about	fond of	pleased about	sick of	used to
awful at	content with	glad about	ready for	slow at/in	worried about

18 Verb + Preposition Combinations

admit to	believe in	dream about/of	pay for	succeed in	think about
advise against	choose between	feel about	plan on	talk about	wonder about
apologize for	complain about	insist on	rely on	thank someone for	worry about
approve of	decide on	object to	resort to		

19 Modals and Their Functions

FUNCTION	MODAL OR EXPRESSION	TIME	EXAMPLES
Ability	can can't	Present	Sam **can swim**. He **can't skate**.
	could couldn't	Past	We **could swim** last year. We **couldn't skate**.
	be able to* not be able to*	All verb forms	Lea **is able to run** fast. She **wasn't able to run** fast last year.
Permission	can can't could may may not	Present or future	**Can** I **sit** here? **Can** I **call** tomorrow? Yes, you **can**. No, you **can't**. Sorry. **Could** he **leave** now? **May** I **borrow** your pen? Yes, you **may**. No, you **may not**. Sorry.
Requests	can can't could will would	Present or future	**Can** you **close** the door, please? Sure, I **can**. Sorry, I **can't**. **Could** you please **answer** the phone? **Will** you **wash** the dishes, please? **Would** you please **mail** this letter?
Advice	should shouldn't ought to had better** had better not**	Present or future	You **should study** more. You **shouldn't miss** class. We **ought to leave**. We'd **better go**. We'd **better not stay**.
Necessity	have to* not have to*	All verb forms	He **has to go** now. I **had to go** yesterday. I **will have to go** soon. He **doesn't have to go** yet.
	have got to* must	Present or future	He's **got to leave**! You **must use** a pen for the test.
Prohibition	must not can't	Present or future	You **must not drive** without a license. You **can't drive** without a license.

*The meaning of this expression is similar to the meaning of a modal. Unlike a modal, the verb changes for present tense third-person singular.

**The meaning of this expression is similar to the meaning of a modal. Like a modal, it has no -s for third-person singular.

FUNCTION	MODAL OR EXPRESSION	TIME	EXAMPLES
Possibility	**must** **must not** **have to***	Present	This **must be** her house. Her name is on the door. She **must not be** home. I don't see her car. She **had to know** him. They went to school together.
	have got to* **may** **may not** **might** **might not** **could**	Present or future	He**'s got to be** guilty. We saw him do it. She **may be** home now. It **may not rain** tomorrow. Lee **might be sick** today. He **might not come** to class. They **could be** at the library. It **could rain** tomorrow.
Impossibility	**can't**	Present or future	That **can't be** Ana. She left for France yesterday. It **can't snow** tomorrow. It's going to be too warm.
	couldn't	Present	He **couldn't be** guilty. He was away . . .

*The meaning of this expression is similar to the meaning of a modal. Unlike a modal, the verb changes for present tense third-person singular.

20 Spelling Rules for the Simple Present: Third-Person Singular (*He, She, It*)

1 Add **-s** for most verbs.

work	work**s**
buy	buy**s**
ride	ride**s**
return	return**s**

2 Add **-es** for verbs that end in **-ch**, **-s**, **-sh**, **-x**, or **-z**.

watch	watch**es**
pass	pass**es**
rush	rush**es**
relax	relax**es**
buzz	buzz**es**

3 Change the **y** to **i** and add **-es** when the base form ends in **consonant + y**.

study	stud**ies**
hurry	hurr**ies**
dry	dr**ies**

4 Do not change the **y** when the base form ends in **vowel + y**. Add **-s**.

play	play**s**
enjoy	enjoy**s**

5 A few verbs have **irregular forms**.

be	**is**
do	**does**
go	**goes**
have	**has**

21 Spelling Rules for Base Form of Verb + -ing (Progressive and Gerund)

1 Add **-ing** to the base form of the verb.

read	read**ing**
stand	stand**ing**

2 If the verb ends in a **silent -e**, drop the final **-e** and add **-ing**.

leave	leav**ing**
take	tak**ing**

3 In **one-syllable** verbs, if the last three letters are a consonant-vowel-consonant combination (CVC), double the last consonant and add **-ing**.

```
C V C
↓ ↓ ↓
s i t       sit ting
```

```
C V C
↓ ↓ ↓
p l a n     plan ning
```

EXCEPTION: Do not double the last consonant in verbs that end in **-w**, **-x**, or **-y**.

sew	sew**ing**
fix	fix**ing**
play	play**ing**

4 In verbs of **two or more syllables** that end in a consonant-vowel-consonant combination, double the last consonant only if the last syllable is stressed.

admít	admit**ting**	*(The last syllable is stressed, so double the -t.)*
whísper	whisper**ing**	*(The last syllable is not stressed, so don't double the -r.)*

5 If the verb ends in **-ie**, change the **ie** to **y** before adding **-ing**.

die	**dying**
lie	**lying**

> **Stress**
> ′ shows main stress.

22 Spelling Rules for Base Form of Verb + -ed (Simple Past and Past Participle of Regular Verbs)

1 If the verb ends in a **consonant**, add **-ed**.

return	return**ed**
help	help**ed**

2 If the verb ends in **-e**, add **-d**.

live	live**d**
create	create**d**
die	die**d**

3 In **one-syllable** verbs, if the last three letters are a consonant-vowel-consonant combination (CVC), double the last consonant and add **-ed**.

```
C V C
↓ ↓ ↓
h o p       hop ped
```

```
C V C
↓ ↓ ↓
g r a b     grab bed
```

EXCEPTION: Do not double the last consonant in **one-syllable** verbs that end in **-w**, **-x**, or **-y**.

bow	bow**ed**
mix	mix**ed**
play	play**ed**

4 In verbs of **two or more syllables** that end in a consonant-vowel-consonant combination, double the last consonant only if the last syllable is stressed.

prefér	prefer**red**	*(The last syllable is stressed, so double the -r.)*
vísit	visit**ed**	*(The last syllable is not stressed, so don't double the -t.)*

5 If the verb ends in **consonant + y**, change the **y** to **i** and add **-ed**.

worry	worr**ied**
carry	carr**ied**

6 If the verb ends in **vowel + y**, add **-ed**. (Do not change the **y** to **i**.)

play	play**ed**
annoy	annoy**ed**

EXCEPTIONS:

lay	la**id**
pay	pa**id**
say	sa**id**

23 Spelling Rules for the Comparative (*-er*) and Superlative (*-est*) of Adjectives

1 With **one-syllable** adjectives, add *-er* to form the comparative. Add *-est* to form the superlative.

cheap	cheap**er**	cheap**est**
bright	bright**er**	bright**est**

2 If the adjective ends in *-e*, add *-r* or *-st*.

nice	nice**r**	nice**st**

3 If the adjective ends in **consonant + y**, change **y** to **i** before you add *-er* or *-est*.

pretty	prett**ier**	prett**iest**

EXCEPTION:

shy	shy**er**	shy**est**

4 In **one-syllable** adjectives, if the last three letters are a consonant-vowel-consonant combination (CVC), double the last consonant before adding *-er* or *-est*.

```
C V C
↓ ↓ ↓
b i g        bigger        biggest
```

EXCEPTION: Do not double the last consonant in adjectives that end in *-w* or *-y*.

slow	slow**er**	slow**est**
gray	gray**er**	gray**est**

24 Spelling Rules for Adverbs Ending in *-ly*

1 Add *-ly* to the corresponding adjective.

nice	nice**ly**
quiet	quiet**ly**
beautiful	beautiful**ly**

EXCEPTION:

true	tru**ly**

2 If the adjective ends in **consonant + y**, change the **y** to **i** before adding *-ly*.

easy	eas**ily**

3 If the adjective ends in *-le*, drop the **e** and add *-y*.

possible	possibl**y**

4 If the adjective ends in *-ic*, add *-ally*.

basic	basic**ally**
fantastic	fantastic**ally**

25 Spelling Rules for Regular Plural Nouns

1 Add *-s* to most nouns.

book	book**s**
table	table**s**
cup	cup**s**

2 Add *-es* to nouns that end in *-ch*, *-s*, *-sh*, or *-x*.

watch	watch**es**
bus	bus**es**
dish	dish**es**
box	box**es**

3 Add *-s* to nouns that end in **vowel + y**.

day	day**s**
key	key**s**

4 Change the **y** to **i** and add *-es* to nouns that end in **consonant + y**.

baby	bab**ies**
city	cit**ies**
strawberry	strawberr**ies**

5 Add *-s* to nouns that end in **vowel + o**.

radio	radio**s**
video	video**s**
zoo	zoo**s**

6 Add *-es* to nouns that end in **consonant + o**.

potato	potato**es**
tomato	tomato**es**

EXCEPTIONS:

kilo	kilo**s**
photo	photo**s**
piano	piano**s**

26 Contractions with Verb Forms

1 SIMPLE PRESENT, PRESENT PROGRESSIVE, AND IMPERATIVE

Contractions with *Be*

I am	=	I'm
you are	=	you're
he is	=	he's
she is	=	she's
it is	=	it's
we are	=	we're
you are	=	you're
they are	=	they're

Simple Present	Present Progressive
I'm a student.	I'm studying here.
He's my teacher.	He's teaching verbs.
We're from Canada.	We're living here.

I am not	=	I'm not		
you are not	=	you're not	or	you aren't
he is not	=	he's not	or	he isn't
she is not	=	she's not	or	she isn't
it is not	=	it's not	or	it isn't
we are not	=	we're not	or	we aren't
you are not	=	you're not	or	you aren't
they are not	=	they're not	or	they aren't

Simple Present	Present Progressive
She's not sick.	She's not reading.
He isn't late.	He isn't coming.
We aren't twins.	We aren't leaving.
They're not here.	They're not playing.

Contractions with *Do*

do not	=	don't
does not	=	doesn't

Simple Present	Imperative
They don't live here.	Don't run!
It doesn't snow much.	

2 SIMPLE PAST AND PAST PROGRESSIVE

Contractions with *Be*

was not	=	wasn't
were not	=	weren't

Simple Past	Past Progressive
He wasn't a poet.	He wasn't singing.
They weren't twins.	They weren't sleeping.
We didn't see her.	

Contractions with *Do*

did not	=	didn't

3 FUTURE

Contractions with *Will*

I will	=	I'll
you will	=	you'll
he will	=	he'll
she will	=	she'll
it will	=	it'll
we will	=	we'll
you will	=	you'll
they will	=	they'll
will not	=	won't

Future with *Will*

I'll take the train.
It'll be faster that way.
We'll go together.
He won't come with us.
They won't miss the train.

Contractions with *Be going to*

I am going to	=	I'm going to
you are going to	=	you're going to
he is going to	=	he's going to
she is going to	=	she's going to
it is going to	=	it's going to
we are going to	=	we're going to
you are going to	=	you're going to
they are going to	=	they're going to

Future with *Be going to*

I'm going to buy tickets tomorrow.
She's going to call you.
It's going to rain soon.
We're going to drive to Boston.
They're going to crash!

4 PRESENT PERFECT AND PRESENT PERFECT PROGRESSIVE

Contractions with *Have*

I have	=	I**'ve**
you have	=	you**'ve**
he has	=	he**'s**
she has	=	she**'s**
it has	=	it**'s**
we have	=	we**'ve**
you have	=	you**'ve**
they have	=	they**'ve**
have not	=	**haven't**
has not	=	**hasn't**

> You**'ve** already **read** that page.
> We**'ve been writing** for an hour.
> She**'s been** to Africa three times.
> It**'s been raining** since yesterday.
> We **haven't seen** any elephants yet.
> They **haven't been living** here long.

5 MODALS AND SIMILAR EXPRESSIONS

cannot **or** can not	=	**can't**
could not	=	**couldn't**
should not	=	**shouldn't**
had better	=	**'d better**
would prefer	=	**'d prefer**
would rather	=	**'d rather**

> She **can't dance**.
> We **shouldn't go**.
> They**'d better decide**.
> I**'d prefer** coffee.
> I**'d rather take** the bus.

---

27 Capitalization and Punctuation Rules

	USE FOR ...	EXAMPLES
capital letter	• the first-person pronoun *I*	Tomorrow **I** will be here at 2:00.
	• proper nouns	His name is **Karl**. He lives in **Germany**.
	• the first word of a sentence	**When** does the train leave? **At** 2:00.
apostrophe (')	• possessive nouns	Is that **Marta's** coat?
	• contractions	**That's** not hers. **It's** mine.
comma (,)	• after items in a list	He bought **apples, pears, oranges,** and **bananas**.
	• before sentence connectors *and, but, or,* and *so*	They watched TV**, and** she played video games. She's tired**, so** she's going to bed now.
	• after the first part of a sentence that begins with *because*	***Because*** it's raining**,** we're not walking to the office.
	• after the first part of a sentence that begins with a preposition	***Across from*** the post office**,** there's a good restaurant.
	• after the first part of a sentence that begins with a time clause or an *if*-clause	***After*** he arrived**,** we ate dinner. ***If*** it rains**,** we won't go.
exclamation point (!)	• at the end of a sentence to show surprise or a strong feeling	You're here**!** That's great**!** Stop**!** A car is coming**!**
period (.)	• at the end of a statement	Today is Wednesday**.**
question mark (?)	• at the end of a question	What day is today**?**

28 Pronunciation Table

▶ A|01 These are the pronunciation symbols used in this text. Listen to the pronunciation of the key words.

VOWELS				CONSONANTS			
SYMBOL	KEY WORD	SYMBOL	KEY WORD	SYMBOL	KEY WORD	SYMBOL	KEY WORD
i	beat, feed	ə	banana, among	p	pack, happy	z	zip, please, goes
ɪ	bit, did	ɚ	shirt, murder	b	back, rubber	ʃ	ship, machine, station,
eɪ	date, paid	aɪ	bite, cry, buy, eye	t	tie		special, discussion
ɛ	bet, bed	aʊ	about, how	d	die	ʒ	measure, vision
æ	bat, bad	ɔɪ	voice, boy	k	came, key, quick	h	hot, who
ɑ	box, odd, father	ɪr	beer	g	game, guest	m	men
ɔ	bought, dog	ɛr	bare	tʃ	church, nature, watch	n	sun, know, pneumonia
oʊ	boat, road	ɑr	bar	dʒ	judge, general, major	ŋ	sung, ringing
ʊ	book, good	ɔr	door	f	fan, photograph	w	wet, white
u	boot, food, student	ʊr	tour	v	van	l	light, long
ʌ	but, mud, mother			θ	thing, breath	r	right, wrong
				ð	then, breathe	y	yes, use, music
				s	sip, city, psychology	t̬	butter, bottle

29 Pronunciation Rules for the Simple Present: Third-Person Singular (*He, She, It*)

1 The third-person singular in the simple present always ends in the letter *-s*. There are, however, three different pronunciations for the final sound of the third-person singular.

/s/	/z/	/ɪz/
talks	loves	dances

2 The final sound is pronounced /s/ after the voiceless sounds /p/, /t/, /k/, and /f/.

top	tops
get	gets
take	takes
laugh	laughs

3 The final sound is pronounced /z/ after the voiced sounds /b/, /d/, /g/, /v/, /m/, /n/, /ŋ/, /l/, /r/, and /ð/.

describe	describes
spend	spends
hug	hugs
live	lives
seem	seems
remain	remains
sing	sings
tell	tells
lower	lowers
bathe	bathes

4 The final sound is pronounced /z/ after all **vowel sounds**.

agree	agrees
try	tries
stay	stays
know	knows

5 The final sound is pronounced /ɪz/ after the sounds /s/, /z/, /ʃ/, /ʒ/, /tʃ/, and /dʒ/. /ɪz/ adds a syllable to the verb.

miss	misses
freeze	freezes
rush	rushes
massage	massages
watch	watches
judge	judges

6 *Do* and *say* have a change in vowel sound.

do /du/   does /dʌz/
say /seɪ/   says /sɛz/

30 Pronunciation Rules for the Simple Past and Past Participle of Regular Verbs

1 The regular simple past and past participle always end in the letter *-d*. There are three different pronunciations for the final sound of the regular simple past and past participle.

/t/	/d/	/ɪd/
raced	lived	attended

2 The final sound is pronounced /t/ after the voiceless sounds /p/, /k/, /f/, /s/, /ʃ/, and /tʃ/.

hop	hopped
work	worked
laugh	laughed
address	addressed
publish	published
watch	watched

3 The final sound is pronounced /d/ after the voiced sounds /b/, /g/, /v/, /z/, /ʒ/, /dʒ/, /m/, /n/, /ŋ/, /l/, /r/, and /ð/.

rub	rubbed
hug	hugged
live	lived
surprise	surprised
massage	massaged
change	changed
rhyme	rhymed
return	returned
bang	banged
enroll	enrolled
appear	appeared
bathe	bathed

4 The final sound is pronounced /d/ after all **vowel sounds**.

agree	agreed
die	died
play	played
enjoy	enjoyed
snow	snowed

5 The final sound is pronounced /ɪd/ after /t/ and /d/. /ɪd/ adds a syllable to the verb.

start	started
decide	decided

Glossary of Grammar Terms

action verb A verb that describes an action.

    Alicia **ran** home.

adjective A word that describes a noun or pronoun.

    That's a **great** idea.
    It's **wonderful**.

adverb A word that describes a verb, an adjective, or another adverb.

    She drives **carefully**.
    She's a **very** good driver.
    She drives **really** well.

adverb of frequency An adverb that describes how often something happens.

    We **always** watch that program.

adverb of manner An adverb that describes how someone does something or how something happens. It usually ends in -*ly*.

    He sings **beautifully**.

adverb of time An adverb that describes when something happens.

    We'll see you **soon**.

affirmative A statement or answer meaning *Yes*.

    He **works**. *(affirmative statement)*
    Yes, he **does**. *(affirmative short answer)*

article A word that goes before a noun.
The indefinite articles are *a* and *an*.

    I ate **a** sandwich and **an** apple.
The definite article is *the*.

    I didn't like **the** sandwich. **The** apple was good.

auxiliary verb (also called **helping verb**) A verb used with a main verb. *Be*, *do*, and *have* are often auxiliary verbs. Modals (*can*, *should*, *may*...) are also auxiliary verbs.

    I **am** exercising right now.
    Does he exercise every day?
    She **should** exercise every day.
    They**'ve** learned how to swim.
    They **can** swim very well.
    We **may** go to the pool tomorrow.

base form The simple form of a verb without any endings (-*s*, -*ed*, -*ing*) or other changes.

    be, have, go, drive

capital letter The large form of a letter. The capital letters are: *A, B, C, D, . . .*

    Alicia lives in the **U**nited **S**tates.

clause A group of words that has a subject and a verb. A sentence can have one or more clauses.

    We are leaving now. *(one clause)*
    When he calls, we'll leave. *(two clauses)*

common noun A word for a person, place, or thing (but not the name of the person, place, or thing).

    Teresa lives in a **house** near the **beach**.

comparative The form of an adjective or adverb that shows the difference between two people, places, or things.

    Alain is **shorter** than Brendan. *(adjective)*
    Brendan runs **faster** than Alain. *(adverb)*

comparison A statement that shows the difference between two people, places, or things. A comparison can use comparative adjectives and comparative adverbs. It can also use *as . . . as*.

    Alain is **shorter than** Brendan.
    Alain isn't **as tall as** Brendan.
    He runs **faster than** Brendan.

consonant A letter of the alphabet. The consonants are:

    b, c, d, f, g, h, j, k, l, m, n, p, q, r, s, t, v, w, x, y, z

continuous See **progressive**.

contraction A short form of a word or words. An apostrophe (') replaces the missing letter or letters.

    she's = she is
    hasn't = has not
    can't = cannot
    won't = will not

count noun A noun that you can count. It has a singular and a plural form.

    one **book**, two **books**

definite article *the*

This article goes before a noun that refers to a specific person, place, or thing.

> Please bring me **the book** on the table. I'm almost finished reading it.

dependent clause (also called **subordinate clause**) A clause that needs a main clause for its meaning.

> **When I get home**, I'll call you.

direct object A noun or pronoun that receives the action of a verb.

> Marta kicked **the ball**. I saw **her**.

formal Language used in business situations or with adults you do not know.

> Good afternoon, Mr. Rivera. Please have a seat.

gerund A noun formed with verb + *-ing*. It can be the subject or object of a sentence.

> **Swimming** is great exercise.
> I enjoy **swimming**.

helping verb See **auxiliary verb**.

imperative A sentence that gives a command or instructions.

> **Hurry!**
> **Don't touch that!**

indefinite article *a* or *an*

These articles go before a noun that does not refer to a specific person, place, or thing.

> Can you bring me **a book**? I'm looking for something to read.

indefinite past Past time, but not a specific time. It is often used with the present perfect.

> **I've** already **seen** that movie.

indefinite pronoun A pronoun such as *someone, something, anyone, anything, anywhere, no one, nothing, nowhere, everyone,* and *everything*. An indefinite pronoun does not refer to a specific person, place, or thing.

> **Someone** called you last night.
> Did **anything** happen?

indirect object A noun or pronoun (often a person) that receives something as the result of the action of the verb.

> I told **John** the story.
> He gave **me** some good advice.

infinitive *to* + base form of the verb

> I want **to leave** now.

infinitive of purpose *(in order) to* + base form

This form gives the reason for an action.

> I go to school **(in order) to learn** English.

informal Language used with family, friends, and children.

> Hi, Pete. Sit down.

information question See *wh-* **question**.

inseparable phrasal verb A phrasal verb whose parts must stay together.

> We **ran into** Tomás at the supermarket.

intransitive verb A verb that does not have an object.

> We **fell**.

irregular A word that does not change its form in the usual way.

> **good** → **well**
> **bad** → **worse**

irregular verb A verb that does not form its past with *-ed*.

> **leave** → **left**

main clause A clause that can stand alone as a sentence.

> When I get home, **I'll call you**.

main verb A verb that describes an action or state. It is often used with an auxiliary verb.

> She **calls** every day.
> Jared is **calling**.
> He'll **call** again later.
> Does he **call** every day?

modal A type of auxiliary verb. It goes before a main verb or stands alone as a short answer. It expresses ideas such as ability, advice, obligation, permission, and possibility. *Can, could, will, would, may, might, should, ought to,* and *must* are modals.

> **Can** you swim?
> Yes, I **can**.
> You really **should** learn to swim.

negative A statement or answer meaning *No.*

> He **doesn't** work. *(negative statement)*
> **No**, he **doesn't**. *(negative short answer)*

non-action verb (also called **stative verb**) A verb that does not describe an action. It describes such things as thoughts, feelings, and senses.

> I **remember** that word.
> Chris **loves** ice cream.
> It **tastes** great.

non-count noun A noun that you usually do not count (*air, water, rice, love,* . . .). It has only a singular form.

> The **rice** is delicious.

noun A word for a person, place, or thing.

> My **sister, Anne,** works in an **office**.
> She uses a **computer**.

object A noun or pronoun that receives the action of a verb. Sometimes a verb has two objects.

> She wrote **a letter to Tom**.
> She wrote **him a letter**.

object pronoun A pronoun (*me, you, him, her, it, us, them*) that receives the action of a verb.

> I gave **her** a book.
> I gave **it** to **her**.

paragraph A group of sentences, usually about one topic.

participial adjective An adjective that ends in *-ing* or *-ed*. It comes from a verb.

> That's an **interesting** book.
> She's **interested** in the book.

particle A word that looks like a preposition and combines with a main verb to form a phrasal verb. It often changes the meaning of the main verb.

> He looked the word **up**.
> *(He looked for the meaning in the dictionary.)*
> I ran **into** my teacher.
> *(I met my teacher accidentally.)*

past participle A verb form (verb + *-ed*). It can also be irregular. It is used to form the present perfect. It can also be an adjective.

> We've **lived** here since April.
> She's **interested** in math.

phrasal verb (also called **two-word verb**) A verb that has two parts (verb + particle). The meaning is often different from the meaning of its separate parts.

> He **grew up** in Texas. *(became an adult)*
> His parents **brought** him **up** to be honest. *(raised)*

phrase A group of words that forms a unit but does not have a main verb. Many phrases give information about time or place.

> **Last year**, we were living **in Canada**.

plural A form that means two or more.

> There **are** three **people** in the restaurant.
> **They are** eating dinner.
> **We** saw **them**.

possessive Nouns, pronouns, or adjectives that show a relationship or show that someone owns something.

> Zach is **Megan's** brother. *(possessive noun)*
> Is that car **his**? *(possessive pronoun)*
> That's **his** car. *(possessive adjective)*

predicate The part of a sentence that has the main verb. It tells what the subject is doing or describes the subject.

> My sister **works for a travel agency**.

preposition A word that goes before a noun or a pronoun to show time, place, or direction.

> I went **to** the bank **on** Monday. It's **next to** my office.
> I told him **about** it.

Prepositions also go before nouns, pronouns, and gerunds in expressions with verbs and adjectives.

> We rely **on** him.
> She's accustomed **to** getting up early.

progressive (also called **continuous**) The verb form *be* + verb + *-ing*. It focuses on the continuation (not the completion) of an action.

> She**'s reading** the paper.
> We **were watching** TV when you called.

pronoun A word used in place of a noun.

> That's my brother. You met **him** at my party.

proper noun A noun that is the name of a person, place, or thing. It begins with a capital letter.

> **Maria** goes to **Central High School**.
> It's on **High Street**.

punctuation Marks used in writing (period, comma, . . .). They make the meaning clear. For example, a period (**.**) shows the end of a sentence. It also shows that the sentence is a statement, not a question.

> "Come in**,**" she said**.**

quantifier A word or phrase that shows an amount (but not an exact amount). It often comes before a noun.

> Josh bought **a lot of** books last year, but he only read **a few**.
> He doesn't have **much** time.

question See *yes/no* question and *wh-* question.

question word See *wh-* word.

reciprocal pronoun A pronoun (*each other* or *one another*) that shows that the subject and object of a sentence refer to the same people and that these people have a two-way relationship.

> Megan and Jason have known **each other** since high school.
> All the students worked with **one another** on the project.

reflexive pronoun A pronoun (*myself, yourself, himself, herself, itself, ourselves, yourselves, themselves*) that shows that the subject and the object of the sentence refer to the same people or things.

> He looked at **himself** in the mirror.
> They enjoyed **themselves** at the party.

regular A word that changes its form in the usual way.

> play → play**ed**
> fast → fast**er**
> quick → quick**ly**

sentence A group of words that has a subject and a main verb. It begins with a capital letter and ends with a period (**.**), question mark (**?**), or exclamation point (**!**).

> **Computers are** very useful**.**

EXCEPTION: In imperative sentences, the subject is *you*. We do not usually say or write the subject in imperative sentences.

> **Call** her now!

separable phrasal verb A phrasal verb whose parts can separate.

> Tom **looked** the word **up** in a dictionary.
> He **looked** it **up**.

short answer An answer to a *yes/no* question.

> A: Did you call me last night?
> B: **No, I didn't. or No.**

singular one

> They have **a sister**.
> **She** works in **a hospital**.

statement A sentence that gives information. In writing, it ends in a period.

> Today is Monday**.**

stative verb See **non-action verb**.

subject The person, place, or thing that the sentence is about.

> **Ms. Chen** teaches English.
> **Her class** is interesting.

subject pronoun A pronoun that shows the person or thing (*I, you, he, she, it, we, they*) that the sentence is about.

> **I** read a lot.
> **She** reads a lot too.

subordinate clause See **dependent clause**.

superlative The form of an adjective or adverb that is used to compare a person, place, or thing to a group of people, places, or things.

> Cindi is **the best** dancer in the group. *(adjective)*
> She dances **the most gracefully**. *(adverb)*

tense The form of a verb that shows the time of the action.

> **simple present:** Fabio **talks** to his friend every day.
>
> **simple past:** Fabio **talked** to his teacher yesterday.

third-person singular The pronouns *he*, *she*, and *it* or a singular noun. In the simple present, the third-person-singular verb ends in *-s*.

> **Tomás works** in an office. *(Tomás = he)*

time clause A clause that begins with a time word such as *when*, *before*, *after*, *while*, or *as soon as*.

> I'll call you **when I get home**.

time expression A phrase that describes when something happened or will happen.

> We saw Tomás **last week**.
> He'll graduate **next year**.

transitive verb A verb that has an object.

> She **paints** beautiful pictures.

two-word verb See **phrasal verb**.

verb A word that describes what the subject of the sentence does, thinks, feels, senses, or owns.

> They **run** two miles every day.
> I **agree** with you.
> She **loved** that movie.
> We **smell** smoke.
> He **has** a new camera.

vowel A letter of the alphabet. The vowels are:

> **a, e, i, o, u**

wh- question (also called **information question**) A question that begins with a *wh-* word. You answer a *wh-* question with information.

> A: **Where** are you going?
> B: To the store.

wh- word (also called **question word**) A word such as *who, what, when, where, which, why, how,* and *how much*. It often begins a *wh-* question.

> **Who** is that?
> **What** did you see?
> **When** does the movie usually start?
> **How** long is it?

yes/no question A question that begins with a form of *be* or an auxiliary verb. You can answer a *yes/no* question with *yes* or *no*.

> A: **Are** you a student?
> B: **Yes**, I am. **or No**, I'm not.
> A: **Do** you come here often?
> B: **Yes**, I do. **or No**, I don't.